HeartWorn Memories

Heart Worn Memories

by

Susie Nelson

Heart worn memories
Worn in between — dreams of old used to be's
And how it was, just you and me
Heart worn memories.

Looking back when I was small
Dad, we had it all
Even when our troubles seem to fall
We always could laugh it off.

Heart worn memories
Vague, but seen
Leaves only heart worn memories.

So the times may have escaped us
But never can erase us
And surely won't replace us.

But only leaves
Heart worn memories
Only leaves
Heart worn memories.

Heart Worn Memories

a daughter's personal biography of

Willie Nelson

By

Susie Nelson

EAKIN PRESS

FIRST EDITION

Published by
Eakin Publications, Inc.
P.O. Box 23069
Austin, Texas 78735

Manufactured in the U.S.A.

ISBN 0-89015-608-5

Library of Congress Cataloging-in-Publication Data

Nelson, Susie.
    Heart worn memories.

    Includes index.
    1. Nelson, Willie, 1933– 2. Country musicians—United States—Biography. I. Title.
ML420.N4N44 1987 784.5'2'00924 [B] 87-15576
ISBN 0-89015-608-5

To Rebecca and Anthony

Contents

Willie Nelson, superstar.

— Photo by Rick Hensen

Acknowledgments

I would like to give special thanks to Ms. Dale Vinicur of the Country Music Foundation in Nashville and to John Wheat of the Barker Texas History Center at The University of Texas–Austin for their generous and tireless research on my behalf. Special recognition also goes to Harold Eggers for dealing with myriad details involved in researching, writing, and publicizing a book.

I was told recently that I had a "remarkable spirit." If that is true, and I hope it is, I got it from my mother, Martha Jewel Scott.

My publisher, Ed Eakin, stayed with me to the bitter end, and I thank him for it.

My two children, Rebecca and Anthony, have always given me inspiration to follow my dreams, and Uncle Robert Murphy took care of the homefront with devotion beyond measure so I could work on this book.

Last, but not least, I want to thank:

John Henry Faulk, who took a great interest in my story and stayed right along with me as I struggled through this complicated project, and who always gave me the love and confidence I needed along the way;

Bob Rosenbaum, my friend and mentor, who has been my guiding point and was invaluable as a critic, collaborator, and scholar of the trade;

and my loving father, Willie Nelson, whose greatness as a human being has touched the hearts of all, but whose greatness has been known to me since I was a little girl. We had our difficult times, but I never questioned his love for Lana, Billy, and me.

Special Credits

I would like to recognize the following for devoting their time and interest in my book:

Ralph Emery	Daniel Schaefer
Mike Tolleson	Alan Mayor
Terry Lickona	Rick Hensen
Darrell Royal	Wesley Rose
Don Holland	Willie Raycheck
Hank Cochran	Morris Russell
Fred Foster	Bonnie Garner
Buddy Lee	Ritchie Albright
Tony Conway	Rick Blackburn
David Zentner	Connie Lincoln
Hal Smith	Honey Younger
Grant Turner	Pamela Lewis
Johnny Cash	Pam Williams
John Prine	Leon Carter
Joe Allison	Hal Durham
Johnny Rodriguez	Ron Bledsoe
Mel Tillis	George Hughes
Mickey Newberry	Mae Boren Axton
Billy Deaton	Shirley Nelson
Owen Bradley	Bobby Bare
Hayes and Faye Jones	Ott Devine
Rev. Wayne Duncan	Tom T. Hall
Buddy Killen	Tompall Glaser
Maggie Cavender	Townes Van Zandt
Ray Pennington	Eldon Stafford
Charlie Williams	Mr. and Mrs. Oakley
Faron Young	Susanna Clark
Ray Price	Moi Harris
Chet Atkins	John Lomax III
Bill Ivey	Joel Cherry
Diana Johnson	Joel Katz
Kyle Young	Carolyn Mugar

ONE

Picnic 1980

"So my dad is important."

"**S**o you are important. My dad's an important man."
You may not believe this, but I didn't realize that I was the daughter of *the* Willie Nelson until his Fourth of July picnic in 1980. And a lot of the time I still have trouble remembering that Dad and Willie Nelson, the superstar Willie Nelson, are one and the same.

☆ ☆ ☆ ☆

I left home to get married when I was sixteen. Got married in order to run away from home, if you want to know the truth. That was back in 1973. Before Dad had made it big. Before everyone in Texas knew that the Fourth of July was synonymous with a Willie Nelson picnic.

I knew Dad was a singer and a songwriter. But he'd played one-night stands in small clubs for the most part back then. He was a headliner, that's true. But the biggest places he played were honky-tonks like Big G's in Round Rock and Randy's Rodeo in San Antonio.

He held his first picnic the summer before I left. It was in a pasture of caliche and Johnson grass on a ranch in Dripping Springs, about twenty-five miles west of Austin and just off the road to Johnson City. The temperature reached 102 that day. Some estimates placed the crowd at more than 60,000. It had been hot, crowded, and fun.

I was glad I had gone to that one. But I hadn't been to one of Dad's large concerts, let alone one of his picnics, for seven years.

And there I was. Eight months pregnant with my second child and sitting backstage looking out at a sea of people. Everywhere you could see, there was nothing but people. Old couples and teenagers,

1

cowboys and accountants, off-duty cops and hippies. People everywhere. And they had all come to see Dad.

The funny thing was that I hadn't wanted to be there in the first place. If Tony, my second husband, hadn't insisted, and if my next-door neighbor hadn't been so excited, I wouldn't have been there at all. You see, Tony (Tony Brewster) didn't know my dad as my dad. He'd been a Willie Nelson fan from long before I met him, but he'd never been to a picnic and was all fired up to go. So was Steve Miller and his girlfriend Marty, who lived next door. They were from Pennsylvania. They'd heard about Willie Nelson picnics but they'd never been to one, or anything like one.

I agreed, reluctantly. I called up Gay Crawford, Dad's secretary. For tickets, or backstage passes, or anything like that, we kids called Gay, or Mark Rothbaum the business manager. If we ever called Dad for something like that he'd just tell us to call Gay anyway.

So I called Gay and arranged for the tickets and the backstage passes. And then I remembered that I was eight months pregnant, that it was going to be hot, and that it would probably take hours and hours to drive there. I remembered the 1973 picnic, where everybody sat on the hoods of their cars, drank beer, and smoked dope while they waited for the traffic to crawl along close enough to park.

I sure didn't want to go through anything like that again. Not when I was carrying 150 pounds on my five-foot-one-inch frame. What I really wanted to do was stay home in Round Rock in my nice, clean, air-conditioned house.

But I'd said I'd go. If I backed out I would never have heard the end of it from Tony—and we weren't getting along so great as it was. And besides, I didn't want to disappoint my friend Marty.

I flat wasn't going to drive out there, however. No way.

I called Gay again and explained my situation. Was there any way, I wondered, that I could catch a ride on one of the helicopters that would be ferrying the stars, the sidemen, the bodyguards, and whoever else couldn't risk getting stuck in traffic?

"Sure honey," Gay said, "Why didn't you ask sooner?" She told me to be at the Austin Hilton around noon.

Space was limited, however, so only Marty and I could go. Steve and Tony would have to drive out. They didn't seem to mind. They loaded up the car with two of the biggest ice chests full of beer you have ever seen, rolled a couple of joints, and headed towards Briarcliff, Texas, and my dad's Pedernales Country Club. They planned on having a big old time. And I guess they did.

But Marty and I drove to Austin, hurrying through the holiday traffic so as not to miss our ride. I didn't know what the big deal was. Shoot. I'd been watching Dad sing ever since I could remember. But Marty was excited, and her getting excited was starting to get me excited too.

Besides, I'd never ridden in a helicopter before. As we took off from the Hilton and headed west over the Hill Country, you could see the traffic building. We flew over Highway 71 and it was thick — remember, this was about noon, and the music had already started. As we swung over 2322, the ranch road that takes you into Briarcliff, it was bumper-to-bumper and hardly moving all the way. When we got to the country club itself, the place was covered with people — solid, swarming people, moving around like a fire ant mound you'd kicked the top off of.

When the helicopter landed, a group swarmed around it like fire ants. But a whole lot friendlier. They crowded around, holding their pens and pieces of paper or something else to write on, pushing to see who was going to get out.

"Who's in there?" they'd ask. "Anybody important?"

I kind of got a rush watching all those people crowd over to meet me. But the question brought me back down to earth. "Anybody important? Not this time," I thought as I tried to maneuver out of the helicopter. There's just no way for a pregnant woman to do that gracefully.

Nope. Nobody important. Just a woman in a red dress with a belly so big she looks like a balloon about to float up over everything and everybody.

About that time, the crowd saw Dad standing with Earl Campbell, the football player, over by another helicopter, so they took off in that direction.

I led Marty over to the stage, where I told one of the security people that I was Susie, Willie Nelson's daughter, and could he please get Poodie Locke for me.

Poodie is Dad's bodyguard and has been for a long time. Poodie always takes care of us. A lot of the people who work security at concerts are on power trips. Not everybody — I have met a lot of nice security people. But there was a good chance that even with my backstage pass stuck on my red dress, even with my saying I was Willie Nelson's daughter, they wouldn't believe me and wouldn't let me in. Their job is to keep the backstage clear of people who don't belong there and they were, by God, going to keep it clear, even if it meant keeping a few legitimate folks out in the process.

So over the years I have learned that the simplest thing to do is ask for Poodie. Poodie came and took us to our seats. He asked us if we wanted anything to drink and in general was just as sweet as he always is.

We had gotten settled in pretty well when Dad came on stage and hit the first chords to his standard opening song, "Whiskey River."

And the place went wild.

"Whiskey river take my mind . . ."

All 60 or 70,000 people were on their feet cheering and waving.

"Don't let her mem'ry torture me."

I saw hand-lettered signs out in the crowd: WE LOVE YOU WILLIE.

"Whiskey river don't run dry . . ."

WILLIE FOR PRESIDENT.

"You're all I have, take care of me."

It was like a great outpouring of love, a river of love, coming down that hill.

"Well, Dad," I thought, "you're important—an important man."

And he loved them right back. Just like he loved his children—Lana, Billy, and me. Just like he loved Paula Carlene and Amy.

Well, maybe not the same. But just as much. I'm sure of that.

☆ ☆ ☆ ☆

I sat there dazed. I finally realized what everybody else in Texas, in the world, already knew.

So this is what he'd been doing all those years. So this is what he was after when he left me with Mama. This is the dream he'd been following when he'd be gone for a month or more at a time, leaving us kids with Shirley on the farm in Ridgetop, Tennessee.

The scaffolding for the sound equipment and the lights made a giant picture frame as I looked out at a landscape filled with swaying, clapping, shouting people, all of them focused on my dad. There were old farm and ranch ladies there, old enough to be my grandmother, sitting next to young girls who'd taken their tops off because of the heat and were bouncing to the music, their breasts following about a half beat behind, bouncing free for all the world to see. The older women's husbands were sitting there in tight-lipped concentration, watching the stage and trying not to peek at the swinging tits.

Joints were being passed around openly, and the air was heavy with marijuana smoke. Beer cans tipped up and new tops popped, tequila and bourbon bottles passed from hand to hand. The teetotaling Baptist and bearded hippie, along with the corseted grandmother in a flower print dress and the late-blooming flower child, enjoyed the music together—all the music, but especially Dad's. And they didn't get in each other's way.

I'd watch Dad sing and see how happy he was, and I'd think back to one of the bygone times—times that hurt.

He'd take the hat he was wearing and throw it to the crowd, as he usually does at his concerts. Someone in the crowd would throw a hat up to him and he'd wear it for a while, and then he'd throw it out and another one would come up and so on.

I'd watch him throw those hats, and then I'd think about the time we had to leave Tennessee and move to Austin.

I was mad. I was pissed off. The move meant no more cheerleading for me. It meant bye bye cheerleaders' camp. It meant I had gone to summer school to bring that math grade from a D up to an A for nothing. So I'd show them. I made up my mind that I just wasn't going to like school. And I finally quit when I was sixteen. Quit, got married, and ran off to Las Vegas.

Dad introduced another act and went over to the edge of the stage. That's the way he does at one of his picnics. He'll sing a song or two and then introduce the next act. Maybe he'll sing a number with them, maybe not. He'll get over to the side of the stage and sign autographs while he's waiting for the next turn. Of course, he'll do a full set plus one of his two-hour encores at the end of the show too, just like always.

As Dad signed autographs, the men were reasonable. They'd hand him a piece of paper, or maybe a hat or a beer can. But the women might want him to sign a tattoo, which just happened to be on the left cheek—and I don't mean the one located near the nose. Or on a breast or the inside of a thigh.

I just couldn't believe some of the places Dad was signing his name. I got up and walked over near him and watched some more. He never slowed down.

"Dad," I said, "you ought to be ashamed of yourself."

"Just doin' my job, angel, just doin' my job." And he looked up at me with the famous Willie Nelson glint in his eye and smiled and went right back to what he was doing.

So I went back to my seat and thought some more.

I thought about how much he meant to everybody. About how the Willie Nelson picnic was the highlight of the year for a lot of the folks out there in the crowd.

I thought about how I'd always wanted a normal home. A home for my dad to come back to after work every day. Just like the kids on TV had. Just like I thought all my friends at school had.

But I could see now that my dad was somebody special.

So what if he couldn't seem to stay married for much more than ten years at a time.

So what if he found himself in other women's arms when he was on the road. The way women throw themselves at him, he'd have to be inhuman not to yield to temptation some of the time. And Dad is nothing if not human.

I looked out at him singing and the crowd being attentive and cheering and pouring love down on him and him giving it back just as much and just as strong. I looked at him and thought to myself, "You've been pissed off all these years for nothing. Look at what this means to him. Look at what he means to all those folks out there. He's had a vision all these years, and this is it. He never stopped chasing it, never gave up on it, no matter how tough things were."

I did feel hurt and lonesome and scared when Dad would go on the road and leave us with Mama. My mother is Martha Matthews, Dad's first wife. She has that Cherokee blood and a taste for the bottle. When Dad first started playing with Ray Price and the Cherokee Cowboys, Mama worked as a cocktail waitress at Tootsie's and the 101 Club in Nashville. I was three or four at the time. Well, Dad would leave for thirty days on the road — or longer. And Mama would work until late at night and come home drunk, most likely. Those were scary times, sometimes. And I missed my dad.

Then I thought about life with Dad and Shirley, his second wife, on the farm outside of Ridgetop. For a while there, Dad stopped going on the road. He never stopped writing songs, of course, but we all lived together, like one big family — Shirley, my older sister Lana, my younger brother Billy, and lots of cows, horses, pigs, and chickens. The sign on the mailbox said "Willie Nelson and Many Others."

Those were the happiest years of my life, and I was really mad when they ended.

I thought about living with Dad and his third wife, Connie. How I was always rebellious and unhappy and felt unwanted and unloved. And how I got out of there as soon as I could, the only way I knew how — by getting married.

The memories faded in and out as I watched Dad and the crowd, and I thought, "But look at all he's done. Look at who he is."

Dad never denied us. He was always affectionate and loving whenever we saw him. Now that he was Super Willie, he could really help us kids out financially, but he had always done the best he could. And it's not like he ever left us completely, ever left us forever. I mean, there I was, twenty-three years old, pregnant with my second child, married to my second husband, had left home when I was sixteen — a runaway, for all practical purposes — and I was sitting backstage at Dad's Fourth of July picnic.

"Girl," I told myself, "look at all the things your dad's done to make you proud of him. Look at all the opportunities he has given you. And what have you done? All you've done is get into sorry marriages and get pregnant."

☆ ☆ ☆ ☆

Marty and I stayed until it started to get dark, somewhere around 8:30 or 9:00. Nine hours of picnicking was plenty for me and my almost-to-be-born baby. The concert was nowhere near over. Dad wouldn't get up for his last set until midnight or so and there was no telling how long he would play — probably as long as there was anybody there to listen.

I was exhausted. I couldn't stay to the bitter end.

We caught a helicopter to take us back to Austin. As I flew over the Hill Country with the green of the cedar trees turning pink from the setting sun, I took stock of the day. Or tried to.

First thing was that I was going to stop feeling sorry for myself. I was going to get out and do something with my life besides keep house for a man I couldn't get along with any more.

And that was the second thing. Some way or another, after I had the baby, I was going to face facts and get Tony out of the house.

I wasn't sure how I was going to do that. I mean, I had been through one divorce by the time I was nineteen, and I sure didn't want to go through another one. But I was bound and determined that something had to change.

I didn't know what my problem was, but I sure didn't know how to pick men. I guess I just didn't look deep enough inside them. Or something. Maybe it goes back to never feeling really wanted, really loved. I don't mean by Dad. He just wasn't around that much. I usually figured that I'd have to settle for a guy because I couldn't do any better. I wasn't worth any more.

Don't get me wrong. Tony was a big, good-looking guy. He was a salesman and could give you a real believable line. But he figured he didn't have to work — he was married to Willie Nelson's daughter, wasn't he? She should be able to support the household. What money he did make he spent on drugs. Dad has always told his band, "If you're wired, you're fired," and you could say I finally felt the same way about Tony.

And a temper. I guess that came from his Italian mother. He'd walk around the house wiping window sills and table tops with a white glove and raise seven kinds of hell if it came up dirty. One time he blew his stack because I hadn't vacuumed the sofa. Another time, he knocked the bejeezus out of me because I put onions in his tuna sandwich.

So as the helicopter went "whup whup" on its way to the Hilton, I thought about what I wanted. I wanted a husband to take care of me, to give me the comfortable, safe, normal home I'd only experienced briefly as a child. If either of my husbands had done that, I would have been content to stay Susie Homemaker forever.

But they didn't. And this one was worse than the first. If I was going to have to take money from Dad in order to live and feed my kids, I for damn sure didn't need him. I was going to live life my way, do things for me, Susie Nelson.

Just what I was going to do was another thing. But as I sat there that afternoon and early evening watching my dad, I said to myself: "You're a Nelson too. Maybe you have some talents you don't know about. You can't tell, because you haven't ever tried. You've been too busy believing all those folks who've been saying that you weren't good for anything. But let's go find out. Let's see if there's anything to this heredity business."

☆ ☆ ☆ ☆

I look back on the Willie Nelson 1980 Fourth of July picnic as a big turning point in my life.

I'm sure a lot of these thoughts had been going on in my head before that afternoon. I'd been married to Tony for three years, so I didn't just all of a sudden decide he was a turkey.

I had taken a few steps towards a life of my own.

I'd begun taking dance lessons before I'd gotten pregnant, and the instructor, Lillian Coltzer, gave me a lot of support. I'd never really had any support before, at least not immediate praise for something I had done. I liked it, both the dancing and the praise.

So I had already started doing things to get beyond the Susie Homemaker role I had gotten myself into.

It was seeing Dad that afternoon, seeing his talent and what it meant for him and for the people who came miles and miles and sat hours and hours in the hot Texas sun, that really brought everything to a head, that crystallized my resolve to get on with my life, to make something of myself.

It's been over six years since that afternoon and a lot has happened to me since then. My husband was killed in an automobile accident the day before New Year's Eve of 1980. I took up dancing very seriously and have since begun a singing career.

But one of the main things I have done is to learn more about my dad. The revelation when he sang that afternoon — so this is what it's all been about — kept at me. I wanted to find out more and more about who he is and how he got that way so I could understand him better. And understand myself better.

The place I started is the same place he started — in a little Central Texas farming community about twenty miles north of Waco. It's called Abbott.

TWO

The Nelsons of Abbott, Texas

"A nice, clean, little red-headed, freckle-faced boy."

One of the things almost everybody always says about Dad is that he has never forgotten where he came from.

That accounts for, they say, the modest, unpretentious way he acts on stage — or anywhere else, for that matter. It explains his limitless patience in signing autographs, and he'll sign his name until the last hat, beer can, or breast is gone. It's the reason he's a soft touch for almost every benefit that comes along and the reason he spends so much time and energy on Farm Aid. And, they say, it's the secret for his appeal to so many different people of all ages and from every walk of life.

If it's true that Dad never forgets where he came from, then maybe, I thought to myself, I had better go take a look at exactly where it was he did come from.

With that in mind, I got in my Volvo and drove north on IH-35 to see for the first time the town where my dad grew to manhood. As I drove, I sorted through what I already knew.

☆ ☆ ☆ ☆

Willie Hugh Nelson was born in Abbott, Texas, on April 30, 1933, a double Taurus and the second child of Myrle and Ira Nelson. Dad's older sister, Bobbie Lee Nelson, was born in 1930, within a year after Ira and Myrle had settled in Abbott.

The family was originally from Searcy County, Arkansas, which is in the northern part of the state, not too far from the Ozark National Forest. Ira married Myrle Greenhow at Pindall in 1929 and soon thereafter moved to Abbott along with Ira's parents.

Times were tough then. The Depression was closing in on Texas, and the pressures of raising two small children in a brand new town, with there never being enough for a little bit extra, was more than Myrle could handle. When Dad was still in diapers, his mother just up and left. She and Ira were divorced soon after, and she moved near some relatives in Oregon and ultimately married a man named Ken Harvey. We grandkids always knew her as Mother Harvey.

Ira, or Pop as we called him, didn't stick around too long either. He'd gotten a job driving a gravel truck and was making a haul outside of Abbott when he saw two girls walking down the road. As one of the girls told the story, "He pulled up in this truck and offered us a ride. I didn't want to get in, but my girlfriend did." He married the girl who didn't want to get in not long after, and Pop and Lorraine (that was his new wife's name, Lorraine Moon) moved to Fort Worth.

Aunt Bobbie and Dad stayed in Abbott and were raised by Pop's parents. So when you talk about where Dad came from you have got to begin with his grandparents, Mama and Daddy Nelson.

☆ ☆ ☆ ☆

William Alfred Nelson married Nancy Elizabeth Smothers in 1900. They homesteaded forty acres and had three children — Clara, Rosa, and Ira.

A photograph of them taken not long before they moved to Abbott shows a strong, attractive couple. Daddy Nelson, thickset and capable, is dressed in bib overalls and a fedora and is watching something off to his right. Mama Nelson, wearing a house dress and apron, her right hand reaching up to rest on her husband's broad left shoulder, looks directly at the camera, her head half-cocked and a look of gentle inquiry on her strong, attractive face. It's a picture of a loving couple secure in the knowledge that they can handle whatever life has in store for them.

I never met Daddy Nelson, but I knew Mama Nelson. She spent one summer with us when we lived at Ridgetop. Billy and I would sit with her on the porch swing, one on each side, and she would sing us "The Numbers Song": "5111, 12333, 34555, 548, 5888, 54333, 5646, 54321." I can still remember the melody.

By the time the family moved to Abbott, Daddy Nelson had learned the blacksmithing trade and he set up shop in town, making his money repairing farm machinery and shoeing an occasional horse or mule. Mama Nelson worked in the lunchroom of the elementary school, and she taught music in her home.

And both went to church. Mama and Daddy were devout Methodists and regular churchgoers. They lived right across the street from the Abbott Methodist Church and were there whenever the doors were open — weeknight prayer meetings, Sunday school, gospel sings, church suppers, regular services. They never missed a one. Neither did Aunt Bobbie or my father.

Both Mama and Daddy Nelson loved music too, especially gospel songs. They took lessons through the mail, Mama for the piano and Daddy Nelson for the guitar. One of Dad's earliest memories is of watching the two of them studying their lessons from the Chicago Musical Institute under the kerosene lamp "into the wee hours of the morning."

Even though times were hard, they had somehow managed to get a piano. Mama would teach Aunt Bobbie each lesson after she had mastered it. I guess Aunt Bobbie must have started playing by the time she was three or so, and by the time she was six or seven she played the piano for the church.

Daddy Nelson got Dad his first guitar, a Sears and Roebuck Stella that cost five or six dollars, and taught him a few chords before he died in 1939 when Dad was six.

One of the highlights of the week for Daddy Nelson was to go the ten miles to Hillsboro for the Wednesday night gospel sing at the county courthouse. And he'd usually take Dad and Aunt Bobbie. Dad remembers that there would be anywhere from twenty-five to thirty-five singers there. All of the good gospel singers in the area, plus a piano player or two, would try to get there and outdo each other — in a friendly Christian way, of course.

They'd sing songs out of the old Stamp Quartet songbooks, and they all could sight-read. They'd spend the night harmonizing, just knocking each other out. Dad says that to this day that was some of the most beautiful singing he has ever heard. He still loves gospel music and always ends his shows with one or two — "Precious Memories" or "Amazing Grace" or other favorites.

☆ ☆ ☆ ☆

Abbott This Exit.

The green interstate sign broke through my memories. I was going to get to see where Dad had grown up. I was going to get to see Willie Nelson's hometown.

I turned off IH-35 and followed the signs to the right, over the railroad tracks and past some shacks and small frame houses.

And that was it.

"Where the hell's the town?"

Then I remembered Dad saying that Abbott was so small, both city limits signs are on the same post.

I finally found the main street, all three blocks of it. There's a barber shop and a post office and a gas station and a church. There'd have to be a church.

Oh yes. And there's a store too. It's called the Willie Nelson General Store now. But years ago, back when Dad was a boy, Bill Fritz owned the store. That's where the teenagers and young men would hang out and drink a soda water—it was six miles to the nearest beer—and talk about girls while they smoked cigarettes or took a chew of tobacco.

I knew about some of the people to see and I had called in advance to set appointments for interviews. And I found others who had known Daddy and Mama Nelson, Aunt Bobbie, and Dad. All in all, I made three trips to Abbott to talk to the people who had known Dad when he was a boy.

I found out that the folks who said that Dad never forgot where he came from were right.

Dad has stayed in touch with the friends he grew up with. He's always stopping by to visit. Sometimes these middle-aged men will up and drop what they are doing and go swimming with Dad in Blair Creek, just like they did when they were kids. Of course, as one of his friends named Eldon Stafford told me, "Willie don't do me like you do, honey. Call and tell me he's comin'. He just shows up. Sometimes I'm at home and sometimes I'm not."

Dad even had a picnic at Abbott. It was on November 4, 1973, the fall after his first Fourth of July picnic. Dad had just been inducted into the Songwriter's Hall of Fame in Nashville, and the Abbott PTA sponsored the "Abbott Homecoming" to honor Abbott's "most famous native son."

It was really put on by Dad to benefit the Abbott PTA. Eldon and another friend from the old days, Morris Russell, told me how Dad had come through one day looking for a place to put on the concert. They tried Spivey's Crossing on the Brazos, but the man who owned the land said, "No, nothin' doin'."

The people in Abbott were a little scared of all the hippies who might show up. But Eldon and Morris finally did find a place for the concert. It was in a field of Johnson grass north of town, a field fenced in by a bois d'arc hedgerow. In fact, Dad and Eldon and Morris used to hunt quail there when they were boys. Eldon and Morris probably still do.

Anyway, Morris called down to Austin to tell Dad about the new place. "You know, what surprised me is that Willie answered the phone," he recalled.

It was an all-day sing with dinner-on-the-ground. The acts that played included Waylon Jennings, Sammi Smith, Billy Joe Shaver, Kinky Friedman, Jerry Jeff Walker, Johnny Bush, and Asleep at the Wheel. Daddy gave Morris a job selling tickets. Morris said he had a lot of fun doing it but that security was so slack most folks got in for free. He doubts that anybody made any money, with the possible exception of the PTA.

But the highlight of the concert, according to Eldon, was Mama Nelson. Dad was playing on the back of a flatbed cotton truck in the middle of the field, and he stopped to give Mama Nelson a bouquet of red roses. "With tears in his eyes," Eldon told me. "Your daddy sure did love Mama Nelson." Mama came up to get them and the first thing she told Dad was, "You need a haircut."

☆ ☆ ☆ ☆

Abbott is in Hill County, about ten miles south of Hillsboro, the county seat, and twenty miles north of Waco, home of Baylor University and the Texas Ranger Museum, among other things.

The 1980 census gives Abbott a population of 359. Hill County as a whole reached its peak as far as population goes in 1910, when it had more than 46,000 residents. In 1930 the county's population was still comparatively high, above 43,000. Now it's down around 25,000. So Abbott probably had more people when Dad was a boy, but it would never be confused with being a big city.

Abbott is on the blackland prairie, which is a swath of rich, easy-plowing soil that runs in a crescent from the Red River on the north to the Rio Grande. The prairie varies in width from fifteen to seventy-five miles wide, generally getting narrower as you go south. It was the leading cotton producing area of Texas until the rise of irrigated, mechanized farming in West Texas. Cotton is still important there.

In Dad's day it was cotton and corn, with some cattle, but cotton was the mainstay of the economy. In fact, the first house the family lived in when they came to Abbott was across from the gin. Daddy Nelson repaired the plows and cultivators for the cotton farmers, and the kids worked in the fields when it was time to pick.

Picking cotton was hard work. You really had to pick three hundred pounds of cotton in a day. At anywhere from fifty cents to a dollar a hundred pounds, it was easy to see you weren't going to get rich filling a cotton sack. Dad tells the story that one time as a young teenager he made two dollars chopping cotton during the day and eight dollars playing rhythm guitar in a Bohemian polka band that night. From that day on, he figured that as long as he was playing music, he had it made.

The rich land in Hill County and the neighboring areas had attracted a fairly wide mixture of ethnic groups. The largest Czechoslovakian settlements in Texas were in the area, and you can still go to towns like West or Praha and hear Czech spoken. Mexicans lived across the street, and Dad picked cotton with blacks. The wide spectrum of different peoples and their customs who lived around Abbott and Central Texas is probably one of the reasons for Dad's unprejudiced attitude.

Even though it was the Depression and times were hard, people weren't totally isolated. For one thing, Abbott was on the Interurban line, an electric railroad that ran from Dallas to Waco. As Frank Clements, the barber who had come to Abbott in 1932, told me, you could ride the Interurban to West for a dime. You could go to the movies for fifteen cents. And you could get a hamburger and a coke after the show for another fifteen cents. "We used to go three or four times a week until we got TV." Mr. Clements was giving a haircut while he talked to me and he never once stopped cutting while I was in his shop. Not bad for an eighty-six-year-old man.

So that's the town where Dad was born and where he lived until he went into the Air Force when he was seventeen. A town of 500, maybe 700 people. A town where you rang up a telephone operator and asked her to connect you with Mrs. Russell or Mr. Stafford. A town where you could walk to just about every corner in ten minutes or so. A town with a cotton gin and an elementary school, a store and a blacksmith shop, a barber shop and a high school, an Interurban station and churches.

I'll say, there were churches. There was the Methodist church where the Nelson family went and the Baptist church where Morris Russell and Mr. Clements went. And then there were the Catholics and the Church of Christers.

☆ ☆ ☆ ☆

Mama and Daddy Nelson were hard-working, God-fearing folks with their feet planted firmly on the ground, the blackland ground of Central Texas. Everybody I talked to remembered them as nice, decent people. Daddy Nelson was a "hefty fellow," Morris Russell's eighty-eight-year-old father told me, "but a real good man."

I wish I'd had a chance to meet him. I picture him as just like Dad, and my great-aunt Rosa says that was what he was like.

Mama Nelson was remembered as a sweet, honest, religious woman. "But not stern," said Wayne Duncan, the preacher. "We used to go down to Granny Nelson's house for a Sunday dinner of fried chicken," Reverend Duncan recalled. "And I'd talk to Willie about fishing, or frogs and snakes."

They lived at first in the small frame house across from the cotton gin, then moved about a block to a larger house across from the Methodist church and just below the Tabernacle. The walls were papered with cardboard and newsprint to keep out the Texas wind, or at least to slow it down a bit. They kept hogs and chickens, and they had a milk cow that Dad sometimes rode like a horse.

Mama Nelson used to tell us stories about when Dad was a little boy. "Oh your daddy was such a fine boy," she'd say in her quiet voice, "just like you, Billy," and she'd give my brother a hug. "But sometimes Mama Nelson would have to get on him."

Billy and I would look at each other and giggle.

"Why, one time, Willie and a few of his little friends went down to the well. After a bit, everybody came back but Willie. So we all went looking for him. He wasn't even as big as you, Billy. So me and your Aunt Bobbie went looking for him all one afternoon. Guess where we found him?"

"Where, Mama Nelson?" we asked.

"Under the bed, fast asleep."

Another time, Dad made her mad. "I don't remember what he did, but I went to get the belt. Every time I'd go to whip him he'd crawl under the bed as far as he could go and wait for me to go off into the other room."

"What happened, Mama Nelson?"

"Oh, I couldn't stay mad at the little fellow for long." She'd pat me on the leg. "But your daddy, he's sure one sneaky fella."

Everybody in the family worked. Dad would run errands for a nickel or dime—a quarter if he was lucky. He'd shine shoes in the barber shop, although after he got a little older, he asked Mr. Clements if he could play his guitar for the customers instead.

Mr. Clements asked him how much he wanted, and Dad said he'd like about two dollars. Mr. Clements said, "Well, we'll see."

So Dad played all afternoon.

According to Mr. Clements, he only knew two songs and he wasn't very good with either one of them. When the afternoon was over, Mr. Clements gave him fifty cents.

"I thought it would be two dollars," said Dad.

"Shoot, Willie," said Mr. Clements, "*I* didn't make two dollars today."

Even after Daddy Nelson died, Mama Nelson was able to keep things going. She made about fifty dollars a month at the cafeteria and supplemented that by giving piano lessons. And, of course, Aunt Bobbie and Dad helped with whatever they were able to bring in.

Church was one of the cornerstones. Mama and Daddy Nelson's quiet, unshakable belief gave them the strength to carry on in spite of economic hardship, in spite of having to raise their grandchildren at an age when they had every right to start slowing down a little bit. Belief gave Mama Nelson the strength to carry on after Daddy Nelson died. And that belief was passed on to Dad and Aunt Bobbie, although I can't help but wonder what Mama Nelson would think of Dad's belief in reincarnation.

One of the major bits of Abbott's Willie Nelson lore has to do with the church, with Sunday school, to be exact. It seems that one Sunday his Sunday school teacher noticed that one of Dad's black Sunday-go-to-meeting socks had a hole in it. So she sent him home to change.

Dad must have had only one pair of black socks or else he was too lazy to change. In any event, he got some black shoe polish, colored his skin to match, and went back to the church. The teacher never said another word about it—then. Later on she'd tell the story often. According to Eldon Stafford, that teacher thought the sun rose and set on Willie Nelson.

When she was in her eighties, she went to hear Dad play at the Convention Center in Waco. She went backstage to see him but, of course, the security guard stopped her and wouldn't let her in. So she told that guard to go tell Dad she wanted to see him. The guard went backstage, and pretty soon he came back and escorted her to see Dad.

Another time, the daughter of the Sunday school teacher saw Dad performing and went up to talk to him after the show. Dad said that he'd like to write her mother a note, but he couldn't find anything to write on. He finally wrote his old Sunday school teacher a note on a beer can. And you know what? She kept that beer can until the day she died. And her daughter has it still. It has become a family heirloom.

Reverend Duncan remembers Dad in church, remembers that Dad had a tendency to doze off during the sermon, but that he'd perk right up when the singing started.

Music was the other cornerstone. Aunt Bobbie remembers Daddy Nelson "pushing" her to play the piano at the gospel sings, telling her that "you might be able to make yourself a living doing this someday." And by the time Aunt Bobbie was in her early teens, not only was she the church piano player, she also went along with Reverend Duncan and his wife to revival meetings.

According to the preacher, Aunt Bobbie "could play the boogie woogie, but she could also play good music." And they'd take her to a weeklong revival and pay her the same as they made themselves — about twenty or thirty dollars for the week.

Dad was encouraged to perform too. He says that his first public performance was at the age of four or five. It was at an all-day, dinner-on-the-ground church meeting where he recited a four-line poem he had written himself:

> What are you looking at me for?
> I ain't got nothing to say.
> If you don't like the looks of me,
> Look the other way.

According to Dad, he picked his nose before the recitation and it bled all over the white suit he was wearing. So his first public performance was something less than an unqualified success. But I think it's prophetic that the poem is about independence and nonconformity, about doing things his own way and not caring what other people think. And I think it's also prophetic that it was at a picnic. It seems the seed for doing things his own way at outdoor concerts was planted as long ago as 1937.

☆ ☆ ☆ ☆

Dad says he can't remember when he started to write poetry, what he called songs without melodies. He just knows that he's been doing it for as long as he can remember.

The fact that he started writing at such an early age is one of the reasons for his belief in reincarnation. As Dad sees it, he had a safe, happy childhood. In fact, he sometimes goes so far as to say that he was spoiled by Mama and Daddy Nelson. But his poetry was about trouble and heartbreak. Since he didn't know anything about the pain and sorrow of living in a vale of tears from firsthand experience, Dad figures that he must have learned about it in a previous life. How else could a happy four-, five-, or six-year-old child know to write about such things?

I don't know the answer to that. Maybe Dad's right.

Mother Harvey, Dad's real mother, had a book of fifteen of Daddy's handwritten poems. His friends say that he was always rhyming things, always reciting his poetry to them.

And he sang all the time. Morris Russell, who was a Baptist, says that he could sit in his church and hear Aunt Bobbie and Dad singing in the Methodist church across the street. And Mr. Clements let him entertain in his barber shop, limited repertoire and all.

☆ ☆ ☆ ☆

One thing people point out about Dad's music is that he seems to have been influenced by so many different styles. Almost all of those influences originated in Abbott.

The gospel music influence goes without saying. But he surprised everybody by putting out the *Stardust* album, which features a lot of music from the twenties and thirties. He said that Aunt Bobbie would buy songbooks that had songs like "Moonlight in Vermont" and "Stardust" in them, and he would hang around and try to pick his guitar and sing along with her. "I thought they were some of the most beautiful songs I'd ever heard. I still do," he told me.

There was also the radio. Dad would listen to Ernest Tubb and Bob Wills, or Little Jimmy Dickens—"take an old, cold tater and wait"—and Frank Sinatra. He'd put that honky-tonk western sound, and that swing sound, and Sinatra's phrasing into the mix with the

Stamp Quartet's gospel songs and Hoagy Carmichael's haunting ballads.

The Hispanic rhythms to Dad's guitar work came from the Mexican family that lived across the street. And the blues? The feeling that made "Night Life" a classic? Says Dad, "I first heard the blues picking cotton in a field full of black people. One would sing a line at this end of the field, another at that end. I realized they knew more about music, sound, feeling than I did. I felt inferior. Plus, they could pick more cotton."

An interviewer once asked Dad why he incorporated so many styles and influences into his music and he answered, "My grandmother told me music was anything that is pleasing to the ear." He's found a lot of things that are pleasing to his ear.

☆ ☆ ☆ ☆

So I learned about Dad's early years. And I saw a lot of things that seemed to be the start of directions he would follow all his life. His independence and nonconformity. His loyalty to family and friends. And his music.

Young Willie Nelson? He was quiet and well mannered. He was shy but determined. He was loved. He was, says Reverend Duncan, "a nice, clean, little red-headed, freckle-faced boy."

THREE

They called him Booger Red

"Hell, yes. Anybody who fought bumblebees would get stung."

D ad's life wasn't just the church and the house with Mama Nelson and Aunt Bobbie, of course. He had school, and work, and friends. Especially friends.

When I went to Abbott to talk to the people who knew him as a boy, I'd ask them what Dad was like. Everybody I asked always mentioned that he was quiet and polite. "He was never mouthy. He always thanked you and was very appreciative of anything you did for him."

That makes sense, because that's the way he is today. For a time, I went with the co-pilot of Dad's Lear, and he told me Dad always acted like he worked for them. "It was like he hated to ask us to do anything for him."

Another thing about Dad in his youth was that he always hung out with older boys. Of course, in small towns, age differences don't mean as much as they do in big cities. They were like older brothers to him, and they probably gave him the older male companionship he missed while growing up in the house with just Mama Nelson and Aunt Bobbie.

Dad spent as much time as he could hanging out at the store with the older boys and young men. Billy Polk, the stepson of storeowner Bill Fritz, named him Booger Red. And the nickname stuck.

☆ ☆ ☆ ☆

"What did boys do for fun back then?" I asked Eldon Stafford.

"We hunted a lot. We'd hunt just about anything. At night we'd all hang out at Bill Fritz's store. And we'd go out around town and hunt sparrows out of the trees. Then we'd bring them back and feed

21

them to the alley cats. Willie would carry a paper sack to put them in. He was the official bird toter."

They'd hunt squirrels and rabbits, but those went into the dinner pot and weren't to be wasted on cats. "Your daddy's got quite a memory," Eldon told me. "He remembers that we went squirrel hunting down on Cobb Creek the day before I went into the service for World War II. I no more remembered that than . . . I guess that's how he remembers all them songs."

Morris Russell recalled the time that he and Eldon and Dad were hunting in a hay field. They were all carrying shotguns and they heard something in the bushes. Willie ran around the other side to see what it was. He had the hammer back. And he fell down. Morris always remembered how scared he and Eldon were that the hammer had been back. Luckily, the gun didn't go off. And the thing that had caused the whole commotion was a cat.

Hunting and fishing, frogs and snakes. Dad and his friends did most of the things typical country boys would do.

"What about girlfriends?" I asked.

You know that when you get a bunch of teenage boys hanging out together they're going to talk about girls a lot. In fact, Dad once said that in Abbott "after dark everyone just hangs out, sitting around, smoking cigarettes, and talking about girls."

But nobody would tell me anything about his girlfriends. They would kind of hint about one special one, and then refuse to tell me any more about her. Eldon did admit that after he got to be sixteen or so, "Willie had an eye for the ladies." And Morris recalled that Aunt Bobbie and Dad used to throw a lot of parties where they would play spin the bottle. But I never did find out who any of his steady girlfriends were or even if he ever had any.

☆ ☆ ☆ ☆

What I did find out about was bumblebee fights. Evidently, back in the forties in Abbott, Sunday afternoons revolved around bumblebee fights. Kind of the way Sunday afternoons now are for professional football games.

How did you fight bumblebees?

That's what I wanted to know.

First, you whittled a paddle out of a thin board. Shingles or boards from apple crates were preferred. Then you bored holes in it so the air would go through and you could hit the bee and not fan it back.

Once armed, all you needed were the bumblebees. And the boys found them by asking the farmers who came into the store. During the week, Billy Polk would ask anyone who came in the store if they had run into a bumblebee nest when they were haying or working in the fields. Bumblebees live in holes in the ground, I was told, and they are black and yellow and about as big as a man's thumb. They are bigger and slower and easier to see than a honeybee, but they're pretty mean just the same.

So on Sunday afternoons, the gang of them would go out to the field where they knew there was a bumblebee nest. One of them would go over to the nest and fan a few times over the hole, creating a little breeze in order to draw a few out. You wanted to draw two or three of the bees out, but you didn't want too many more because that was more than you could handle. If you did get too many out of the nest at one time, the others would come over and make a few swings in the vicinity to draw the excess away.

I guess the sport was seeing how many bees you could kill without getting stung. Or maybe the sport was to stand back and laugh at some poor soul who was flailing wildly away at a bunch of bees and yelping every time he got stung. Eldon explained that bees were attracted to motion and dark colors. So they would tell someone who was along on a bumblebee fight for the first time to wear a dark handkerchief. And then they would all die laughing, watching the bees make a beeline for him.

"Then what would you do?"

"Go back to Fritz's store and drink a soda and forget about it until the next Sunday."

"Did you or Dad ever get stung?" I asked Morris and Eldon.

"Hell, yes. Anybody who fought bumblebees was goin' to get stung. Some days we'd come back with both eyes almost swollen shut."

"What did you do about the stings?"

"We put chewing tobacco on them to draw the poison out. A lot of us started chewing tobacco because of bumblebee fights."

"You were a grown man during a lot of this, weren't you?"

"Yep. Might go fight some tomorrow, you can't never tell. Fact, one time when your daddy dropped by to visit I asked him if he thought he could still do it, fight bees that is, and he said 'Hell yes.' "

It sure didn't sound like a lot of fun to me. And Morris agreed that modern kids might not think it was so much fun. But back then, with folks just coming out of the Depression and not too many kids having more than a nickel in their pockets at any one time, fighting bumblebees was fun with a capital F. Especially if that bee was on someone else.

☆ ☆ ☆ ☆

To hear them talk, it sounded like they had a lot of fun back then.

They loved to pull practical jokes. One of their favorites was a game they called pocketbook playing.

The equipment for pocketbook playing consisted of an old, discarded woman's purse and a length of string. They would tie the string to the purse handle and go out to the edge of town where there was a big billboard. They'd throw that purse out in the road and hide behind the sign, with one of them holding the end of the string. A car would drive by and the driver would see the pocketbook and slam on his brakes. While he was slowing down, they'd pull the purse back behind the sign and try to keep from laughing while they watched the driver hunt and hunt for that pocketbook he was positive he had seen lying by the side of the road.

Sometimes they would use a wrench or some other popular tool. "Man, a farmer would burn rubber for a quarter of a mile trying to stop if he saw a tool he could use just lying by the side of the road," Eldon said.

One time they went to play the pocketbook game with a purse but without any string. The older ones convinced Dad and another young kid that since they were young and spry they should be the ones to run out and pick up the purse while the driver was coming to a stop.

All went well for a while. But then one driver was too fast. He and Dad met at the pocketbook. "And he had a big ol' six-shooter hanging down by his side," said Eldon. "Willie said a few words to him and the man went on his way. And you know, to this day I don't know what Willie said to him."

Another practical joke they liked to play was putting a car up on blocks.

"How'd that work?" I asked.

"Oh, you'd jack a car up just enough so's you could get blocks under the rear axle, but not enough so that it looked like the tires were off the ground."

"And then what would you do?"

"Nothin'. Just go on about your business. Of course, when the driver came out and tried to drive off, he'd end up real mad. You'd sure get cussed at, if he had an idea of who did it."

And apparently Halloween was a real big old time. If you can believe Eldon and Morris, it would take half a day to clean up the main street so that traffic could move along it, what with all the old cars, trash cans, outhouses, and whatnot all the kids would pile in it. One time they even took a wagon apart and put it together on top of one of the churches.

☆ ☆ ☆ ☆

I guess Fritz's store was the hangout for most of Abbott. In the summertime, one of the big things to do was to go to the town of West, which was about five or six miles down the road, to play baseball. All of the younger kids would hang out by the store and mob anybody like Eldon or Morris, who had a car, in hopes of getting a ride to West and back.

Eldon, who played baseball about three or four times a week after he got out of the service, was used to carrying a car full of younger kids the round trip. Dad was usually one of them. He would always be quiet and polite about asking for a ride, they say.

But even though he was quiet, almost shy, Dad was almost always willing to take a dare.

It seems that one night after a baseball game in West, Dad was in the car with Eldon about to head back to Abbott when they passed St. Mary's Catholic Church and saw that there was a wedding dance going on.

"Let's go in," said Dad.

"Willie, you're crazy. We can't go in there all sweaty and dirty in our baseball uniforms. They's people wearing good suits and nice dresses and all. You can't go in there."

"Can too."

"Bet you a quarter you can't."

"You're on."

"But here's what you have to do. When you get up to the second floor, you have to stick your head out the window and wave so's I know it's you. And you have to turn your baseball cap around backwards and then walk through the length of the whole dance hall."

"For a quarter?"

"Yep."

"Okay." Dad got out of the car and tucked his shirt into his pants as best he could and went in the church door. Pretty soon Eldon saw Dad's head at the second-story window, where the social room of St. Mary's was, and he waved and turned his hat around backwards. Then he disappeared.

"You know what happened," says Eldon, "is that he thought he'd just have to walk through the room once and go out the other door. But the other door was locked, so he had to walk back through the room the same way he came in order to get out. And by that time, every eye in the place was looking at him, wondering just who in the hell that was."

"But he got his quarter."

"Yeah. He sure did. See, you have to understand that we went to wedding dances a lot because they didn't cost nothin' to get in. If it was a pay dance, we would wait until half time. Then we could get in free."

Pranks and practical jokes were one thing, but formal sports also kept everyone busy.

Dad played baseball, football, basketball, and ran track. He was a four-letter man, which wasn't bad for somebody who only stood five feet nine inches tall and weighed about 130 pounds when he graduated from high school.

Dad says he wasn't that great, but he loved to play. "When you lived in Abbott, all you had to do to make the roster was be standing there when the team came out."

I don't know how good he was, but he is remembered as being real good in running, high jumping, and pole vaulting. He also was pretty good in baseball, because he almost had a baseball scholarship.

Dad has kept up his interest in sports over the years. When we were living in Tennessee, on the farm in Ridgetop, we all had horses to ride. Dad also learned karate then, way back before the martial arts were fashionable. He started his golf too, out in the cow pasture, wiping the balls off when they landed in cow patties and teeing them up again. And whenever the band plays Las Vegas or some other long gig, they'll get up a baseball team and play other teams from the casinos. But as far as I know, running is something he left alone after high school and didn't pick up again until he moved back to Austin in 1972 and started working out with Longhorn football coach Darrell Royal.

☆ ☆ ☆ ☆

Growing up in Abbott was a lot of fun for Dad. But it was also a lot of work. Times were hard, and everybody worked at whatever they could get.

Dad would go stay the night with Morris Russell and they would work on the various farms in the area, including working for Morris's father.

Morris likes to tell about the time he and his father and my dad were picking corn — called pulling corn — by hand. They had a tractor and a trailer, and Mr. Russell would pick the whole day as the two boys took turns driving the tractor and picking.

Morris told Dad to take the first turn driving the tractor. After about two hours or so, Morris asked Dad if he wasn't ready to pull corn for a while.

Dad said that he wasn't quite ready.

Another hour or so passed with Dad driving and Morris and his father pulling corn. Finally, Morris said that it was his turn to drive and Dad's turn to get down and pull some corn.

Dad said that he just didn't feel like pulling corn that day.

"Dammit Willie," said Morris, "you're sure a sorry outfit. You aren't ever going to amount to nothing."

He tells that story with a smile now, but I'll bet he was hot at the time. Dad has never bragged about what kind of a worker he was. In fairness, Morris points out that he didn't like work then either. None of the kids did. It was just something they had to do.

Picking cotton was a widespread activity in that region, and I haven't heard anybody who has ever done it say that they liked it.

"It's tough," says Eldon. "Sore fingers and an aching back."

Or as Dad says, "It's a real bad paying job. Just as hard as you could make it. If you were like me, you picked awhile and sat on your sack awhile, and it wasn't as bad as it was for some."

One story goes that when Dad was picking cotton for a farmer named Walter Plunkett, he told him that he wasn't going to make his money picking cotton, he was going to make it singing.

And that proved to be right—but it took him quite a while. One of the things he did was work as a relief telephone operator. The woman who ran the central switchboard liked to go out on Saturday nights, so either Dad or Aunt Bobbie would take over for her. This was when Dad was eleven or twelve and his voice was just starting to change, so he always figures that everybody thought he was a girl. After just one night a week on the switchboard, he says he knew everything that was going on in the county.

☆ ☆ ☆ ☆

There was music.

Dad's first music gig was playing rhythm guitar in John Rajcek's polka band. With all the horns and accordions and whatnot making as much noise as they did, nobody could hear Dad well enough to tell if he was any good or not.

A couple of years later, when Dad was thirteen and Aunt Bobbie was sixteen, the two of them started playing with Bud Fletcher, who Aunt Bobbie dated and married not long after. His band was called "Bud Fletcher and His Texans." It was quite a family affair because Dad's father, Pop Nelson, would drive down from Fort Worth on the weekends and play a little fiddle.

In later years, Dad would always say that once he started playing with Bud Fletcher, his best course in school was baseball. "That's when I started drinking beer and hanging out in beer joints and playing music and not wanting to get up in the morning and go to school."

Dad and Aunt Bobbie had always stayed with their music. They would ride the Interurban all the way to Waco to perform on "Mary Holiday's Amateur Talent Show," which was held on Saturday mornings and broadcast live on radio WACO. Aunt Bobbie was still playing at revivals and giving piano lessons, and Dad was playing wherever he could.

When they played with Bud Fletcher, they had a regular Sunday morning sign-on show with KHBR radio in Hillsboro, the county seat. Dad says that they'd come dragging in after playing and driving all night. It being Sunday, they were followed by preachers—most of whom would direct their preaching to the band. "You could tell they thought we were nothing but wicked hillbillies," he said.

The band played in most of the beer joints on the highway to Waco. One place, Albert Morales's place, had a black cook who was famous for his cheeseburgers. People would drive from miles around, from as far away as Hillsboro, to have one of Blackcat's cheeseburgers. A lot of the time Dad would catch a ride down there with Eldon and play with the band. Eldon would stop back by for a cheeseburger after his baseball game and pick Dad up and give him a ride home.

One time Eldon stopped in for his post-game cheeseburger and Dad was singing a song called "Ragmop." When he finished singing, a customer stood up and called out, "Willie, would you sing it again for three dollars?"

"For three dollars I'll sing it all night."

☆ ☆ ☆ ☆

Dad's childhood sounds like it came from the pages of *Tom Sawyer* or *Huckleberry Finn* in a lot of ways.

Many of the things that are associated with Dad were formed during those Abbott years. His religious beliefs. His friendliness and politeness. His strong loyalty to family and friends. Even his movie roles—he claims that ever since he went into Hillsboro on Saturday afternoons to see Lash Larue and Rocky Lane, Roy Rogers and Gene Autry, he wanted to be in cowboy movies.

Throughout his growing-up years, there was always music and songwriting. Dad estimates that he probably wrote six or eight songs a day when he was in his teens. He wore his hair longer than most boys back then, and people would tell him that he was going to be one of those "long-haired musicians," although I doubt that anybody had any idea of just how long his hair was going to get.

You can see just about all the signs of the man in the child. Just about all except his love for the road. Mama Nelson thought that driving six miles to West to play in a beer joint was on the road. And she didn't like it.

Dad says that he would stand in the cotton fields and watch the cars go by on the highway and think that he had to get out of there.

After he graduated from high school, ol' Booger Red did get out of there. He joined the Air Force.

"I was young and dumb and that was the easiest way out of the house."

☆

FOUR

Marryin' Martha and movin' on

"... and every night was like Custer's Last Stand."

N ow we're getting to one of the most important events in Dad's life, at least as far as I'm concerned. And that is his meeting and marrying Martha Matthews — Martha Jewel Matthews.

To me, that was the second most important thing that he ever did — the first most important being that they had another child after my sister Lana was born. Of course, Lana and my brother Billy have different ideas about what the first most important thing was.

☆ ☆ ☆ ☆

Dad didn't marry Mama right out of high school. In fact, he didn't even meet Mama until after he had tried a little baseball and attempted a military career.

One of his dreams was to play professional baseball. He got as far in that direction as a tryout for a baseball scholarship at nearby Weatherford Junior College. But he was still playing in honky-tonks and beer joints, and the two hours of sleep he'd had the night before his tryout didn't help his reflexes any.

After blowing his chances for a baseball scholarship, Dad joined the Air Force. His basic training was at Lackland Air Force Base in San Antonio. He remembers that it was in December and it rained almost all of the time. To make the experience more memorable, they lived in pup tents with mud floors. After basic, he was stationed at Sheppard Air Force Base in Wichita Falls, where he at least got to live in a barracks.

But Dad didn't find a home with Uncle Sam. He learned to appear at morning roll call and then, when they went back inside to get their canteens for the day's training, he would slip out the back door and hide under the barracks all day. He says that since it was a time of

31

peace, he never could see any sense in the discipline, the marching, and the yelling. But I don't think Dad would have seen any sense in all of that under any circumstances.

From Wichita Falls, Dad was sent to Biloxi, Mississippi, to go to radar mechanics school. Evidently, he considered that senseless too, because after a month or so the Air Force sent him to air police school. Maybe they figured that the best way to get him to obey orders was to be responsible for enforcing them.

Whatever they thought, it didn't work. At the time, Dad was just eighteen. He stood at about five feet nine inches and weighed maybe 130 pounds with his hair wet. Somehow, I just can't see him rousting some big, drunk airman who was misbehaving on a weekend pass. And Dad couldn't either. "Shoot," he says, "I was on their side."

Since he washed out as an AP, the Air Force made one last stab at finding a place for him. They tried to make him a medic. But a back injury he had gotten loading hay bales years ago started to act up again, and he ended up being hospitalized. The main thing he remembered about the medical treatment he received courtesy of the Air Force was that a dumb nurse, a lieutenant—those are Dad's words— would make him get up at 6:00 A.M., make his bed, and then let him lie back down.

According to what Mama always told me, Dad preferred to sleep until two or three in the afternoon. "Trying to get him up in the morning was the damnedest thing you ever saw. He could sleep through a damn tornado. I remember when you and Billy were babies, he'd come home in the middle of the night and get you and Billy and put you right in the middle of our bed. Along about five or six in the morning, I'd wake up soakin' wet from my ass to my elbows. And there'd be your daddy with the two of you lyin' across him. He'd be soakin' wet, too, but sound asleep. I'd wake him up and he would hold you both while I changed the sheets. Then the three of you would lie back down and he'd be asleep again in less than five minutes."

Mama claims that Jesus Christ Himself could have come down and asked Dad to stand at attention and he'd have stood up just long enough to acknowledge His presence and then "laid right back down to rest." So no mere lieutenant was going to change his ways.

Dad was not a military man. Finally, the Air Force agreed and gave him a medical discharge. His career in the armed forces didn't make it through the year.

☆ ☆ ☆ ☆

Dad returned to Abbott and went back to the honky-tonks. He would spend his nights picking and his days at one short-term job after another, from making saddles to trimming trees.

The tree-trimming job almost ended in tragedy. While cutting branches away from high-tension lines, Dad's partner was about forty feet up and needed another rope. Dad took it up to him, but rather than climb back down the tree, he decided to shinny down the rope. He'd only gone about four feet when he got his finger hung up. He couldn't go up or down, and he was too far away from his partner to reach him. So his partner did the only thing he could—he cut the rope. Dad fell the forty feet through the branches and electric wires and was able to get up and walk.

Walk is exactly what he did. He walked home and hasn't trimmed a tree since.

At one point, he enrolled at Baylor University with the intention of getting a degree in business. He may have registered as a business major, but he spent his time playing dominoes. Since Baylor didn't have a dominoes major, the administration suggested that he look elsewhere.

And that was the end of Dad's formal schooling. It was also the end of his hopes for being a professional athlete.

As a boy, Dad dreamed of being a singing cowboy like Gene Autry, or a professional baseball or football player, or a musician—a singer like Ernest Tubb or a bandleader like Bob Wills.

With college a bust and baseball out of the picture, it looked like music was meant for him.

But another thing happened. He met a sixteen-year-old carhop from Waco. That meeting ultimately produced three children and, if you believe what a lot of people say, enough heartbreak to inspire most of the songs that got him elected to the Songwriter's Hall of Fame.

Mama was the only child of Etta and W.T. Matthews. She did have a half-brother named Gerald Bass from her mother's earlier marriage, but Gerald was twelve years older and they never lived in the same household. For all practical purposes, Mama was an only child.

Nannie and Pa, as we grandkids called them, named their only daughter Martha Jewel and treated her like a precious gem. Nannie sewed all of Mama's dresses—and they were beautiful. Pa was a plumber, and every extra penny he made crawling under people's houses to fix their stopped-up pipes was spent on things to make their little jewel sparkle.

By the time she was a teenager, Mama was traffic-stopping good-looking. She was tall, five foot seven, with raven hair so black it had a blue sheen to it. Her eyes were like chips of anthracite coal. I'll bet the men who stopped by the Lone Oak Drive-In for a cheeseburger and large root beer prayed that she'd be the one who took their order.

And when she was dressed up in her poodle skirt that swirled when she spun around, I'll bet she didn't have any trouble filling up her dance card either.

Mama loved to dance. She was the original party girl. She used to go dancing in all the honky-tonks along the highway between West and Waco. If Nannie or Pa tried to ground her, make her stay in her room for a night, that didn't stop Martha Jewel Matthews. She'd no sooner go to her room and shut the door than she'd be out the window and in a friend's car, on her way to the 31 Club in Waco.

That's where she met Dad. He was playing and she was dancing, and from all that I hear, it was an instant mutual attraction.

According to Mama, she went up to the bandstand and asked him if he wanted to dance.

"I don't know how," Dad answered.

That didn't stop Mama, and it wasn't long until she had him out on the floor.

The old saying that opposites attract couldn't have been more true in this case. Dad was quiet and reserved, shy really, always polite and appreciative of anything you did for him. Mama was loud, aggressive, the life of the party. With her it was "my way or no way," which is understandable since she was an only child—and a spoiled one at that.

Understanding her was one thing and being able to live with her, at least without a blow-up, was another. Dad always says that "my first wife was a full-blooded Cherokee, and every night with us was like Custer's Last Stand."

You can lay a lot of blame for the fights between Mama and Dad on Mama being spoiled. But she came by some of that spark, to put the best name on it I can think of, naturally.

Her parents were a lot like Mama and Daddy Nelson. They were survivors—hard-working Christian people with a strong sense of duty and family responsibility. And down through the years Nannie and Pa took care of us three grandkids, took care of us a lot. But while Nannie was a lot like Mama Nelson, she also had a temper. Nannie would tell you to kiss her ass in a New York minute, in just those words. And she'd mean it too.

But the spark in Mama that wasn't inherited came from her taste for beer. Now I'm sure you've all heard the myths about Indians and firewater. I don't know if they're literally true in all cases. But they sure do fit my mama. After she had had a few beers, it didn't take much to put her on the warpath.

Mama didn't develop her drinking habits until she and Dad got to Nashville, however, and until then there was no denying that these opposites had attracted. After a three-month courtship that consisted mainly of Mama being at the 31 Club whenever Dad was playing there and Dad filling up on cheeseburgers at the Lone Oak whenever he could get to Waco, they ran away to Cleburne and got married by a justice of the peace.

Martha Jewel Matthews married Willie Hugh Nelson in February 1952. Mama was sixteen and Daddy wasn't quite nineteen.

☆ ☆ ☆ ☆

Eighteen-year-old guitar pickers and sixteen-year-old carhops don't make a lot of money, so the newlyweds lived with Mama Nelson in Abbott. Dad would work at anything he could get to try to make ends meet while he continued to play the guitar at nights.

Mama didn't think much more of Dad's employment record than she did of his sleeping abilities. "He lost more damn jobs in one month than most people have in a lifetime. All he wanted to do was pick that damn guitar." Evidently, when Mama would get on him bad enough, Dad would go find a job. But as soon as he'd made enough to keep her quiet, he'd go back to hanging out with musicians and picking that guitar.

The young couple continued like that for a while, sometimes living with Mama Nelson in Abbott, sometimes living in Waco with Nannie and Pa. Mama continued to get work as a carhop or a waitress. In fact, Mama has been a waitress of one kind or another all her life.

But she never lost her taste for dancing. So the new couple spent their evenings in the same joints—Daddy picking and Mama dancing.

☆ ☆ ☆ ☆

Dad got itchy feet and decided he wanted to try his luck somewhere other than in the Waco area. So he and Mama moved to San Antonio, where he met another guitar picker named Johnny Bush. Johnny and Dad have stayed friends since, and Dad always opens his shows with "Whiskey River," which Johnny wrote.

Dad and Johnny spent their evenings picking in the honky-tonks and dance halls around San Antonio, sometimes even taking turns on the same guitar. But Dad thought it would be a good idea to bring his night life and day jobs closer together.

An ad for a disc jockey at KBOP radio in Pleasanton, a town about thirty miles below San Antonio, looked like just the ticket. After all, hadn't Dad had radio experience with Bud Fletcher and His Texans in Hillsboro? The only thing was, they did that show live, singing into microphones. Somebody else did the engineering. And somebody else was the announcer.

But Dad applied for the job anyway. He'll try just about anything once.

The man who owned the station, Dr. Ben Parker, asked Dad if he'd had any experience.

"Sure," he answered.

Then Dr. Parker asked Dad if he was familiar with the control board.

"That's an RCA board, isn't it?" asked Dad. As he tells the story he always points out that anybody could see it was an RCA board because it had RCA Victor written all over it. "I don't know that board," said Dad, "I've only worked on Gates boards." He'd remembered that KHBR had a Gates board. He also figured that Dr. Parker would have to show him how to work the Victor board because it looked different than the Gates.

Dr. Parker showed him how and then gave him a live, on-the-air tryout. Part of the tryout included a fifteen-minute newscast. And right in the middle of the newscast Dad had to do a commercial for the Pleasanton Pharmacy that went like this: "The Pleasanton Pharmacy's pharmaceutical department accurately and precisely fills your doctor's prescription."

Dad says it took him about thirty-five minutes to finish a fifteen-minute newscast. When he finished, it was obvious that he hadn't spent too much time around radio stations.

But Dr. Parker hired him anyway.

Dad worked at KBOP for a year. And Dr. Parker and Dad are still good friends. Not long ago, Dad played a benefit for a museum Dr. Parker opened—the Pleasanton Cowboy Longhorn Museum. He flew in from Las Vegas to play, and, so the story goes, he got two speeding tickets during the thirty-mile drive between San Antonio and Pleasanton.

After a year at KBOP, Dad figured he'd gone about as far as he could there, so he moved to Denton and got a job selling ads for another radio station.

But he didn't like selling as well as he liked being on the air. So he and Mama moved to Fort Worth, where he worked as a disc jockey at several stations.

It was during this period that he first met Paul English, a "scrawny kid just out of high school." Paul's brother played in a band with Dad. Paul had opened a leather shop after graduating from high school. One day, the band was doing a live thirty-minute set on Dad's radio show and they needed a drummer. So Paul's brother called him up and told him to come down to the radio station. When he got there, he found out that they wanted him to play drums.

Paul played the trumpet. He had never played drums in his life. The only reason he was called was because he owned his own shop and could get off work. None of the drummers they knew could leave their jobs at a moment's notice. So Paul learned to play the drums through on-the-job training.

After six weeks of playing on free thirty-minute live sets, the band finally got a paying gig. So they all asked Dad who they should get for a drummer. "I think we ought to use Paul," he answered, "he's been working for nothing for six weeks."

☆ ☆ ☆ ☆

My older sister Lana had been born in Hillsboro just before they settled in Fort Worth. There was Dad with a young wife and infant, working as a disc jockey during the day, and playing about three or four nights a week for eight dollars a night in some of the roughest bars in Texas.

Some of them were located on a stretch of road in Fort Worth called the Jacksboro Highway, known by some as the Jaxbeer Highway. The road is lined with honky-tonks with names like the County Dump, which is right next door to the Tarrant County dump, and the

Bloody Bucket. Not far away is another area known by the locals as the Northside Bar Circuit. The two have schooled some of the best blues, rhythm and blues, and honky-tonk country musicians in Texas.

The customers were workingmen looking for energetic relaxation — mechanics needing a diversion after a day of tearing diesel engines apart, cowboys wanting to make the most out of their time in the big city, plus the usual assortment of gamblers, hustlers, and general sharp operators. They knew what they wanted and they wanted it right then. They weren't much on subtlety. And they had no patience with anyone who got in their way.

Fights were a nightly occurrence, and in some joints they happened almost on the hour. Killings were commonplace enough to scarcely raise eyebrows. Several owners of the places where Dad played had enough concern for the welfare of their entertainers to thoughtfully stretch chicken wire in front of the stage so that only the hardest of thrown beer bottles could get through. And at one of these clubs, the only reason the band was hired at all was to cover the noise from the crap table.

While all this was going on, Dad was teaching Sunday school at the Metropolitan Baptist Church. So was Mama, for that matter. But then someone in the congregation learned that he was spending his nights working in night clubs and saloons in Fort Worth and around North Central Texas.

That didn't sit too well with this upright Christian, and he complained to the pastor. The preacher came to Dad and said that there had been a report that he was singing in dens of iniquity to all those crazy people who frequented such hellholes.

He admitted that that was true. "But," Dad said later, "the funny part of it was that I was singing to the same people on Sunday mornings that I was singing to on Saturday night."

The pastor told him that he couldn't do both. He either had to quit the honky-tonks or quit the church. Well, the eight dollars a night that the clubs were paying was a whole lot more than what the church was paying. Dad thinks the person who had complained was a heavy contributor to the collection plate every Sunday, and he figures that the pastor said to himself, "Do I want this broke picker or do I want this person who throws money into the church?"

"I'm not saying that this is what happened," says Dad, "but, if it did, then he took his money and I took mine."

Dad took the incident as an attack on him personally. He couldn't see why it was okay for plumbers and electricians to do their work and be accepted as church members, but he had to choose between his work or the church.

The episode turned him off of organized religion. He has never belonged to a church since, even though there was a time when he thought about becoming a preacher.

Mama and Dad and Lana stayed in Fort Worth for almost two years. For a while, Dad had a radio show on KCNC called "Western Express." Every afternoon he had a kiddie segment where mothers would call in and request songs to help their toddlers take their afternoon naps. One of the songs he played a lot, especially on the kiddie segment, was "Red Headed Stranger," recorded by Arthur "Guitar Boogie" Smith.

I can attest to the fact that he thinks it's a good lullaby because he sang us to sleep with it for years.

But by the beginning of 1956, Dad got the urge to roam again. He'd felt that he was stuck in a rut in Fort Worth. To add to his dissatisfaction, Pop's wife Lorraine was getting to him and Mama. Maybe the warm sunshine of Southern California would get things going his way.

FIVE

Trying the West Coast

"He was clean, just so clean . . . and he looked like hunger."

California sunshine looked like the answer. How to get there was the question.

Mama and Dad didn't have a car. At least not one that could make the trip.

Dad saw an ad for a car forwarding agency that wanted people to drive cars to California. A car forwarding agency lets you drive a car to a particular city and all you pay for is the gas. In those days they wanted you to show them $50 cash so they could feel fairly confident you'd be able to buy enough gas to get there.

Dad only had $25. So he went around to one of his friends and asked if he could borrow the fifty, just to "show it to them." After the very short-term loan of $50, Mama and Dad and Lana, who was not yet two years old, started out towards San Diego, California, with $25 for gas and food. They made it, but not without having to siphon off gas out of a county government storage tank.

☆ ☆ ☆ ☆

Mama got a job in San Diego waiting on tables, but Dad couldn't find a thing.

It didn't set well with either of them for Dad not to be working, so he decided to hitchhike up to Portland, Oregon, where his mother Myrle lived with her second husband. Maybe things would be better there.

Dad left Mama and Lana in San Diego and started hitchhiking to Oregon with $10 and a suitcase. He got to Orange, California, just as it was getting dark. He was hungry, tired, and near broke.

There was a country night club nearby, and he counted up what money he had—just enough for one beer. He nursed that beer the whole night long and managed to keep from being thrown out. As the band was packing up at the end of the evening, Dad got to talking with them, wondering if they knew anybody who might give him a job. They told him that they didn't know of a thing. But one girl told Dad to stick around. She would make some phone calls and see if she couldn't find something.

The search came up empty. Well, as Dad tells the story, that old suitcase was getting heavier and heavier every mile. And this girl seemed real nice, someone you could trust. So Dad gave her Mother Harvey's address in Portland and asked her to send the suitcase up there. Dad never saw the girl or the suitcase again.

He set out on foot with just his clothes and no money. He slept underneath the freeway overpasses, using old newspapers to keep warm. Somewhere along the way he managed to pick up an old coat. Besides providing warmth, the coat proved to be an invaluable place to hide cans of vienna sausages and jars of peanut butter that he liberated from various grocery stores along the way.

☆ ☆ ☆ ☆

Dad finally made it to Portland.

Not only that, but he got a job as a disc jockey with KVAN radio in Vancouver, Washington, right across the Columbia River from Portland.

He sent for Mama and Lana. They lived with Mother Harvey and Ken for a while. Then they got a place of their own. Mama was pregnant with me, so she sent for Nannie and Pa to come up from Waco and help her out with the new baby.

And I came. On January 20, 1957. I was born in the hospital in Vancouver, Washington.

Nannie says that it was cold and snowing the day they brought me home from the hospital. "Snow up to your ass," she told me.

Nannie and Pa loved us. That was one thing they made sure we knew. They were simple people, like I said, and they didn't have much money. But they loved us, and they showed it to us every day.

Pa told me he would set me up in my high chair in the kitchen, and then he'd say, "Give Pa a kiss." I'd shake my head "No." And he'd ask again, "Please give Pa a kiss." And I'd shake my head "No." Then he'd ask again. And I'd finally give him a kiss.

Pa got a job with a plumbing outfit. That's one good thing about having a trade like plumbing or auto mechanics — you can usually find a job no matter where you end up.

But one of the main things that Pa did was cook. Nannie wouldn't cook, and Mama wasn't the cook back then that she is today. So Pa was the cook. Not only that, Pa washed the diapers. He'd get in the bathroom and scrub those diapers out just as good as any woman ever did it.

Nannie was a good housekeeper. It wasn't like she didn't do anything or was lazy. Not at all. Nannie kept house and made us clothes and things to play with. And she did know her baking, I have to admit.

Between Nannie and Pa, we were well taken care of.

Which isn't to say that everyone was overjoyed to see me. Mama told me that not long after they brought me home from the hospital she found me crying in my crib with a red pepper in my mouth. Lana had put it there.

Lana also got Mama to change my name from Deana to Susie. I had been named after a friend of Mama's, but Lana had a doll named Sue and that's how I came to be named Deana Sue Nelson. For the longest time I resented that name. Susie sounded to me like something you'd call a milk cow or something.

☆ ☆ ☆ ☆

That's the way things went for a while. Dad working at the radio station during the day and playing around Portland and Vancouver whenever he could get a gig. Mama waiting tables. Pa working as a plumber. And Nannie and Lana and me at home, for the most part.

Finally, though, Nannie and Pa moved back to Texas. They'd helped Mama cope with me, the newborn. And the weather had gotten to them.

I've always thought it was funny that Mama and Dad had started out for warm, sunny Southern California and had ended up in the cold and rainy Pacific Northwest. Don't get me wrong. It's beautiful country, with the forests of Douglas fir, the snow-capped mountains, and clear rivers and streams everywhere. But if you were born and raised in Central Texas, the gray skies and rain and snow would just wear you down. Nannie and Pa must have felt they were living in a sauna, only the steam was cold.

There were enough folks in the area who liked country music to keep Dad busy. I don't mean that he was making a lot of money. Disc jockeys on local radio stations weren't paid very much then — they aren't paid a whole lot now — and Mama still had to work.

But between his radio job and his playing in the clubs, Dad was working as a musician.

And then Mae Boren Axton came to call.

If you're not into country music, that might not mean anything to you. But this lady is a pistol. If I didn't know better, I'd swear she was Mae West's sister.

Mae Axton, some people call her Mama Axton, is a songwriter of some renown. In fact, when she came to Vancouver in 1957 — not long after I was born — she had just had quite a bit of success with a song recorded by an up-and-coming singer out of Memphis, Tennessee, named Elvis Presley.

The song? It was called "Heartbreak Hotel."

After a hit like that, Mae Axton wasn't living on lonely street.

You may know Mae Axton as the mother of singer-songwriter-actor Hoyt Axton, who wrote "Joy to the World" and starred in the movie *Gremlins*.

Mae was in the area doing some promotional work for Hank Snow. She had been up in Vancouver, British Columbia, to accept a song-writing award and had about two weeks before she had to be back home. Hank had a tour of the Northwest coming up, and he talked her into doing some pre-tour publicity for him. She knew the manager of KVAN and arranged for an interview. The manager assigned Dad to do the job.

Mae described the meeting to me, calling Dad "the kid who interviewed me. This skinny, shy kid."

Dad may have been skinny and he may have been bashful, but he knew how to get someone's attention too. According to Mae, Dad was interviewing her about Hank and she was doing her job as a promoter, when all of a sudden Dad told her, "I play every song of yours that comes in."

Mae said to herself, "Boy, this kid's all right!"

Dad followed that up by saying, "I read every story that you write that I can find in the magazines."

Mae told me that really knocked her out, that he knew she wrote short pieces for *Country Song Line-Up* and other magazines.

After the interview, as Mae started out to the airport, Dad said, "I know you have a plane to catch, but I'm trying to write some songs.

I don't know whether I have a chance or not. Would you have time to listen to one?"

Mae told me, "You know, I looked at him after he said all that. He was clean, just so clean, but he had patched jeans, really worn, and he looked like hunger. And I said, 'Son, I'll take time.' "

So Dad played her a song on an old reel-to-reel tape recorder in the lobby of the KVAN radio station in Vancouver, Washington.

Says Mae, "I couldn't believe what I heard."

"What did you do?" I asked her.

"Well, I just listened. And then Willie turned it off and I asked him if he had any more."

"Yes, ma'am," he said.

"I listened to a couple more and I said 'Son, I got to leave. I have a plane to catch. But let me tell you something. Two things I want to tell you. One is that if I could write half as good as you, I'd be the happiest woman in the world.' And remember, I had just written 'Heartbreak Hotel.' Willie just looked at me and I said, 'Number two. I don't know anything about you except this one thing. But you quit this job and go to Texas or Tennessee and you write.' I just told him what he needed somebody to tell him."

Mae finished up by giving Dad her unlisted number on the back of her business card and telling him that she could always raise a few hundred dollars if he needed it.

But in all the struggling years he never asked her for money. Not until a couple of years ago at some press conference or award ceremony when Dad asked her to tell about the Vancouver interview and then got her to tell about the offer of a loan. When she got to that part he said, "I need two hundred dollars now," and held out his hand.

He did follow her other advice, although not immediately. As with most things, Dad had to do it his own way.

☆ ☆ ☆ ☆

One of the first things he did was record a song. He released "No Place To Go," with the flip side being a song called "The Lumberjack," written by a friend named Leon Payne.

Except for Leon's contribution, it was a one-man production. Dad wrote it, sang it, released it on the Willie Nelson label, published it through Willie Nelson Music, and promoted it himself on his radio show, selling the records for a dollar apiece, along with a free, autographed 8×10 photograph of the artist, singer, record company president, and publisher.

He had an initial pressing of 500 copies and eventually sold about 2,000.

Also during this period he teamed up with another songwriter named Jack Rhodes and wrote "Too Young To Settle Down." I don't know whether it was recorded then, but the title sure was the truth. It wasn't too long before we hit the road again, heading back towards Texas and to Fort Worth.

☆ ☆ ☆ ☆

The trip back to Texas took us through Denver, Colorado, where Dad got a job picking at a honky-tonk called Heart's Corner. That stay lasted six weeks, and the man who owned the place rented Dad a guitar.

Then we went to Springfield, Missouri, where Dad met an old friend of his named Billy Walker. Billy was working for the Ozark Jubilee at the time. Mama and Billy's wife were old friends too. She was the one Mama had named me for, before Lana got into the act.

Meeting someone she knew from home was a welcome relief for Mama. It gave her something familiar to hang on to after all the moving around that she and Dad had done ever since they'd gotten married.

The Walkers invited us to stay with them for a few days. And Billy even set Dad up for an interview with Si Simon, the man who ran the Jubilee.

The interview didn't work out. I guess Mr. Simon thought Dad was "ahead of his time" or something. Dad worked as a dishwasher until he could raise enough to pay for the gas to get us back to Texas. Come to think of it, that experience may have burned Dad out on kitchen work. I've never seen Dad wash a dish in my life. Or cook either.

We finally got back to Nannie and Pa's house in Waco, then we moved to Fort Worth. Mama was pregnant with Billy by this time. And she was on Dad all the time: "Why don't you get a real job?" That kind of thing.

So Dad tried. Lord did Dad try. He quit the music business and made a real effort at living the life of a straight-time, daytime father of three.

Songs for sale

"I tried to be like everybody else, but it just wasn't me."

D ad took Mae Axton's advice, at least part way. He returned to Texas. But it took another two years before he got to Tennessee.

During that time, my brother Billy was born, Dad tried to be something other than a musician, and he sold his first songs.

But Dad was still scrambling. And that meant we were all still scrambling. He may have been gradually learning more about how the music business worked, at least as far as writing and performing were concerned, but he hadn't learned even a little bit about how to handle money.

☆ ☆ ☆ ☆

When we first got back to Fort Worth, where Pop and Lorraine Nelson lived, Dad tried to quit music.

He started selling encyclopedias.

Dad borrowed an old panel truck from a friend of his and began hawking *Encyclopedias Americana* door-to-door. He claims that he didn't have time to learn the sales pitch, so he just took the type-written spiel with him.

He'd tell prospective encyclopedia owners that he was new at the job and in order for them to be sure that they all understood one another, that Dad wasn't misinterpreting anything in any way, the company had asked him to read from the prepared script.

So he'd read them the pitch.

And the customer would come back with, "Shoot, I can't afford it."

And Dad would say, "Well, let me see what the company says about that." And he'd read the rebuttals on the back of the sales pitch.

The same look of honesty that Dad had used back in Abbott to keep the man from pulling his six-shooter during the purse prank must have worked here too, because Dad made three sales that first night. In fact, he was so good that it didn't take the company long before they made him an office manager.

But convincing folks to buy something they couldn't afford really got to Dad—that and the fact that he'd rather be picking and singing. So he quit his job as an up-and-coming supersalesman and went back to the honky-tonks. As he told a reporter from *Time* magazine later on, "I tried to be like everybody else, come home at five and turn on the TV, but it just wasn't me."

So before long he was playing the clubs again, even going as far back as the Nite Owl and Scotty's Place. He played at Scotty's one time when Mama was along, and Eldon Stafford and Morris Russell made a special point of driving over to hear him play. They had kind of lost touch with Dad after he went into the Air Force. And that was the only time either of them saw my mother.

Folks who aren't musicians, or who don't know musicians, probably can't understand how Dad could quit his job and go spend all his time in honky-tonks—either playing, trying to line up a gig, listening to someone else play, or just getting to know other musicians.

But I understand it. I've been around musicians all my life. And once it gets in your blood, you're a goner. You're not good for anything else. A musician is what you are, and a musician is all you're ever going to be.

Money is nice, but money isn't the driving force. Paul English explained it this way to a magazine interviewer one time: "Back home, if we ain't cold, we ain't wet and we ain't hungry, we classified it as a good time." Dad always claimed that as long as he got paid more than he could make picking cotton, he was ahead of the game.

I once asked him not long ago if he ever thought he'd be where he is today when he was a kid. He said, "Shoot, I never thought I'd be where I was twenty years ago when I was a kid."

Music had a hold of Dad and wouldn't let go. But he wasn't doing as well in Fort Worth as he had been before he left for the West Coast.

So we hit the road again.

☆ ☆ ☆ ☆

Our first stop was in Waco, but with there being five of us now, Mama and Daddy and us three kids, there just wasn't room at Nannie and Pa's house.

On top of the no-room problem, Dad was serious about wanting to make it in the music business and there just weren't enough contacts around Waco.

So we went to Houston. But we didn't have any money, as usual.

Dad did have his songs. And Mae Axton had given him about as strong a statement of encouragement as you could get.

One of the songs he had ready at this time was "Family Bible," which he dedicated to sweet Mama Nelson. It was a song inspired by the memory of Mama and Daddy Nelson studying the Bible by kerosene lantern light — when they weren't studying their music lessons from that mail-order school out of Chicago.

> I can see us sitting 'round the table
> When from the Family Bible Dad would read,
> And I can hear my mother softly singing
> Rock of Ages, Rock of Ages, cleft for me.

He had hoped that Frankie Miller, who was on the Starday label out of Nashville, would record the song, but Don Pierce, the man who ran Starday, wouldn't let him do it.

So Dad took his song to a musician he knew named Larry Butler, who headed a band that played at the Esquire Club on the Hempstead highway. Dad asked him for a job, but Larry said that he didn't need anyone at that time. Then Dad asked him if he wanted to buy songs, and he played him several.

Larry Butler wouldn't buy them. Not because they weren't good, but because they were too good. In fact, he was appalled at the idea that Dad would even think about selling his songs. If he needed the money that bad, Larry told Dad, he would loan him some.

And he did. And that was how we got the money for our apartment in Pasadena, just outside of Houston.

But kids need food to eat and milk to drink in Houston just like they do in Fort Worth. And apartments need the electricity and gas turned on and a phone put in if you want to be reached by people who might offer you a job. It wasn't long before Dad needed money again.

This time he ran into a guy he had known before named Paul Buskirk. Paul owned a recording studio, and Dad approached him to see if he wanted to buy any of his songs.

He did. He bought "Family Bible." Actually, three people — Paul, Walt Breeland, and Claude Grey — went in together. And Claude Grey recorded it. How much did Dad get? All of $50, that's how much.

As a number of people have observed, Dad may be one hell of a songwriter, and now a performer with unprecedented charisma, but he is definitely lacking in the business department. It seems like when the Lord was putting Dad together and He was going down the check-list, He must have said: Good Heart—OK. Musical Talent—Check. Sense of Humor—OK. But when He came to Business Acumen, He thought: Nope. Don't want to give the boy too much.

Paul English claims that he's learned an awful lot from Dad over the years, particularly about tolerance and how to be polite to the fans, but as he told an interviewer one time, "I never took any of his heed in business. I think that Willie's a lousy businessman."

He sure doesn't seem to be able to handle money. When he has some, he'll either spend it or give it away to someone who looks like he needs it more. Even when he was doing fairly well in Portland, with a radio show and regular gigs in the dance halls, we were always on the edge of being stone-broke. We could barely get back to Texas.

And then he followed the same pattern in Houston: $50 for "Family Bible." But there was some good that came out of it. Along with his recording studio, Paul Buskirk had a music school. And he hired Dad to teach guitar.

☆ ☆ ☆ ☆

There was only one problem. Dad didn't know how to read music.

Paul Buskirk said not to worry. He'd teach Dad himself.

Dad got his first lesson on a Wednesday and gave his first lesson that following Monday. Mama said that it drove her crazy, the five of us in that small apartment in Pasadena and Dad practicing every minute.

But it worked. Dad managed to stay one lesson ahead of his students. And they never could tell because Dad already was an excellent guitar player. He had just learned to play by ear and couldn't read music, that's all.

But he learned. They say that you learn more about a subject by teaching it than by being taught. So maybe learning to read music by being a music teacher was one of the ways Dad developed his ability to handle more complicated arrangements than a lot of country performers use.

Bit by bit Dad started getting established in Houston. He got a job as the Sunday morning sign-on DJ for KCRT radio (now KIKK).

A six-night-a-week job opened up at the Esquire Club, and he began recording for Pappy Dailey in Houston.

The first record he did for Pappy Dailey was a 45 with "The Storm Has Just Begun" on one side and "Man With the Blues" on the other. The label lists the artists as "Willie Nelson with the Reil Sisters."

The other 45 that he recorded for Pappy Dailey had "What a Way To Live" on one side and "Misery Mansion" on the other.

So things were on the upswing, at least to some extent. Dad had a DJ job, he was playing regularly, he had a fairly steady job teaching the guitar for Paul Buskirk's music school, he had recorded two 45s. And he was writing songs.

One of the songs that he wrote while we were living in Houston was a tune called "Night Life."

A magazine writer named Bob Allen once asked him if he remembered how he wrote any of his songs. Dad said yes, he remembered where he was and how he did it for a lot of them. And one of the ones he remembered was "Night Life."

"I wrote 'Night Life' while I was living in Houston, just before I went to Nashville," he said. "I was driving back and forth to Pasadena, over to a place across town called the Esquire Club. It was about a thirty-mile drive over there and I had plenty of time to think. So I wrote it on my way over there. I got there and tried to remember it through the evening. And then going home that night, I remembered it again, and I went home and wrote some more. When I got home, I finally got around to working it out and writing it down."

It's easy to understand how "Night Life" could come to him while he was driving to work six nights a week at the Esquire Club:

> When the evening sun goes down
> You will find me hangin' 'round;
> The night life ain't no good life,
> But it's my life.

One of the famous stories about Dad's lack of business acumen involves "Night Life." He sold it for $150.

☆ ☆ ☆ ☆

"Night Life" went on to be one of the most recorded songs in history. More than seventy artists, including Ray Price and B. B. King, have recorded it, selling a total of more than 30 million records.

Dad gave up the writer's royalties to "Night Life" to the three guys who paid for the recording session. But he had the record.

And when he got to Nashville, he had that to show people what he could do. In fact, in 1975, when Dad was a guest on Ralph Emery's radio show, he described going down to Ralph's late-night record show when he first got to Nashville—along with just about every other would be-picker and songwriter in Nashville—and being totally ignored by Ralph.

"You blew me off completely," Dad told him. "That's why I've hated you for years. But I had a copy of my record 'Night Life' right there in my chubby little fist."

☆ ☆ ☆ ☆

I don't know how long Dad had thought of going to Nashville. Maybe it dates back to that Vancouver interview of Mae Axton. Maybe even before that. Maybe even to the first time he heard Ernest Tubb on Mama Nelson's old Philco radio.

But it was becoming clear that the way he had been doing it wasn't getting him very far very fast. Even when he was working steadily, he seemed to go through money as if he would catch some deadly disease if he kept it too long.

Mama was giving him an earful of his shortcomings whenever he got home. That was a constant part of our homelife. I was eight years old before I knew that people's parents were supposed to get along.

Dad could see himself becoming a perpetually drunk, perpetually broke club singer. Always being pulled every which way between a bitching wife, hungry kids, teaching music, being a disc jockey. Barely hanging on and always one step away from having to sell Bibles, or vacuum cleaners, or even worse, encyclopedias.

I think that is what he had on his mind when he wrote "Night Life." The last verse says:

> Listen to the blues that they're playin'
> Listen to what the blues are sayin'
> My, it's just a scene
> From the world of broken dreams;
> The night life ain't no good life,
> But it's my life.

I think he felt that if he stayed in Houston and kept on the way he was going, he'd just be one more addition to the world of broken dreams. Because he couldn't quit. When you hear Dad sing that song, he always sings that last line, "But it's my life," with force and conviction—almost defiance. He was a musician, and that's all there was to that.

It was time, Dad probably thought, to go to the center of the action and be nothing but a singer and songwriter. No more teaching guitar. No more spinning records. Just head for the big time and do it until it worked.

Like I said, I don't know how long Dad had been thinking along these lines. But the manager of KCRT, a man named Larry Gloger, sped his thinking by firing Dad from the Sunday morning sign-on show.

I don't know why. It certainly wasn't a major blow as far as the family income was concerned. But Dad said that it hurt his ego, and that's why he left town.

Maybe he took it as a sign that now was the time for him to do what he had been thinking about for so long. It was time to go to Nashville and give it his best shot, no holds barred.

When I look back and try to imagine what it must have been like to do that, I think that it must have taken quite an act of faith.

But then, faith was one of the few things a Methodist boy raised by Mama Nelson in the Depression-era farming community of Abbott, Texas, would have plenty of.

☆ ☆ ☆ ☆

Dad took us to Nannie and Pa's in Waco. He told us he would send for us as soon as he could.

And then he pointed his second-, third-, or fourth-hand 1946 Buick northeast and drove to Nashville.

That firing by the station manager of KCRT may have been a sign after all, because that car didn't break down until it got inside the Nashville city limits.

SEVEN

Nashville

"Son, take this money ... and keep your song."

D ad tells a story about that old 1946 Buick. He was about three payments behind on it when he left Texas, and when he got to Nashville it just completely quit running. Dad called back to Texas to tell the dealer where the car was, and he found out that the car lot had gone out of business. "And so," he says, "the car just set there and settled into the earth and as far as I know, it's there still."

☆ ☆ ☆ ☆

Dad had come to Nashville to make it as a singer and songwriter or die trying. And from some of the stories I've heard, he came pretty close to the latter.

Back then, Nashville was already the most important center for country music. It wasn't anything like it is now, of course. In fact, when I interviewed people in Nashville who knew Dad, I was fascinated to hear about how different things used to be. There was a camaraderie among record producers of different labels that just isn't there now. The emphasis was on cutting singles, not albums, because, as Ralph Emery told me, jukeboxes kept country music alive. Record companies didn't promote artists with tours the way they do now, and of course the money was nowhere near the same. Back then, a big country hit sold three or four hundred thousand copies.

There was also a good side to the way things were different. If a company, or even a company's regional representative, liked a song, they would keep pitching it, trying to get it air-play, for six months, a year, or maybe even longer. Ralph told me he was married to Skeeter Davis when she cut "The End of the World," and it was out for nine months and sold just 80,000 before RCA started pushing it. The same

53

thing happened with Patsy Cline's release of the Harlan Howard-Hank Cochran hit "I Fall To Pieces." It was out for six months before anything started to happen. Today, if a record doesn't make a big move in three weeks, it disappears like it never happened.

The Nashville of the late fifties and early sixties may have been kind of amateurish by today's standards, but it was still the capital of country music. Oh, there was some country being recorded out in California around Bakersfield, and you could get records cut in Fort Worth, or Houston, or even Portland, Oregon. But Nashville was it. Nashville was the home of the Grand Ole Opry, which began broadcasting as the WSM Barn Dance in 1925. The Opry was a country institution, and it still is today.

☆ ☆ ☆ ☆

Dad wasn't the only would-be picker in the world who had figured out that Nashville was the place to be if you wanted to make it in country music. The town, or at least the part of the town that figured in the music business, was literally crawling with men and women who had come from all over the South and West to try to make it big. And the place that most of them congregated was at Tootsie's Orchid Lounge.

Tootsie's was just a beer joint. But the thing that made it more than just another beer joint was that it was across the alley from Ryman Auditorium, home of the Opry.

The Opry had virtually no backstage area, dressing rooms, or air conditioning. Moreover, the Opry format involved having each singer or group do no more than two or three numbers and then not re-appear for an hour or two. This meant that there was a lot of time to kill. And what better way to kill it than by grabbing a few cool beers, or maybe something stronger, with your friends while you waited?

Fans, as well as hopeful artists and writers, knew this. So they would all gather at Tootsie's as a way to make contact with established performers, or record producers, or promoters. Tootsie's developed into the informal headquarters of the music business in Nashville.

The place had a back room, and it was there that songwriters and musicians showed their stuff. They would stay there until two o'clock closing, when Tootsie would sweep the beer bottles off the tables and stick you with her big hat pin if you gave her any lip. Some guys would just leave their instruments and amps set up in that back room.

And then everybody would usually go down to Ralph Emery's all-night radio show on WSM and watch him spin records in the hopes that maybe they'd get interviewed, or one of their demos would get played, or at least they could talk to others in the same boat and maybe learn something that could help them out further down the line. Maybe someone would have a bottle and they could go up to his room and spend the night singing songs to each other.

That's the way you paid your dues and got into the music business then.

Dad fit right in. After all, hadn't he just written a song that he hoped would tell the world that the night life was his life? The people Dad met and hung out with back then read like a country music honor roll: Hank Cochran, Mel Tillis, Harlan Howard, Roger Miller, Billy Walker, Ray Price, Faron Young, Marty Robbins, Grady Martin, Boots Randolph...and on and on.

It was hard to break in, though. There was an establishment in Nashville then, just like there is now, and there were sure a lot of people who didn't know where their next meal was coming from. For a while, Dad was among them. As he told an interviewer not long ago:

> Sometimes I get to thinking back about my early days when I was scratching to make ends meet. There were days I would start out trying to peddle my songs without a penny in my pocket. I mean I was flat broke.
>
> I would go into Tootsie's to see if anyone was in there who might be interested in my songs. I would be so hungry my stomach would be growling. When the waitress would ask me for an order, I would have to fake it because I was broke.
>
> I would tell her I was waiting for someone else and would order when he got there.

☆ ☆ ☆ ☆

One of the first people that Dad met when he came to town was Billy Walker—"The Traveling Texan," the same Billy Walker we had stayed with in Missouri, on our way back from Oregon.

Billy had moved from the Ozark Jubilee to the Opry and he was also recording for Starday — the label Dad had hoped would let Frankie Miller record "Family Bible."

Billy tried to get Dad on as a staff writer at Starday. But Don Pierce, the owner, didn't like the songwriter any better than he had liked the song.

According to Wesley Rose, who ran his father's publishing company, Acuff-Rose (the company that signed Hank Williams when he got to town just after World War II), Dad once sang "Hello Walls" to somebody and asked him if he thought he should pitch it to Mr. Rose. "Hell no," was the answer. The funny thing, according to Mr. Rose, was that he met Willie after Faron Young had cut the song, because he wanted to meet the man who had written it.

As with most things in this life, Dad went through a lot of might-of-beens and if-onlys, both on his part and on the part of a lot of record producers and recording artists. I'm sure that just about everybody else who was in Nashville during those days has a whole lot of if-onlys to tell about too.

But it wasn't all missed opportunity.

☆ ☆ ☆ ☆

One night Dad was at Tootsie's. Naturally. And just as naturally, there were a bunch of songwriters in the back room taking turns playing. In walked Hank Cochran, the songwriter who had just written "I Fall To Pieces" with Harlan Howard.

Hank was regarded as one of the best songwriters and *the* best song pitcher in Nashville, whether it was his material or someone else's.

A few guys got up in order to let Hank sit down. And some of them left because they couldn't stand the competition. At least, that's the way I was told the story. But Dad, being the new boy in town, didn't know who the hell Hank Cochran was, so he just kept his seat and waited until his turn with the guitar came.

His turn came pretty quick, because most of the folks in the circle had already sung a few tunes and were glad to let somebody else have the limelight now that Hank was there. Dad took the guitar and started playing. And he kept on and on. Some things never change. Once Dad takes the stage, it's hard to get him to stop singing.

Anyway, he sang a bunch of his songs, like "Touch Me," "Night Life," and "Funny How Time Slips Away."

After he finally finished, Hank Cochran introduced himself and complimented him on his songs.

"How would you like a writing contract with a publishing company?" asked Hank.

Dad would like that just fine, thank you.

"Well, you come on with me tomorrow," Hank told Dad.

At this time, Hank was the premier songwriter and pitchman for Pamper Music Company, a publishing company that had its offices in Goodlettsville, about twenty miles north of Nashville.

Hal Smith, the owner of Pamper, had heard of Dad already. Word about this new guy in town had spread quickly. It's funny, but everybody I talked to said they all knew that Dad was a great talent the minute they heard him. The songwriters and artists loved his songs, and most of the musicians really enjoyed his singing. In fact, it's hard to find anybody who didn't immediately fall in love with his singing.

The problem, they all say, was that they didn't know if he was commercial. He was ahead of his time. The record companies were scared to put any effort behind him.

Hank drove Dad up to Goodlettsville to play for Hal Smith, then Hank took Dad home and went back to get the verdict. Was Dad in or not?

Hal sadly began to explain to Hank that he loved Dad's music and he thought that he was a wonderful talent—but he just couldn't hire him. The budget wouldn't stand it. Hal had just doubled Hank's salary with a $50-a-week raise (this was his weekly draw against future royalties) and there just wasn't any more to go around.

Hank sat there and thought for a bit, not saying a word. Then he asked Hal if he gave up his $50 raise would he have enough money to hire Dad?

Hal smiled and said, "Sure Hank, if you're willing to do it."

So that's what they did. And that's the way Hank told me the story.

Dad was waiting for the word in a broken-down, three-room trailer on the wrong side of the tracks in Nashville.

Mama and we three kids had arrived from Waco by this time, and Mama was holding down two jobs waiting tables—one during the day and working at Tootsie's at night.

The name of the place was Dunn's Trailer Park. The little cracker box cost $25 a week, but Dad always said that $3 a week was more than it was worth. There was a sign out in front that said "Trailers, For Sale or Rent," and if that sounds familiar, it's because Roger Miller used those words in his hit "King of the Road."

Coincidentally, it was also the same trailer that Hank and his wife had lived in when they first came to Nashville. So Hank didn't have any trouble finding his way when he drove back from Pamper to tell Dad the good news.

And it was real good news, the first truly good news Dad had had while trying to make it in the music business. Mama told me she cried and cried because she was so happy for him. Dad cried because it looked like all of his scrambling and dragging us around the country, never knowing if he could buy us enough gas to get to our destination, was going to pay off. Hank cried because Mama and Dad were crying.

I don't remember, but I'll bet all three of us kids cried too.

So Mama and Hank and Dad headed off to Tootsie's to spread the good news and maybe get in a little celebrating.

But it wasn't too long before reality set in.

The salary was better than nothing, but it wasn't like bringing in an oil well. Mama was still going to have to work.

☆ ☆ ☆ ☆

Mama continued to work at Tootsie's and Dad went to work for Pamper, writing songs and cutting demos.

A lot of record producers I talked to said that Dad's demos were some of the best of his recordings they had ever heard. It would usually be just Dad and his guitar, maybe with a bass or a drummer. In fact, Fred Foster of Monument Records said that the reason Dad finally made it big is because he started cutting records that sounded like his demos from the old days.

Dad wrote a lot of his songs in a garage on the Pamper property in Goodlettsville. According to him, "There was a door, a window, and a guitar, and that was about it." They were out there one day, and Dad started talking to the walls. He called Hank over to help him but Hank had to answer a phone call. By the time Hank got back, Dad had written all of the lyrics to "Hello Walls" on a piece of cardboard.

The story goes that a few nights later, Hank and Dad were down at Tootsie's back room and Faron Young was there. Hank asked Dad to play "Hello Walls," and Faron liked it a lot.

By this time, Dad had also gotten a job with the Bobby Sykes band, and they were playing around the general Nashville area. One night, not long after the time he had sung "Hello Walls" with Faron in the room, they were on the same show with him.

Faron asked Dad to teach him that song he liked so well. So Dad taught Faron "Hello Walls" and another called "Congratulations." And

Faron went into the studio the next week and cut the two singles back-to-back.

Things were moving pretty fast. Patsy Cline recorded "Crazy," Billy Walker recorded "Funny How Time Slips Away," which Dad had written especially for him, and Ray Price recorded "Night Life." All four made the country Top 20 in 1961, and "Crazy" and "Hello Walls" also made the pop Top 20. "Hello Walls" sold two million copies before it was all over.

☆ ☆ ☆ ☆

Country music likes to parody a lot of its best songs, and with "Hello Walls" a big hit, it became fair game. It's an easy song to make fun of, and Dad always says that he has a series of house songs ready. Things like "Hello Roof" and "Hello Car."

But the song that made it onto a record was called "Hello Fool," and Ralph Emery was the man who recorded it. An announcer at the Opry during those days, Ralph came out of the Opry house one day and ran into Hank Cochran standing there with a little guy next to him. He had the lyrics to "Hello Fool" written down on a paper sack.

Ralph took it to Joe Allison of Liberty Records and Joe said, "Let's do it." It went to number four on the *Billboard* country charts and Ralph thought, "Hell. This is easy." He thought he had a new career. But he hasn't had a hit since.

Joe later told Ralph that he was going to sign Dad to a recording contract. Ralph had heard Dad sing on the Opry, and he joined Lorraine as one of the few people who didn't think he could sing.

But Joe ignored Ralph's opinion and signed Dad anyway. Ralph now says that Joe was right, that some of Dad's best records were done by Liberty. But he likes to point out that he signed with Liberty first. (Dad later had two Top-10 hits with Liberty: "Willingly" and "Touch Me.")

Not long after "Crazy" and "Hello Walls" were recorded, but before they started to really move, Dad heard that Ray Price's bass man, Donny Young—now known as Johnny Paycheck of "Take This Job and Shove It" fame—had quit.

Dad didn't know how to play bass. But then, he didn't know how to be a DJ either. So just as he did with Dr. Parker in Pleasanton, he told Ray that he could play and then went out and got a bass and learned real quick. "If he ever knew I didn't know how to play," says Dad, "he was kind enough not to mention it."

☆ ☆ ☆ ☆

So there we were. Mama was working at Tootsie's and around. Now Dad was on the road with Ray Price and the Cherokee Cowboys, making $25 a night.

But things were piling up. Late in the year, after "Hello Walls," "Congratulations," and "Crazy" had really started to hit, Dad got back into town and found a mountain of bills, the car needing work, and very little food in the house.

He went down to Tootsie's to hunt up Faron Young. He found him and asked him if he wanted to buy the writer's interest in "Hello Walls" for $1,500.

"No, Willie," he answered, "I'm not going to take advantage of a little young boy like you by buying your song. I just got a check from Capitol for a lot of money, and I know you're fixin' to get one too."

Dad told him that he needed the money now.

"How much do you need to get you through this rough piece you're going through?"

"$500."

Faron reached into his pocket and peeled off five $100 bills and gave them to Dad. Faron told him, "Son, take this money and go feed your family and pay your bills and keep your song."

And Dad did.

About a month later, Dad was back off the road again and Faron was back sitting in Tootsie's again.

All of a sudden, Dad came running into the room like a rocket. He grabbed Faron and kissed him right on the mouth. And he gave him his $500 back.

Dad had gotten his first royalty check for "Hello Walls." It was for $3,000. And it was the biggest chunk of money he'd ever seen at one time in his life.

☆ ☆ ☆ ☆

Nineteen sixty-one had been quite a year. Dad went from being so broke that he couldn't manage to buy a cup of coffee and a doughnut, to bringing home a six-figure income.

He got to spending it in wild and crazy ways. He was still fronting Ray Price's band for about $25 a night, for instance, but he would go from gig to gig by airplane and stay in penthouses. This was while the boss, Ray Price, one of the biggest stars of country music at the time, was riding on the bus with the band.

He did do things for us and Mama, though. One of the first things he did after the money started coming in was buy Mama a new car. He bought it with his first check for "Hello Walls."

Actually, it was a used car. But it was a Cadillac. It was Ray Price's 1959 Cadillac. Black, with those big fishtail fins.

Mama would get drunk and drive that car like a bat out of hell all over the place. It was a wonder she didn't get killed.

It's a wonder we all pulled through. Because while Dad's career was taking off, our family was falling apart. Mama continued to work at Tootsie's, and she started drinking. Not only that—Mama started to meet some friendly folks. And Dad was gone more and more.

Things started to fall apart for real the minute we hit Nashville.

☆

EIGHT

Things fall to pieces

"You dream about me and I'll dream about you."

We arrived in Nashville in the wintertime and moved into that ugly green crackerbox trailer at Dunn's Trailer Park.

I remember that it snowed. That was the first time I remember seeing snow, although Nannie always told me that there was snow on the ground when Mama and Dad brought me home from the hospital after I was born.

I don't remember this, but Mama always told me a story that Dad came home drunk one night and it was snowing, and Dad lay down and rolled around on the ground, hollering "Snow, snow, sno-oo-oow" loud enough for everybody to hear.

They probably didn't worry about it much, though. They were used to crazies around there. Just another fool picker from Texas.

☆ ☆ ☆ ☆

With Dad putting all of his time into pitching songs and trying to break into the music business, Mama had to work two jobs. She had a day job at the Wagon Wheel, a down-and-out kind of bar on Broadway across the street from Tootsie's. And nights she worked at Tootsie's.

Dad was doing his "contacting" at Tootsie's back room, Ralph Emery's late-night record show, and other places around town.

Mama wanted Dad to make it, of course, and she would do her best to pitch his songs too. But it was mainly Dad who did it, who kept at it until people like Faron Young heard his material and folks like Hank Cochran went to bat for him.

A lot of times, of course, Dad would be singing in Tootsie's back room while Mama would be waiting tables in the front.

A little later, after Dad had signed with Pamper and was working with Ray Price, we had a live-in babysitter and housekeeper named Sue. She was a Tootsie's regular, and she and Mama got to be good friends.

Sue told me that she was in Tootsie's one night and heard this guy she had never seen before singing a song called "Darkness on the Face of the Earth."

"I've got to tell Dynamite," that was her name for Mama, "I've got to tell Dynamite about this."

So she went into the front and found Mama and said, "Dynamite, you've got to hear this. There's some fool in there singing about the sun being scattered all over the ground."

Mama laughed. "Honey, that's my old man."

☆ ☆ ☆ ☆

Just because Mama wanted Dad to make good didn't mean she had a whole lot of patience with him staying out late—sometimes for days at a time—and coming home drunk. Not while she was holding down two jobs and caring for three kids.

And Mama wasn't one with a whole lot of patience. She didn't have any inhibitions about telling you just what she thought, either.

The situation was ripe for marital friction. So Mama and Dad started fighting. And some of those set-tos have become legends.

Probably the most famous of the fights that Mama and Dad had was the one about the sheet.

The story goes that Dad came in drunk after a couple of days straight out on the circuit "contacting." After he passed out on the bed, Mama, so the story goes, sewed him up in the sheet and then worked him over with a broom handle.

Most of that's true. Except for the fact that she tied instead of sewed him up—took all four corners and tied them in a knot. She then took us kids and all of Dad's clothes and left him there, naked, with no telephone and too shy to go up to the neighbors in the buff. Left him and didn't come back for four days.

Another legendary fight had Dad sitting at the breakfast table nursing a monumental hangover when Mama got so mad that she threw a fork at him. It hit him in the side and stuck there, quivering like a tuning fork. That's Mama's idea of working things out. Her way or the highway.

Isn't it always ironic that when people have hard times together, and then start to make headway, to see some glimmerings of light at the end of the tunnel, the wheels start to come off the wagon?

That's what was happening to Mama and Dad. Just when things were finally falling in place for him, things started falling apart at home.

One day Dad came home drunk after being gone for days, and Mama was really hot. She waited until he undressed and climbed into bed. Then she got a butcher knife, turned on the lights, and let out a yell.

Dad sat bolt upright in bed and saw his ever-loving Martha, the hot-blooded Cherokee squaw, holding a butcher knife and coming at him with a look that gave every indication she was going to separate him from his red hair.

Dad had seen that look before. He yelled for her to put down the knife, and he kept yelling as he made it through the door and over to the graveyard next door, with Mama in hot pursuit.

It must have been quite a sight. Dad, naked, running through the graveyard and jumping all the white headstones neatly lined up in a row, like a man jumping hurdles in hell. I'll bet he never thought he'd run a race like that when he was on the Abbott High track team.

Mama still laughs to this day when she tells that story. "If you could have just seen your dad running through that graveyard naked. He was so scared and he ran so fast."

Mama finally put the knife down and managed to get Dad home. But Dad wasn't laughing. The next day he was gone again.

☆ ☆ ☆ ☆

That's Dad's way. When things get too hot, he just disappears. He doesn't like confrontations.

Maybe it's because he knows he has a real bad temper and he's afraid of what he might do if he stayed around and tried to deal with the situation. Maybe it's because he knows that he's in the wrong, at least part way, but he knows he's got to keep on that way to get where he wants to go.

I don't know why it is. But a lot of times when I was growing up, I sure wished he would have stayed around and taken charge, set things right.

I am sure that Dad never did anything out of meanness. He never wanted to hurt anybody. I don't think he has a malicious bone in his body.

Dad is a shy and agreeable person. He can't say no, and he'll go along with just about whatever anybody wants—just as long as it doesn't interfere with his music.

Charlie Williams, a former Fort Worth disc jockey who knew Dad well back then, told me a story that shows what I mean. It happened about the time Dad was cutting his first album for Liberty.

He and Roger Miller and Molly Bee went over to Charlie's house. Roger was head over heels in love with Molly, but she had her eye set on Dad. As the evening progressed and folks had a few drinks, Roger called Dad into the kitchen and told him, "That girl, all she does is look at you. Why don't you take her home?"

"Okay," said Dad.

After a bit, Roger called Dad back into the kitchen and said, "Willie, I don't want you to take her home. I'm in love with her."

"Okay," said Dad.

According to Charlie, that happened nine different times through the course of the evening. And all Dad ever said to Roger, who was bouncing back and forth like a ping-pong ball, was "Okay."

That's a basic part of the way Dad is. Whatever suits you plumb tickles him to death. As long as you don't get in the way of his music.

I have always thought that there were two things going on that had Dad carousing the way he did. One was that it was the accepted way to make yourself known in the Nashville music circles those days. Hanging out with other songwriters was what Dad had to do. The other is that Dad was so agreeable that if someone said, let's go to Hank's house and pick some more, or let's go see what Ralph's doing on the radio, Dad would just say "Okay."

But there was one other reason: Mama was no prize herself.

☆ ☆ ☆ ☆

Mama was beautiful.

Sue, the woman who ended up keeping house and babysitting for us, used to call her "blanket ass" and tease her about being pigeon-toed and having skinny legs.

But Mama was beautiful. She had an outgoing personality, and the men were all crazy about her. A stranger was just a friend that hadn't met her yet, as far as Mama was concerned. A true extrovert.

Of course, looking the way she did and being as friendly as she was—she could charm the pants right off of anybody—it was natural that she didn't get along with any of the other girls she worked with. She was too pretty, too dynamic, and they couldn't stand the competition. And it was just as natural that anybody who looked and acted the way Mama did in a beer joint was going to get hit on.

I imagine that Mama spent most of her working time flirting with the customers and trying to keep it from going too far. One of her earlier conquests when she first started working at Tootsie's was Roger Miller.

Poor Roger. He got a crush on Mama and tried his best to get her to come home with him. When he found out that he'd been putting the make on his friend Willie Nelson's wife, he was overcome with remorse and wrote a song, "Sorry, Willie," in apology.

Of course, Mama wasn't the one to tell him who she was.

As things got worse between Mama and Dad, and Dad spent more and more time on the road with Ray Price, she'd stay awhile after work and have a drink or several. And, as Sue said, "Other people took advantage of her weaknesses."

☆ ☆ ☆ ☆

But before things between Mama and Dad got damaged beyond repair, we moved out to a nice red brick house out in Goodlettsville near the Pamper offices.

Sue had kept house and taken care of us kids before, and Mama kept after her to come live with us. Finally, Sue said she would.

She came out and took one look at the trailer and said that if we wanted her to stay, we were going to have to get out of that cracker box. Sue looked in the paper and found an ad for a partially furnished house for rent at $85 a month.

"I had $85," Sue told me, "so I told Willie, 'Let's go.'"

And that's how we got to the nicest house we had lived in up until then.

When I talked with Sue recently, she filled me in on a lot of things that I only had vague memories of.

"What were we like back then?" I asked her.

"Lana was smart, smart, smart. Martha was always talking about how smart Lana was, and when I moved in, I found out she was right."

Lana would come home from second grade, have a snack, and change out of her good clothes.

"Then she'd ask me if there was anything I wanted her to do," Sue remembered. "If there wasn't, she'd go outside and play for a little bit. Then she'd come in and set the table for dinner and then go off and read, or sit at the table and talk with me. She knew all about the stock market and would talk about that day's quotations. Not bad for a girl that was seven going on eight."

"What about Billy and me?"

"You were just little tykes. I remember that you were trying to teach Billy how to talk, not that you could talk worth a durn yourself. You and Billy were always playing. And you'd watch TV. I remember one commercial, it was for the Dutch Maid laundry, and they had these kids all in a big wooden shoe. No matter where you or Billy were or what you were doing, if you heard that commercial you would come running to watch it."

The house was on a little winding road without much traffic. We loved to go for walks with Sue, down the road to the end where there was a little church and a cemetery. We'd have some very important conversations on the way. Sue would ask us where God lived. I always had to answer first, of course. "God lives in Florida."

Lana would just roll her eyes in disgust. But as far as I know, Billy still thinks God lives in Florida.

Easter Sunday fell not long after we moved out there, and that afternoon Dad and Hank and Harlan Howard decided to fly kites.

"They got these spools of crocheting thread, 650 yards to the spool, and used that for the kite strings. Those kites went so high they went plumb out of sight. There were these fools out in the yard flying kites they couldn't even see."

We had a dog, a white Samoyed we called Eskimo. We'd gotten him at the Humane Society. Eskimo would lie there in his cage and constantly move his right paw. It was a nervous tic, probably the result of getting hit by a car or something. But Billy thought he was trying to shake hands.

That dog took care of us. If we were walking down the road to play in the cemetery and a car came along, Eskimo would get between us and the car and herd us over to the side of the road. He'd do the same thing if we were out playing in the yard and a car passed by. He'd just get between us and the road and make sure that nothing happened.

When everything went to pieces and we had to leave Nashville, Mama gave Eskimo to Tootsie.

☆ ☆ ☆ ☆

Dad was on the road a lot, and I was getting to be a real little troublemaker.

One time when he'd just gotten back from a road trip and was sleeping in the back bedroom, Sue was in the living room combing Lana's hair. I was busy teasing and bothering Lana, trying to get attention, I guess. Sue kept telling me not to bother Lana and to let her finish. She would tell me to leave the room and I would, then a minute later I'd be back in aggravating Lana again.

Finally, Sue had had enough and she smacked me on the bottom. I screamed like I'd been shot.

That woke Dad up and he came out and told Sue, "Now Sue, when I'm home, *I'll* correct the children."

We always loved it when Dad came home. He always brought us presents, and we would fight for our turn to talk with him and sit on his lap. But we knew it couldn't last, that he'd have to get back on the bus.

One time we drove Dad out to Hendersonville so that he could get on the road for thirty days or so. As he climbed aboard the bus, carrying his suitcase and guitar, I hollered at him, "You dream about me, Daddy, and I'll dream about you."

When he got back from that trip, he came in at about 5:30 in the morning. Sue, always an early riser, was already up, drinking her coffee.

According to Sue, Dad looked like hell.

"How long have you been up?" Sue asked him.

"Three days. At least," answered Dad. "I had to finish a song."

That's how he wrote "You Dream About Me."

We all liked living in the brick house near Goodlettsville.

But there were signs that told us things weren't going right.

☆ ☆ ☆ ☆

One time, Bobby Sykes, the leader of the first group Dad had played with when he first got to town, had been out to the house for a picking session and stayed the night. He also stayed the next day.

Sue was spending time with him, giving him a manicure and whatnot, and Billy had a jealous fit. He cried all day.

Finally, Mama got home from work and Bobby took Sue out for a night on the town. But they had barely finished their first beer at Tootsie's when there was a call for Sue. It was Mama.

"You've got to come home right now," Mama told her.

"What's wrong?"

"It's Billy. I can't get him to stop crying. I'm afraid he's going to make himself sick."

"Well, he's been crying all day," Sue said. "I guess you'd better send someone down to get me. Or do you want me to have Bobby bring me back?"

"Don't you *ever* bring Bobby back to this house," Mama told her.

The main thing I remember about those days was that Mama and Dad were gone a lot. Even when Dad was home off the road they didn't hang out together very much. Of course, Mama had to work and Dad would want to rest, but they also just weren't getting along.

When they would go out together, they would always get into it. Once they were having dinner at some friend's house, it might have been the Cochrans, and Mama dumped her whole plate of food — mashed potatoes, gravy, and all — on Dad's head.

Like Mel Tillis, who was a Tootsie's regular in those days, told me, "If your mama had been one of those muscle-building ladies like they got now, your daddy would have been a dead man."

Sue told me that she had never seen Dad hit Mama, although she'd seen Mama hit him plenty of times. But she did say that one time Mama came home without Dad and she was all beat up.

"Somebody had just stomped the teewatty out of her. I never knew what had happened, but Martha said that Willie had done it."

The marriage was rolling downhill, picking up speed for a smash-up.

☆ ☆ ☆ ☆

Dad pretty much quit coming home. For all practical purposes, he and Mama were separated.

But Dad doesn't give up things very easily. Believe it or not, he doesn't like change. Dad tries to stay until the bitter end, until there's nothing left.

And one time, just when he was about to leave town with Ray Price again, he decided to stop by Tootsie's and see Mama one more time. He got Hank to go along with him. Hank would stick with Dad no matter what.

Mom, as everybody called Tootsie, greeted them at the door and congratulated Dad for all the success his songs were having.

Things went rapidly downhill from there.

They started upstairs to look for Mama, and just as they got to the top, they saw Mama charming a table full of thirsty men.

When she heard the familiar voice and saw Dad and Hank, all hell broke loose.

Mama reached for any and every thing handy as Hank and Dad backed down the stairs under a hailstorm of glasses and beer bottles.

They ended up at the bar. What do you do at a bar? Have a drink. Of course. So Dad ordered a beer. Meanwhile, Mama was running around upstairs collecting more ammunition, all the empty glasses she could carry, and she returned to the top of the stairs. She started cussing him out every which way, telling him to get his sorry ass out of Tootsie's and out of Nashville and not to come back.

Dad had fire in his eyes, Hank tells me, but in his usual quiet way all he said was, "Let's talk."

Hank meanwhile was tugging on Dad's arm. "Let's go, Willie. She's hot." And he tried to pull Dad out the door.

But Dad wouldn't budge. And Mama wouldn't stop throwing glasses.

Dad started trying to catch the glasses that Mama was throwing. Meanwhile, everybody downstairs in Tootsie's split the scene to watch the action from the safety of the sidewalk.

Finally, a glass ricocheted off the wall and hit Hank in the face, almost cutting his chin off. Blood was everywhere. Hank was moaning with pain and trying to keep the gash closed with his hands. He grabbed Dad by the nape of the neck with one hand and pulled him outside.

"I told you she was crazy. But you just won't listen."

Dad took Hank to the emergency room. The doctor on duty was a young intern who looked barely old enough to be out of high school.

Dad was not confident that this guy could handle the job, so he began questioning him.

"Are you old enough to be doing this sort of thing?" Dad asked.

"Yes, sir . . ."

Totally obnoxious, Dad interrupted him. "Do you have your diploma, boy?"

The intern was hot now, but still professional. "Yes, sir."

"Do you know who this is that you're about to begin work on?" Dad continued.

The young doctor, who had been putting on his sterilized gown and trying to examine Hank, was still professional. "Yes, sir."

Dad wasn't listening. "This is the great Hank Cochran. The man who wrote, 'Make the World Go Away,' 'Little Bitty Tear,' 'I Fall To Pieces.' His face is his life and . . ."

All the while Hank was lying on the table still trying to hold his chin together, with blood just pouring through his fingers. He'd had enough.

"Shut the fuck up, Willie!" he yelled, "Goddammit, I'm bleeding to death!"

Dad let the doctor sew up Hank's chin. By the time they got out of the hospital, Dad was really mad.

"I'm going back over there and shoot the place up."

Hank looked at Dad and said, "Well, Willie, that's just wonderful. But do you mind dropping me off at home first?"

I guess Dad cooled down and found Ray Price and the bus.

Mama was holding court in Tootsie's, a victorious Amazon queen receiving the adulation of her admiring courtiers.

Lana and Billy and I were back home watching the "Ed Sullivan Show" with Nannie and Pa (who had come up from Waco to stay with us) and having a Sunday night treat of ice cream.

Suddenly, a news brief interrupted the show: "Tootsie's Raided." The news camera focused on Tootsie's front door. And who should show up as big as life but Mama herself, along with Tootsie and a few others being herded into the paddy wagon.

Nannie jumped up to turn up the volume and started yelling at Pa.

"My Lord, W.T. Look at what your wonderful daughter has got herself into now!"

That was Nannie's favorite expression when something out of the ordinary happened—which around our house in those days was just about all the time.

Pa got dressed immediately and went downtown to try to bail Mama out. But he couldn't find her.

A day or so later, in walked Mama and two girlfriends, looking as though she had been on a world-record drunk. Nannie began questioning her about where she'd been and what had happened.

Mama started yelling back, cussing Nannie out for even thinking that she had been involved in the raid.

But in walked Billy. "Hi, Mama," he laughed, "You sure looked funny on TV."

Mama's mouth snapped shut. She'd been caught good and proper, and she knew it. She turned and marched down the hall without saying a word and shut the door to her bedroom.

And things just continued to get worse.

☆

NINE

Where did everybody go?

"I always try to give her what she wants, and she wants a divorce."

After the fight at Tootsie's, things just got worse and worse.

Mama had asked Nannie and Pa to stay and help out, to give her some moral support, I guess. She was running around town in that big, black Cadillac that Dad had bought for her from Ray Price.

And she was running around, period. As Mama says, what's good for the goose is good for the gander.

☆ ☆ ☆ ☆

Mama always had been a party girl. With the way things were between her and Dad, she was partying with a vengeance now.

But as Sue, who was still with us, told me, she never had a wreck and she always made it home. It might be daylight, but she'd get there. And if she was too drunk to drive, she'd get somebody to either drive her home in the car or bring her home in theirs.

Dad was on the road a lot now, and when he came home now it was just to visit for a few hours while Mama was at work.

Of course, we were always excited when Dad came to visit. We were so glad to see him, Nannie said we wouldn't even let him sit down. Of course, he'd always bring us presents and we couldn't wait to open them and see what they were.

And then while we were playing with our new toys, Dad and Nannie and Pa would talk. Nannie and Pa always loved Dad no matter what. After all, they knew their daughter — and that it took two to tangle.

So we would play and Dad would eat his favorite beans and corn bread that Pa had fixed. Dad would explain that he loved Mama, but they were two different people and they couldn't get along any more. He would ask them to take care of us, and ask if there was anything they needed. And then he would tell them who to call, and how to get in touch with him, and where he was going to be as best he knew.

But then it would be time to leave. We would gather around him, and he would explain to us how it was time for him to go back to work. All three of us would talk at once, each doing our best to get his attention and tell all the important things we had on our minds.

Dad would listen to each of us patiently. We'd kiss him and hug him and tell him how much we loved him. He would hold us, wrap his arms around all three of us together. And then he would say, "Your great-big-fat-ugly Daddy loves you with all his heart."

Then we would hear the bus pull up in the driveway and we'd know it was time for him to go.

Lana and Billy and I would walk with him all the way to the bus door, with Nannie trailing right behind. The door would swing open, and we would start to cry. And Dad would start to cry. He would hug so tight I couldn't breath, but it was okay, I wanted him to never let go. As we all cried, he would look at Nannie for help, with the tears just streaming down his face.

Then he'd say that he'd be back soon and he would have a present for each of us when he came. That would get our attention and break the spell for a moment. Then Nannie would take hold of our hands, and Dad would stand on the bus steps and look back at us. He wouldn't say anything, just stand there and wave and cry.

And then the door would shut and the bus would start to move.

The three of us would stand there with Nannie in the driveway and watch the bus as long as we could, until it was out of sight.

☆ ☆ ☆ ☆

Sue left too.

It wasn't too long after Nannie and Pa had come up to stay with us.

She had gone to spend a few days with some friends, to take a little break from all the craziness going on around the house, I guess. Anyway, Mama didn't approve of the people she had gone to visit. She called Sue up and told her to come get her things.

Mama could be mean and ugly. She had packed all of Sue's stuff up and put it in the old Studebaker out in the yard. She wouldn't even let Sue come into the house and say goodbye.

So with Sue gone, that left Nannie and Pa to take care of us while Mama worked, just like they had in Portland and again in Waco when Dad had first come to Nashville.

Just like before, Pa did the cooking and Nannie cleaned the house. I asked Nannie why Pa did all the cooking and she said, "Because your grandpa cooks the best and I'm the oldest." At the time that seemed to me to be a pretty good answer. Being three years younger than Lana, I knew all about the privileges that went with being the oldest.

Speaking about cooking, I remember one really funny thing that happened.

We had a bird named Oscar which we all three loved. Pa had taught Oscar how to say "Hello Walls," Daddy's first big hit, and how to say Pa's two favorite words, "Oh shit."

When Pa would come in from work, the first thing he would do was take off his shirt, the second thing was get a Pearl out of the refrigerator, and the third thing was to let Oscar out of his cage. Oscar would settle down on Pa's head and ride around while Pa cooked dinner.

One day Oscar was riding on Pa's head while he did what he did best, which was cook dinner. All of a sudden we heard Pa let out a yell, "Oh shit!"

"Oh shit!" Oscar yelled back.

We didn't think anything about it. That was just Pa and Oscar having their usual conversation.

But Pa kept on yelling. So we went in to see what was going on. Pa had ahold of a dish towel and was trying to swish Oscar out of his hair. Shit was running down Pa's head into his ears and all. Pa was swishing and screaming, and Oscar was shitting and hanging on for dear life.

"Etta! Etta! Come here! This goddamn bird has just shit on my head."

But Nannie couldn't hear because she was outside hanging clothes on the line. Lana was at the dinner table doing her homework like she always did at that time of day. She saw what was going on and broke up in helpless laughter. Billy and I just stood there, halfway in shock and halfway giggling. We didn't know what was going on, but we sure knew it wasn't like anything we had ever seen before — Pa looking helplessly out of the window waiting for Nannie to come in.

☆ ☆ ☆ ☆

Oscar may have been making a prediction. Because things for us started to go to shit in a hurry.

It was somewhere around this time that Mama got word that Dad was going with a lady out in California. The lady's name was Shirley Collie.

Dad was touring on the West Coast with Ray Price, which was convenient for Dad because his record label, Liberty, had a studio in California. Shirley also recorded for Liberty and had heard a bunch of Dad's demo tapes.

Hank Cochran, a friend of Shirley's, was in California at this time. He asked her out to lunch and then mentioned that he would like to drop in on a friend who was recording that day. They went by the Liberty studio, and there was Dad sitting on a stool in a sound room, recording "Mr. Record Man."

"Oh my God," thought Shirley. "That's the same guy I heard on the tapes. He is fantastic."

"Who is that?" she asked Hank.

"Nobody important," said Hank. "Let's go to lunch."

Hank must have seen her reaction and, having his own reasons for inviting Shirley to lunch, figured he had better get her the hell out of there.

Shirley was a singer and yodeler and had been married to Biff Collie for about five years. Biff was originally from San Antonio, but at the time he was a successful disc jockey and had a local TV show.

One Saturday night Biff was working as an announcer at a big country and western dance hall in the Long Beach area, and Shirley went along. Biff introduced her to the Ray Price band just before they went on, and Shirley watched the show from the corner of the stage just behind the curtain.

As Shirley describes it, she was looking out over the band and listening to the music.

"They were good, just so good," she says.

Ray was singing, but gradually her field of vision narrowed down to the red-headed bass player in a green rhinestone Nudie suit. When his turn to sing came, he sang "Busted" and "San Antonio Rose."

And she thought, "He is the greatest thing I have ever seen."

And she fell in love.

She watched Dad through the end of the set, mesmerized. At the break, Dad put his bass down, came over to her, and took both of her hands in his. "You know," he told her, "you ought to record some of my songs. You ought to record 'Lonely Little Mansion.' "

Biff, a great admirer of Dad as a writer, invited him out to their house in San Gabriel on the band's day off. They visited, went bowling, had corn bread and beans, and Biff interviewed Dad for his radio show. Dad ended up spending the night.

During the course of his extended visit, Shirley learned that Mama and Dad were having serious problems. When she drove him back to the motel the next day to prepare for a gig at the Palamino Club, Dad said, just in a general way, "Isn't it funny how sometimes you can fall in love with somebody and you've just got to give up everything so you can be with that person?"

And Shirley remembers answering, also in a general way, that that might be true for some people, but not her. She and Biff had a good, solid marriage. She had her career, she was earning money, she had security, and she loved her husband. She was perfectly happy. No, she couldn't imagine anything that would be better than what she had.

They were talking around their situation, but they both knew that something had happened.

When they got to the motel, Dad asked Shirley if he could call her sometime.

"Sure," said Shirley, "we'd be glad to hear from you anytime. And you're always welcome to stay with us whenever you're in Southern California and have some free time."

A couple of weeks later, Shirley flew to Nashville to record. Joe Allison asked her if she wanted to do a couple of male-female duets with Dad. One thing led to another, and she and Dad recorded "Willingly" and "Chain of Love."

"Willingly" made it to number one in 1962.

Shirley got her copy of the tape and flew back to San Gabriel. When Biff heard it, he said, "Where'd you learn to sing like that?"

Ray Price and the Cherokee Cowboys returned to Los Angeles to perform on the "Town Hall Party," a show that Shirley was a regular on. She had just finished videotaping her segment of that week's show and was leaving to go home when Ray's bus pulled up. As she was getting into her car, Dad stuck his head out of the window and yelled, "I'll call you!"

A few days later, the phone rang. Shirley answered and she recognized the voice instantly.

"Shirley, I love you."

"I love you too, Willie," she answered, "with all my heart."

"I don't have any idea of what we're going to do. But I love you."

☆ ☆ ☆ ☆

As it turned out, they made plans for Shirley to catch up with the band. The next stop for them was a three-day gig in Atlanta, and Shirley flew there to be with Dad.

That was the first time that Shirley had ever lied to Biff. She told him she was going to Atlanta to work, but instead she and Dad spent the time, when Dad wasn't playing, running around like a couple of school kids, looking at the sights, feeding each other slices of pizza, and talking.

Lord, how they talked.

They talked about where they had been and what they had done. They talked about what they wanted out of life and how they were going to try to get it. They talked about their marriages.

Dad made it clear that his marriage was at an end. Mama had filed for divorce a number of times and had never followed through, but it was just a matter of time.

They also talked about us three kids. Or at least Shirley tried to. But, she says, every time she would bring up the subject of us, Dad would withdraw and not say anything. She learned that she would just have to wait his silence out.

Shirley thinks the reason for the silence was a combination of guilt and worry. He was worried about leaving us with Mama. He felt guilty because he wasn't there to take care of us, and because he knew he was getting into something that was going to make it harder for him to see us and make sure we were all right.

But he knew he had to do what he was doing. And Shirley did too.

They spent those three days together without having sex, if you can believe that, and left with their resolve strengthened that they had to be together.

Shirley flew back to California, and Biff picked her up at the airport. As soon as she got in the door, she told Biff she was leaving him. She didn't love him any more, and she was madly in love with someone else. The only thing she could do was leave him.

Biff's reaction was simple and direct.

"You're crazy."

☆ ☆ ☆ ☆

When Biff found out that Shirley was going to leave him for Willie Nelson, he couldn't believe it.

Why, he was just a front man for Ray Price. He didn't have any name, he didn't have any position, he didn't have any money. What he did have was a wife and three small children. Shirley must have flipped out completely.

You have to understand that Shirley was a successful performer in her own right. She had her first professional job at the age of fourteen, singing on the radio in Kansas City. She had been a regular on the Ozark Jubilee and then on the Phillip Morris Country Music Show. In fact, that's where she had met Biff. She had a recording contract. She had appeared on the Groucho Marx show and was a regular on Biff's television show, "Country America," and on "Town Hall Party."

Biff had made quite a thing about her on his show. He called her "my girl Shirl." It was my girl Shirl this and my girl Shirl that. And now my girl Shirl was trying to do something totally out of character. My girl Shirl would never leave him for another man. My girl Shirl would never throw five years of marriage, her career, and everything else she had down the tubes, especially not for a nothing, $25-a-night front man.

She had to be crazy.

So he brought in a psychiatrist.

And the shrink's verdict?

He concluded that whatever else Shirley was or might be, she definitely was not crazy.

So Biff turned to defensive tactics. He kept changing their home phone so Dad couldn't call. But using Hank as a messenger, Shirley managed to keep up with Dad's schedule and Dad managed to learn the new phone numbers.

Finally, Shirley decided that she just had to leave.

Ray Price was about to leave on a thirty-day tour of Canada and Shirley figured that if she was gone for thirty days, Biff would finally get the idea that she was serious.

Dad made arrangements for her to travel on the bus with the Cherokee Cowboys.

Shirley secretly bought a plane ticket to Seattle, picking a departure time when Biff would be on the air. Live. She drove to the airport, watching in the rearview mirror all the way to make sure that she wasn't being followed.

But she got on the plane all right, and she caught up with the band. She and Dad had a romantic interlude, while the band got to pretend they were smuggling a defector from behind the Iron Curtain, hiding Shirley on the bus as they traveled across Canada.

But before they started out, Shirley and Dad went window shopping in Seattle. And Dad bought her a wedding band that she still has to this day. It's inscribed on the inside: "I will love you forever and after forever. Your Willie."

☆ ☆ ☆ ☆

Biff tried without success to catch up with the lovebirds. The hiding was good, except that some way or another Shirley's mother, who lived in Chillicothe, Missouri, found out where they were and called.

Shirley was sick with a strep throat at this time, so Dad did all the talking. Shirley's mother told Dad to take care of her girl and that she would talk to Shirley when Shirley was ready to talk.

Shirley may not have wanted to talk with her mother, but she didn't have much trouble talking with Dad.

I ought to say right here that not everyone from those days in Nashville liked Shirley. She has a strong personality. She knows what she thinks is best for herself and everybody around her. When I was doing research for this book, I ran into a lot of folks who thought that she took too much of a role in Dad's recording sessions, directing how things should be handled and so on. One of the women who worked at Pamper Music said that she was too hard and inflexible for her taste.

Be that as it may, it was on this trip across Canada that Dad decided to leave Ray Price. Or, to be more accurate, Shirley and Dad decided he should leave Ray Price.

As Shirley told me, "Willie was the best. He was too good to go on being just a front man. In my eyes, he was the greatest thing that had ever happened, and I refused to listen to anything negative about him."

So Shirley told Ray that Dad was leaving after the trip was finished.

Dad told him too, but only after Shirley had made the announcement.

Ray tried everything he could think of to talk them out of it. He offered to hire Shirley as a singer. He offered to double Dad's salary. "Then you could be together on the bus," he told Shirley. "You'd never be separated."

"No," said Shirley, "that's not for me. You'll have to ask Willie. But that's not for me."

Dad stuck by his decision to quit too. Although, when you think about it, he didn't really have much choice.

So when the tour was over, the bus stopped in Goodlettsville and let Dad and Shirley off. Shirley stood by the side of the road with the suitcases and watched us kids playing in the yard. She watched Dad go into the house, with us following close behind. And then she watched him come out of the house.

"And I know that the hardest thing he ever had to do in his life was walk out of that house and leave his children and walk up to me standing with the suitcases by the side of the road."

☆ ☆ ☆ ☆

Things were hard for us too.

Nannie and Pa had moved back to Waco. So we moved out of the house in Goodlettsville to a house in town. We had to stay at a night-time babysitting service while Mama worked.

I hated that place.

The old lady who ran it would always greet us with a smile. But that was just an act she put on for the parents. That would change as soon as Mama left.

Billy would grab my hand and start to cry when Mama was gone. The old lady would take us into this room full of other kids, some crying just like Billy, and set us down in front of the TV.

We'd stay there in that big room full of kids, some crying, some sniveling, and some watching whatever was on the TV, until it was time to go to bed.

Then, in a stern voice—a voice like the wicked queen in *Snow White*—she would tell us all it was time to go to bed. And we would go into another big room where we all slept. It was lined with double bunk beds, all in a row.

Lana would get a bed for herself, and Billy and I would sleep together. We would hold each other tight while Billy cried himself to sleep.

In the morning, all the kids ate together in the kitchen. The really little kids would be lined up in rows of high chairs, while us bigger kids would be sitting along the wall waiting our turn to eat.

Breakfast was the same every day. Oatmeal. Nothing else.

I hated it. Billy hated it. He would cry while this ugly old woman kept shoving it into his mouth. He would turn to me for help, but I couldn't do anything.

I would just look at the clock on the wall and count the minutes as they went by slowly, ever so slowly, until Mama would come.

I would watch the clock crawl and I would think about the little brick house in Goodlettsville where we had all been very happy at one time.

I'd remember that Nannie and Lana and I shared a bedroom, that Billy and Pa's room was across the way, and that Mama and Dad slept down the hall.

We didn't have air conditioning, and in the summer when it was hot, we slept with the windows open and you could hear the crickets.

Nannie would lie there and tell Lana and me about the good old days in Waco. Or she would talk about the days in Portland. How beautiful I was when I came home from the hospital — I always liked that part the best.

The hot summer nights would be full of Nannie's gentle reminiscences of how handsome Dad was, what a beautiful, happy couple he and Mama were, how they couldn't stay away from each other, how they loved to go dancing.

She'd talk about how Pa would make snow ice cream for Lana, and about how happy we all were, together.

Then all the crying in the room would bring me back to reality.

And I'd ask myself the same questions:

What happened?

Why didn't Mama and Dad love each other any more?

Why weren't we happy together any more?

Tears would start to well up in my eyes. Then the doorbell would ring and I knew Mama had come . . . at last.

☆ ☆ ☆ ☆

I didn't like our new home either.

We still had the black Cadillac, but the new house didn't have any heat and almost no furniture. We all slept in one room.

I didn't know why.

I remember I woke up one cold morning and went into the kitchen to make sure that Oscar was covered up.

But when I called him, Oscar didn't move.

When I went to touch him, he fell off his perch to the bottom of the cage. Frozen stiff.

I ran crying to get Lana.

Lana woke up and so did Billy. And we went running to the kitchen. I remember it was so cold you could see our breath. I was crying and so was Billy.

Lana took Oscar out of his cage and wrapped him in a cloth. Billy and I got our coats and followed Lana out into the snow and watched her bury Oscar.

I stood there for the longest time after Lana and Billy had gone back inside. Every now and then Lana would yell at me to come in.

But I didn't. I just stood there and looked at the snow. And cried.

I felt so empty, so lonely.

I wanted Nannie and Pa.

I wanted Daddy home again, just like it used to be.

Where had he gone?

Where the hell had everybody gone?

☆ ☆ ☆ ☆

Mama sued for a divorce again and this time she meant it. Sue, the babysitter, was one of the witnesses, and she told me that Mama had Dad sewed up so tight "he couldn't even get his clothes out of the cleaners."

"Why?" I asked.

"I don't know," she answered, "just meanness I guess."

Dad had asked Sue to be a witness and told her to tell the court anything Mama wanted her to say, just as long as the divorce went through.

Sue told me that he said to her, "I've always tried to give her want she wanted, and she wants a divorce."

Everything was over, save a technicality or two, early in 1962.

Mama took us away from Nashville and dropped us off in Waco with Nannie and Pa while she headed off to seek her fortune in Las Vegas.

TEN

Dad and Shirley

"My future tightly clutched within those healing hands of time."

After Dad had left us that last time in Goodlettsville and walked back to Shirley, who was waiting by the side of the road, they went on in to Nashville somehow and stayed at the Downtowner Motel.

Mama was mad at Shirley for taking Dad away from her. Somehow, she had worked it around in her mind that it was all Shirley's fault.

That was Mama's way. She used to blame Hank, or Roger Miller, or Harlan Howard for keeping Dad away from her. Whoever hung around with Dad too much was going to catch it with both barrels from Mama, sooner or later.

So now she blamed Shirley.

☆ ☆ ☆ ☆

Mama still had a sense of humor, though. Sometimes.

She found out that Shirley and Dad were staying at the Downtowner, so she tried to call Dad.

"I'm sorry. Mr. Nelson is not taking any phone calls," said the switchboard operator.

What does Mama do but check into a room next door to Dad and Shirley's.

She made sure Dad knew about it too. So Dad tried to call her.

"I'm sorry. Mrs. Nelson is not taking any phone calls."

Turn about is fair play.

Even though Dad and Shirley were together, he wasn't having an easy time leaving Mama and us kids.

He once said that in order to write songs, he had to dig back into himself and remember a lot of unpleasant things: "There have been times when I dreaded writing the next song, because I already knew what it was going to be about. And I hated to go back to that mentality and live those things again . . ."

One of the songs that Dad wrote about his breakup with Mama was called "The Healing Hands of Time":

They're working while I'm missing you,
Those healing hands of time.
Soon they'll be dismissing you
From this heart of mine.
They'll lead me safely through the night,
And I'll follow as though I'm blind;
My future tightly clutched within those healing hands of time.

☆ ☆ ☆ ☆

Mama took us to Waco to stay with Nannie and Pa while she followed her bartender friend to Las Vegas. And she got a job at a casino as a cocktail waitress.

Dad and Shirley began to make plans for the future.

At this time, they were living on Shirley's money. Dad had blown all of his money from his first royalty checks on airplanes and penthouses while he was traveling with Ray Price. Plus, I found out after I was grown, he was paying Mama $600 a month for child support.

So Shirley pulled all of her savings out of her California bank and had it sent to Nashville. They lived on that and her American Express card while they made plans.

Shirley told me that the idea was always to get married, establish a home, and get us kids to come and live with them.

"We weren't planning on running around like a pair of crazed lovers," she said.

That didn't stop them from having a big party and inviting all their friends — Patsy Cline, Hank, Harlan Howard, Ralph Emery, and all.

But they decided that the first step along the way — to "make things right," as Shirley puts it — was for her to get divorced from Biff.

I don't know whether that was her idea or Dad's, but I kind of suspect it was Shirley's because she is much more concerned with getting papers filled out and satisfying rules and regulations than

Dad is. As near as I can tell, Dad figures that how you feel and what you think is more important than any formal procedure. If two people think they are married, then they are; if two people think they are divorced, then they are. Notarized pieces of paper don't have much to do with what's really important in relationships as far as he is concerned.

But however they made the decision, they decided to go to Reno so Shirley could file.

It took them two weeks to make the drive. The reason was that they fought all the way.

They'd be driving along all lovey-dovey and happy and then Dad would say something like "I don't see why I should have to have a driver's license."

Shirley would be shocked. She saw herself as a solid citizen and pillar of the community. She believed in an orderly society, one with rules and regulations that must be followed.

So she would go through all the reasons why it was necessary to have a driver's license.

They'd pull over to the side of the road and go at it hammer and tongs.

Then, with the air clear for a while, they would be lovey-dovey again and drive on for a bit more. They'd stop for a bite to eat, get back on the road, and then Dad would say, "I don't see why I have to pay income tax." And the whole thing would start all over again.

The scenario is hilarious to me: There they were, arguing just like one was William F. Buckley and the other one was Timothy Leary, en route to get a Reno divorce so they could be together.

And remember, this was in 1962. Nobody had heard of Timothy Leary yet, let alone LSD or hippies. What's really funny is that in those days, Dad was known in Nashville as "old spic and span Willie." But considering his liberal attitude then, maybe the earring and long hair weren't so far away after all.

They finally got to Reno, and Shirley filed for divorce.

But while they were waiting the six weeks required by Nevada law in order to establish residency, two things happened: Biff cross-filed in California, and Shirley began to feel guilty.

☆ ☆ ☆ ☆

Shirley eventually got the divorce. But her lawyer warned her not to go into California for a year. And he also said that she and Dad couldn't get married for a year.

The reason was Biff's cross-action in California. At the time, California law said that there had to be a one-year waiting period from the time a divorce suit was filed until it became final.

Shirley decided to see Biff. Maybe she could explain things to him, make him understand how things were, and get him to drop his suit. Anyway, she would feel better about the whole situation if she could talk with him. After all, she had been married to him for more than five years. She felt she owed him that much.

So she called him. He said that if she'd come on down to San Gabriel for a few days so they could talk, he would think about it.

Shirley flew to California and Dad went to Fort Worth to stay with Aunt Bobbie while they worked it out.

The meeting with Biff was strained but civil. On the second day, while Biff was doing his radio show, the phone rang.

Shirley answered.

"Mrs. Collie?" asked a woman's voice.

"Well, this is Shirley."

"I'm just calling to make sure that you will be arriving on schedule tomorrow."

"What are you talking about?"

"Don't you know that your husband has made arrangements for you to stay with us for a while?"

Trying to be smart, Shirley asked, "Can I bring my guitar?"

"Oh yes. All our patients are allowed to bring some of their most favorite things from home."

Biff was going to have her committed.

In a panic, Shirley called Dad in Fort Worth and told him what was happening and to come get her right away.

Dad got a car from Aunt Bobbie's husband Paul, who ran a used car lot, filled up the back seat with cans of protein drink and vitamins, and drove straight through to San Gabriel, stopping only for gasoline and calls of nature.

He got there late the next morning, leaving state troopers in Texas, New Mexico, and Arizona staring at their radar screens in disbelief, and he called Shirley from a drug store.

Shirley scribbled Biff a quick note saying that she'd be back in a few minutes, drove down to meet Dad, left the car she was driving parked in front of the drug store, and she and Dad never looked back until they had crossed the Arizona line.

Once safely out of California, Shirley called Biff and told him never to call her, write her, or try to find her in any other way again. Ever.

☆ ☆ ☆ ☆

Dad and Shirley stayed in Fort Worth with Aunt Bobbie for a while. They were sort of instant celebrities in the neighborhood. Shirley says that on the first morning, she and Dad were still sleeping when she felt people watching them. She slowly opened her eyes and saw all these little kids, five, six, and seven years old, coming in and out of the room.

She got up and asked Bobbie what was going on. It seems that my cousin Fred was charging all the kids in the neighborhood a nickel to see the famous country and western stars while they slept.

They worked around Fort Worth for quite a while after that, although they were hardly stars. When asked how he had done at the box office, a lot of times Dad would say, "There was one crowded around."

But Dad would play guitar, Shirley would be on bass, and Jimmy Day would play steel as they hit the variety shows and honky-tonk circuit that Dad had played when he was a kid. Sometimes they might be one of the opening acts of a package show. But they were mainly trying to stay busy while they sorted out what they were going to do.

They were both having conscience pangs. Dad had been friends with Biff, and here he had gone and run off with his friend's wife. He even called Joe Allison, who was also a friend of Biff's, to ask him how that would affect his career.

But Shirley took the brunt of the disapproval. She was getting bad-mouthed by everybody for running out on Biff. She was "Bad Shirley" to a lot of people — and still is, to some. All I can say is, they don't know Shirley like I know Shirley.

☆ ☆ ☆ ☆

While they were sorting things out, Dad took Shirley down to Abbott to see where he had grown up. He showed her the house — she still has a nail from it — and showed her his little place under the porch where he could crawl up and be alone. She remembers him talking about eating corn bread and buttermilk.

And they were trying to find us.

Even though Dad paid Mama $600 a month in child support, he didn't know where we were because he sent the money to the court, not directly to us.

Finally, Nannie called and told them we were living in Waco with Pa and her.

Boy, were we glad to see Dad.

That was the first time Shirley got to meet us up close. She says I was out in the backyard in a wading pool and Lana was running around without her bathing suit, with everybody trying to catch her. "She was like a deer."

I don't remember Shirley being there. We were so glad to see Dad that I guess everything else is blocked out of my mind.

Nannie and Pa were glad to see Dad too. For one thing, they always liked Dad. But for another, they weren't getting any of the child support that was being sent to Mama and they couldn't afford to get us all the things we needed.

But then Mama came and got us and took us out to Las Vegas to live with her.

☆ ☆ ☆ ☆

Life with Mama in Las Vegas was interesting, to say the least.

She found an old woman to come live with us and take care of us while she worked. We called her Granny.

Granny was something else. She dipped snuff and drank Country Club Malt Liquor all the time. She would always hum, then spit in the coffee can and take a sip of Country Club. Hum, spit, sip. It used to drive me crazy. I was always afraid she was going to spit on me.

She'd take us down to the 7-11 so she could get more Country Club. For some reason, Billy and I wouldn't wear shoes and we'd hop from one side of the curb to the other all the way to the store and back again.

When we weren't fighting, that is. When we got to be bad, Granny would warn us, "You stop that or I'm gonna tell Marthie." Of course, we didn't pay any attention.

At the store Granny would get more Country Club and snuff. We'd get Big Hunk candy bars. I can still taste that white taffy and all those nuts.

Nannie still made our clothes and would send them up from Waco. Lana was tall with thin legs, and I was short and so chubby my legs would rub together when I walked. We didn't look a thing alike. But Nannie would send us identical dresses. I remember one matched set in bright red with yellow dots. They were awful. Of course, Nannie's choice of material was limited by what Winn's had on sale.

During that time I remember watching Mama primp before she went to work. Billy and I used to bathe together in the bathtub and try to drown each other while Mama got ready for work. Mama would put on her bar makeup, yelling at us all the time. "Hurry up, Billy. Wash. Don't slide down the back of the tub — you'll knock your damn head off."

That was just the way she talked. She never meant anything by it, and she never scared us.

"Susie, make him get down. I'm gonna knock your damn brains out if I see you let him do that again." It was always my fault if Billy got hurt.

We'd stop fooling around when it came time for Mama to put her false eyelashes on. We'd stop everything and watch with awe. We could never figure out how they could stick on. It was like magic.

I'd look at Mama, so tall and pretty, and wonder if I would ever look like her.

☆ ☆ ☆ ☆

Once Dad and Shirley knew where we were, they kept in touch with us as best they could. Dad would come pick us up for visits whenever he was in Las Vegas.

There was always confusion just before he arrived.

"You kids hurry up. Your dad will be here any minute. Susie, shut the door to your bedroom so your daddy doesn't see that damn mess."

"Daddy's here."

"Come give me a kiss. How have you been? Have you been good girls?"

"I have, but Lana hasn't."

"I have too, Daddy."

"I know you have, darlin'. How about you, Billy, have you been a good boy?"

"I don't know." Billy would rub his eyes and look at the floor. "Mama, have I been a good boy?"

"Yes, Billy." Mama would shake her head.

And the presents. There were always presents when Daddy came. It was like Christmas when he visited.

Then it would be time for him to go.

"Daddy's got to go to work so I can buy you more pretty things, but I'll be back real soon. I promise. Will you write me a letter? Lana can help you, can't you Lana?"

Lana, holding back the tears, just nodded.

Then Billy would run to Dad and throw his little arms tight around his neck. He would try to be so big, but soon his ears would turn red and he would start to stutter. And the tears would begin to flow.

Dad and Shirley would never forget to send us CandyGrams on our birthdays. And Dad would write us letters.

Lana kept a letter that Dad wrote to us during this time and put a facsimile of it in her book *Family Album*. It pretty well reflects what Dad was going through:

> As you grow older, you will come to realize that things do not always work out exactly as you want them to. There will be many things that you will want more than anything in the world but for some reason you won't be able to have them. Then you may feel badly and think that life has played a dirty trick on you and you will not be able to understand why. But always stop and remember what daddy told you; happiness does not come from having everything you want, but in understanding and accepting all, and in prayer and the belief that everything always happens for the best.
>
> Always.

Those are things that Dad has told me over and over in different ways through the years, and I think I'm beginning to understand what they mean. Finally. Now that I'm thirty.

We really appreciated hearing from Daddy and we especially liked being able to see him. We enjoyed seeing Shirley too. But Mama made it very clear one day that she didn't want to see Shirley as a stand-in for Dad.

Dad was playing at a club in Las Vegas and was supposed to come pick us up for a visit, but for some reason he was late. We were all excited about getting to see him, but then when he didn't come and didn't come we started getting worried and nervous and bitchy.

Finally, Shirley knocked at the door.

Mama didn't like Shirley, you know, so she loves to tell the story of what happened. One of the things Mama likes to do when she tells the story is mimic the way Shirley talked. She always spoke in a very careful, forceful way, especially when she was in formal or difficult situations. And this one promised to be difficult. Remember, Shirley was the staunch defender of driver's licenses, income tax, and every other paper evidence of civic responsibility and good citizenship.

Mama opened the door and there stood Shirley.

"I have come to pick up the children."

Mama makes Shirley sound like the Duchess of Windsor when she tells the story. And she answers her in the same way.

"Well. You tell *Mr.* Nelson that he if wants to see *his* children he should pick them up himself."

"I *said* I have come to pick up the children. Willie sent me for the children."

That was too much for Mama. She picked up the mop that was standing by the door and began to work Shirley over, swinging it with both hands.

"You tell that goddamn, low-life son of a bitch that if he wants to see his goddamn children he can pick them up his own goddamn self."

Mama was working Shirley over good. Shirley was screaming and trying to fight back. She hadn't expected anything like this.

Lana was crying and yelling at Mama to stop.

"Don't hit her, Mama. Please don't hit her."

Billy was screaming in the corner, not knowing what was going on. His ears were standing straight up and his eyes were as big as a Pekingese lap dog's.

I was in shock, but I watched with both eyes. Even at the age of six, I really liked excitement.

Mama switched to a one-handed grip on the mop so she could hold Shirley by the hair with her other hand to keep her from getting away. She was still swinging the mop handle pretty good with just one hand. And in between yelling at Shirley and telling her how she was going to beat the shit out of her, Mama was yelling for Lana to go get the butcher knife out of the kitchen.

Lana wouldn't go get the knife.

"I'll get it, Mama," I told her, and I ran to get the knife like an obedient little girl.

But by the time I got back, Shirley had broken Mama's hold on her hair and gotten away.

Mama had put on quite a show. And everybody in the whole apartment complex had heard it and come out to watch.

One of the spectators was Chuck Andrews. He was much taken with Mama and came right down after the show was over.

"Ma'am," he told her, "you have one of the prettiest arm swings I have ever seen. Anybody who can swing a mop handle with that kind of coordination ought to be a pretty good dancer. And I sure would like to take you dancing and find out."

They were married three weeks later.

☆ ☆ ☆ ☆

About a year after the trip through Canada, Shirley finally got her divorce from Biff. She knew it one day when seven big moving cartons arrived from San Gabriel. They contained all of the clothes she had left behind.

"When Biff sent those clothes, I knew he had given up hope."

Dad had been asking Shirley to marry him all through this period but she kept putting him off.

I later asked her why and she said she didn't know. She just felt that she would know when the time was right.

She and Dad were playing at the Golden Nugget when the right time came.

They may have been playing to small crowds around Texas, but Dad and Shirley did have a number-one record. So it isn't surprising that they were able to get a job in Las Vegas. They brought eight musicians with them from Texas, including Paul Buskirk, Johnny Bush, and Jimmy Day. Shirley remembers that they rented a kitchenette apartment, and she would cook supper for everybody after the show.

She was sitting in the dressing room at the Nugget when she decided that now was the time. She went down to one of the Las Vegas wedding chapels and made arrangements. Then, as they came off the stage after the last set, Shirley turned to Dad.

"Do you still want to marry me?"

"You bet."

"Then let's do it."

☆ ☆ ☆ ☆

Dad got an offer to run the West Coast office for Pamper Music. They went to California, but the job was all paperwork and sitting behind a desk. That was something that Dad just wasn't cut out for.

So they went back to Nashville.

And they went back with a reasonable amount of money. Shirley was able to keep Dad from blowing all of his royalty money and, in truth, he had probably learned a lesson from what he had done with the first checks. I'm not saying he got business sense — most folks still don't think he has any — but he didn't feel the need to throw it away with both hands.

In any event, they got back to Nashville with the idea of establishing a home, a true family home.

Actually, they were flying back and forth between Nashville and Los Angeles, staying with Hank and his first wife Shirley when they were in Nashville. Dad was doing the paperwork to close down Pamper's West Coast office, changing record labels, and looking for a house.

One crisp Friday afternoon in late November of 1963, Dad and Shirley were out with the real estate agent. They had looked at one house and were going to the second when they went around a curve on Greer Road in the little town of Ridgetop, Tennessee, and saw it. Their dream house.

"Willie," Shirley said, "if that place has a fireplace in the kitchen, that's our house."

They went up and knocked on the door. There were a couple of women in there baking apple pies. A fire was going in the kitchen fireplace.

They put down their earnest money and caught a plane to Los Angeles to close up everything in California.

It was a night flight, but there were no lights. No lights in Dallas. No lights in Los Angeles. It was dark all over the country.

President Kennedy had been shot in Dallas that day.

☆

ELEVEN

Ridgetop and Las Vegas

"If it isn't perfect, Chuck goes into orbit."

D ad and Shirley returned from California to Tennessee, all set to move to their new farm.

It was snowing the day they arrived, but they were bound and determined to get to their new house. With more guts than good sense, they headed out from Nashville to Ridgetop.

It was dark by the time they got there, dark and snowing. And they got stuck.

☆ ☆ ☆ ☆

They got stuck on the hill just before they reached the house. The car wouldn't climb the hill, and they were both exhausted and soaked to the knees from taking turns, one pushing and one driving.

They were taking turns slipping and sliding and getting wetter and colder by the minute when George Hughes, who was to be their neighbor, happened along on his way home. With his help, they pulled the car out on to the crown of the road where it could get some traction.

"I didn't know them from Adam's off ox," Mr. Hughes explained to me when he told me this story. So Dad and Shirley introduced themselves and told him where they were in the process of moving to. They were fixing to be his new neighbors. If they could get up the hill and warm up, that is.

Mr. Hughes looked at them standing there shivering with cold feet and wet clothes and told them to follow him to his house, where they could get warm.

"Ruby," he told his wife when they got there, "we've got some young'uns here that are about froze to death. I'm going to build up a fire so they can thaw out." After he built a coal fire in the big grate, everybody gathered around.

That was how they met the man who ran the farm for them for the next five years.

It was a good thing they met him that night. They had been so eager to get to their new house, they had arrived without anything. No food. No furniture. The electricity wasn't on. The house didn't even have a telephone.

☆ ☆ ☆ ☆

Dad and Shirley may not have known much about farming or about living in the Tennessee mountains, but they sure started trying to learn in a hurry.

It wasn't long after Mr. Hughes had rescued them and taken them home to dry off that Shirley came by on foot to visit.

You see, Mr. Hughes kept hogs. And he had one shoat that had a stripe down its back. Shirley was attracted to that little hog and told Mr. Hughes in her direct way: "I want that pig."

"Well, all right," said Mr. Hughes.

So Shirley paid him, picked the pig up, and carried it in her arms all the way home.

That was the start of the Willie Nelson livestock operation.

Another major step to turn Dad into a gentleman farmer happened on his thirty-first birthday.

Shirley wanted to give Dad something special. Recruiting Mr. Hughes to provide the expert's eye, she set off for the livestock auction to add a heifer to the one-pig herd. She came back 52-head richer — or $8,000 poorer, depending upon your point of view. To top everything off, one of the cows was pregnant and she calved just as the cattle were being unloaded at the farm. So they always figured that they'd gotten one extra — and Dad had a birthday calf to go along with being an instant cattleman.

Shirley wanted to give Dad an extra special party, since he had never had a birthday party before. She also wanted to make it a surprise. So she started cleaning up and fixing up the basement, doing it when Dad wasn't around.

But a couple of days before his birthday, Dad got back to the house unexpectedly, went down to the basement, and found Shirley hard at work.

The surprise wasn't a surprise any more.

But that didn't bother Dad. He was excited and wanted to help. What was needed was paint, thought Dad. Specifically, red paint. On the banister.

So Dad's contribution to his birthday celebration was to paint the banister a deep barn red. And that was okay. In fact, it was probably a good idea. The only problem was that Dad used an oil-base paint. It was in late April and the humidity was high, particularly in the damp of a Tennessee mountain basement, so the paint didn't dry.

Everybody who came to the party, and that was just about everybody that Dad and Shirley knew in Nashville, went home with red paint on the palms of their hands.

But red paint wasn't all that there was.

Shirley made home-brewed beer, and it wasn't subject to the laws regulating maximum alcohol content. This stuff was as strong as nature would allow, which works out to about fourteen percent. A glass of Shirley's home brew carried about four times the wallop of your 7-11 six-pack.

Shirley followed the same principle with her homemade wine— whatever nature created in the way of alcohol content was fine with her. The wine was served out of a homemade leather wine flask. It was made like those leather flasks you can sling over your shoulder on a string and every time anyone wants a sip they can just take the top off and squirt a stream into their mouth.

It was like that, but with a difference. It was big. It probably held a gallon—maybe more.

And it didn't have a top. This meant that once it was filled, somebody had to be carrying it. You couldn't set it down, not without wasting Shirley's good homemade wine. And nobody wanted to do that. If somebody had to carry the wine, then you know other people had to be drinking it. They had to pitch in and lighten the load.

That must have been some party.

Shirley says she spent the whole day in the kitchen frying chicken. There was a never-ending stream of people coming through, going up and down the stairs getting their hands red, eating fried chicken and ice cream and cake, and drinking home brew—and probably some other things too.

Shirley remembers Hayes Jones trying to leave. Hayes was a booking agent who handled Dad for all but his Texas dates. Anyway, Hayes was knee-walking drunk. Actually, he was drunker than that. He'd somehow get vertical and kind of weave in the air in the general direction of his car. Then he'd lose his balance. Down he'd go. Only a few feet closer to his car. Up he'd get again and weave around like a streamer in a light breeze. And down he'd go. Again a few feet closer to his car. He kept repeating the process — like a very large, very drunk, but very determined inchworm.

Shirley's pretty sure that he spent the night in his car, although she couldn't swear to it because she wasn't in such good shape herself. But I can give personal testimony that Hayes survived the party, because I interviewed him for this book in 1986.

☆ ☆ ☆ ☆

They were having a great time getting settled in on the farm at Ridgetop.

But things weren't going so hot in Las Vegas. At least not for Lana, Billy, and me.

Mama had married Chuck Andrews three weeks after the broom-swinging incident with Shirley. And they wasted no time — my first half-brother was born nine months later.

Chuck was a contractor who installed elevators. He was based out of Las Vegas, but his work took him all over the Southwest. In the time that we were with Chuck and Mama, we lived in Los Angeles and Albuquerque, besides Las Vegas.

Chuck was a highly organized kind of person. He liked regular schedules. He would be home at 5:30 and wanted his dinner ready at 6:00 sharp. And he liked his house kept clean. He was the type that would wipe window sills with a white glove on, and if the glove came up dirty, watch out. He slapped Mama more than once because she hadn't done things his way.

Well, Mama didn't like doing things anybody else's way. You probably have gotten that idea by now.

But there she was with the three of us, and one more on the way. And things got even more crowded real quick. Five months after my half-brother Charlie was born, Mama got pregnant with David.

So now Mama was either pregnant or with an infant — or both — and she couldn't work. Not that Chuck wanted her to. No wife of Chuck Andrews was going to have to work.

So she started drinking heavily. And Chuck didn't like his wife drinking, either.

Not that I blame him. Mama was no princess when she was drinking. That was something we all had known for a long time. But because of Chuck's attitude, Mama had to be sneaky. She'd stash her bottles of V.O. in the trash, in among the dirty clothes, under the shoes in the back of our closets, in the lampshades—anywhere that Chuck hadn't thought to look yet. I remember lying in bed trying to go to sleep when Mama would tiptoe into the room and pull a bottle out of the lampshade from the light next to my bed and take a couple of quick nips.

I'd lie there thinking, "Mama, you fruitcake. You're just going to get caught again and Chuck's going to hit you again."

☆ ☆ ☆ ☆

Looking back, I think that one of the biggest reasons for Mama's drinking was the fact that Chuck couldn't stand Billy. He liked Lana and me all right, but he didn't want anything to do with little Billy. Mama always says that Chuck was jealous of Billy, and maybe he was.

Billy probably was jealous of Chuck too. If you remember the story that Sue told about the way Billy had acted when she paid too much attention to Bobby Sykes, you can see that he could have driven Chuck crazy.

I remember one time when Chuck came home from work. Billy was playing with something, a bowl or a flower vase, I'm not sure which. Anyway, he dropped it and it broke. Chuck started screaming at him and picked him up and spanked him hard, real hard.

Billy was crushed, broken-hearted. He became even more quiet and nervous than ever. He would just sit in his room and listen to Dad's records and cry.

Mama couldn't bear to see Billy like that. She wrote Dad and Shirley describing the situation. She didn't exactly come right out and ask if Billy could live with them, but she sure left the door wide open.

And it didn't take Shirley long to respond.

"Do you really think Martha would let Billy come live with us?"

"We can ask," answered Dad. "You call."

Dad never talked to Mama on the phone, or in person, for the longest time after she married Chuck.

So Shirley called. The answer was yes.

Shirley bought Billy a new blue suit and an airplane ticket, and in the spring of 1964, Billy was living at Ridgetop.

☆ ☆ ☆ ☆

Lana and I got some relief in the summer when we got to spend a month at Ridgetop with Dad and Shirley. The farm was so beautiful and peaceful. We couldn't believe it was so nice, after everything we had been through.

But the month was up all too soon, and we had to go back to Mama and Chuck.

Living with Mama's new husband and our new half-brothers and moving around every couple of months or so was hard on all of us, but it was especially hard on Mama. She knew she had really made a mistake this time. The fact that she would let Billy go shows just how bad she knew the situation was.

That's why she drank the way she did. Things were tense all the time around the house, and that's the only way she could get through the day.

"Lana, set the table and don't forget to put the two forks together and the knife on the other side. The last time you did it wrong, and Chuck raised hell for an hour."

"Mama, I always forget."

"Well don't. If everything isn't perfect, Chuck goes into orbit. Susie, come get David and feed him. God. Y'all are driving me crazy. Lana, come stir the gravy."

Lana had to stir the gravy so Mama could take a nip of V.O.

"Granny, didn't you get me another bottle when you went to get the beer?"

"Why, yes I did, Marthie."

"Where is it, goddammit? I can't find it."

Chuck would come home and dinner would be served promptly at 6:00. He never said much at the table. He didn't like conversation at mealtime. We were just supposed to eat. And Mama never ate with us. She just kept serving from the kitchen, chain-smoking cigarettes all the while, and running periodically to one bedroom or another.

☆ ☆ ☆ ☆

Things were heading for disaster in Las Vegas. But in Ridgetop, Dad and Shirley were building a peaceful oasis. And they were becoming farmers, or at least trying to.

One of the things that helped that transformation along was that George and Ruby Hughes's house burned down. It happened one day in June, a month or so after the "surprise" birthday party for Dad.

As Mr. Hughes said, "It burned the whole house, almost everything we had — and it durn near burned us up."

The first person on the scene was Shirley, and Dad wasn't far behind.

A few days later, Dad and Shirley went by to see how the Hugheses were getting along. Their plan was to rebuild on the old foundation, and in the meantime they were looking for a trailer they could put up on the lot to live in during the two or three months they figured it would take to rebuild.

Dad and Shirley asked what kind of luck they had had in finding a trailer. Mr. Hughes showed them what he described to me as a "trashy, no account trailer, but it would have kept the rain off us."

"Mr. Hughes," said Shirley, "you can't live in that."

"I haven't got my insurance money yet, and I don't know if I can afford anything else."

"Don't you worry about money."

A day later, a brand spanking new trailer was delivered to the Hugheses.

So under the experienced eye of Mr. Hughes, the Willie Nelson Ridgetop farm got under way.

When the farm was in full swing it had 600 acres, with 200 head of registered Black Angus, twenty-five brood sows that produced 800 hogs for market each year, six horses, three ponies, and all kinds of chickens, geese, and ducks.

Between growing up in a farming community and having his own place when he was grown, Dad now has a deep affection for farmers and understands the problems they have. That's why he organized the Farm Aid programs and why he stays personally involved in how the money is spent — including signing every check himself.

But when Billy arrived, Dad and Shirley were still learning and Mr. Hughes was just establishing himself as Dad's farm manager and right-hand man.

☆ ☆ ☆ ☆

"When Billy came, he was mine. We went everywhere together."

Shirley couldn't have children herself, and she took to Billy with all the enthusiasm pent-up mothering instincts can bring.

She used to play bass and sing with Dad, but when they decided to have Billy live with them, she retired from the road. Her last show was in Biloxi, Mississippi.

And Billy must have felt like he was in heaven after what he had been through since Dad and Mama had separated.

I almost said hog heaven, so that reminds me of a story.

Among the things that Mr. Hughes did was butcher. He'd kill and butcher fifteen hogs at a time. Ruby would make sausage and Mr. Hughes would smoke the hams.

Billy wanted to help once. Now, Billy was a bit squeamish and he had a queasy stomach. So Mr. Hughes told Shirley that he didn't think Billy ought to come.

"No. Let him go and we'll see what happens."

"All right," said Mr. Hughes, still doubtful.

Butchering hogs is a bloody process. First you shoot them. Then you hang them up by the heels and slit their throats to let the blood drain. Next you scald the whole carcass by dipping it in a big kettle of boiling water. Then you scrape all the bristles off, gut and clean the body, and cut the meat up into hams, roasts, ribs, and so on. What's left over, you grind into sausage.

By the time Shirley came to pick Billy up, he was sick.

"He was green as a gourd and he told me, 'I don't ever want to do that no more.'"

Mr. Hughes had a reputation for curing Tennessee country hams. And when he butchered fifteen hogs at a time, that worked out to thirty hams. But there were generally more people who wanted them than could go around.

One time Joe Allison of Liberty Records called. He was based in Los Angeles and knew a lot of people in the entertainment business, and he used to brag about the Tennessee country hams he could get from his friends Willie and Shirley Nelson.

It seems that he had bragged about the hams to Robert Mitchum. And Mitchum was having a party and wanted one of those famous hams. So Joe asked them to send one by airplane. Not by air freight, mind you. He wanted a seat bought on the plane for the ham.

They bought the ham a first-class seat and sent it off to Robert Mitchum's party.

A couple of days later, Joe called again to say that the ham had arrived and that Robert Mitchum was there in the office. Did Shirley want to talk to him?

"No. What do I want to talk to him for? Just as long as the ham got there okay."

Shirley hung up the phone and thought, "I must be out of my mind. I just passed up a chance to talk to Robert Mitchum, the movie star."

TWELVE

Spic and span Willie

"Things are out of meter . . . he's hard to follow."

All the while that Dad and Shirley were settling into Ridgetop, learning to be farmers and getting Billy to come and stay with them, Dad was still working to get his career as a recording artist and performer off the ground.

☆ ☆ ☆ ☆

Of course, Dad was still writing for Pamper. He would leave Ridgetop with six or eight songs, then he and Hank would cut demos and take them around to the various record companies or pitch them to artists.

It's probably more accurate to say that Dad would write the songs and cut the demos, but he left it to Hank to pitch them. That made a lot of sense, though, when you think about it, since Hank Cochran was recognized as the best song pitchman in the business.

Hank was crazy about Dad's songs. But he also liked the way Dad played and sang.

"Hell," he'd grumble, "Chet ought to just release the demo."

As I mentioned before, a lot of the people in the business think that when Dad's record sales started to take off it was because he was able to record them his way — the way he did those demos for Pamper Music. Ray Pennington, another of Pamper's pitchmen, remembers the first time he heard "Blue Eyes Crying in the Rain":

"When you hear a hit for the first time, you always remember where you were when you heard it. I was beginning to get on I-65. I reached down to turn it up — that's another measure of a good song, you turn it up — and I said, 'That sounds like Willie settin' in his living room. That is a stone smash.' Boy was it."

But I'm getting ahead of myself.

Dad's contract was about up with Liberty. The company flew him and Shirley out to Los Angeles and put them up in the Knickerbocker Hotel, all expenses paid. They stayed in the penthouse for over a week while they thought over Liberty's offer. On the one hand, Dad had had two Top-10 singles with Liberty and had cut eleven singles in all. He also had two albums on the Liberty label.

But his first two releases were the ones that made the Top 10. None of the other singles and neither of the albums were doing well. So, after living high on the hog at Liberty's expense, Dad and Shirley decided to turn down the offer and they returned to Nashville.

Chet Atkins of RCA Victor was interested in signing Dad. He first noticed Dad when Faron Young released "Hello Walls," and he kept up with him from a distance after that. He'd heard him on the radio and in person and he was at some of Dad and Shirley's recording sessions for Liberty. Chet told me he remembers they would come in together and love on each other between takes.

"I thought, 'I wonder how long you can sustain a relationship like that? That's a little unnatural,' " he said.

When Chet heard that Dad wasn't with Liberty any more, he invited him to come to RCA. As Chet remembers it, Dad said "Okay" at first, and then he backed out and signed with Monument.

☆ ☆ ☆ ☆

Fred Foster, the man who owned Monument, told me that his philosophy was to find a singer who was different and readily identifiable.

"I was looking for someone who could be identified the minute the needle hit the groove." One of the artists on Monument who fit that description perfectly was a singer from West Texas named Roy Orbison.

When Fred heard Dad on a demo at Pamper one day, he heard the same kind of thing.

"I heard that phrasing and said to myself, 'This is going to be a gigantic star.' Then I heard he was on Liberty and it depressed me to no end. I probably went out and had a drink."

But good things come to those who wait. Fred had gotten to know Dad slowly and told him that if he ever left Liberty to give Monument a call. And one day Dad called.

The fact that Monument was not a typical, formula Nashville label probably influenced Dad. They had Roy Orbison and Boots Randolph, the saxophone player, and they had just signed Lloyd Price, the rhythm and blues singer who had had a national smash with "Stagger Lee." That, plus the fact that Fred wanted to record Dad with just a small group, and even let him play guitar, probably changed Dad's mind about RCA Victor.

So they went up to Monument's studio, which Fred had bought from Sam Phillips of Sun Records—the Memphis-based label that first recorded Johnny Cash, Carl Perkins, and, of course, Elvis Presley. They cut five sides in that session, heading for an album and hoping for a hit single.

Fred remembers the bassman telling him: "You just can't do this. Willie is all over the place. Things are out of meter. He's hard to follow."

"You *got* to follow," Fred told him.

Fred had signed Lloyd Price and Dad within a week of each other. The plan was to release their singles together and to start the campaign with full-page ads in *Billboard*—in different sections of the magazine because they were targeted for different markets.

It is certainly a big deal for one artist to have a full-page ad in a national trade publication like *Billboard*. Dad was excited. No one else had ever showed that much faith in him. No one else had ever encouraged him to record his songs his way, and then release them just the way he'd cut them in the studio. It looked as if this was going to be the big break he needed to get established as a performer, so that he could play to crowds of more than one around the stage.

The ad company they commissioned, a small agency called Cumberland Advertising, shared Fred and Dad's enthusiasm. The head of Cumberland was a man named Mark Clark Bates. He liked to know about the artists before he designed his ads, so he called Fred one day and asked who this Willie Nelson was.

Fred told him he was a great songwriter and a great singer. Naturally. Bates said he would do something really special.

What he came up with was a color ad—and color ads weren't that common back in 1964—on a coronation theme. He was going to use royal colors, purples and violet shades, and make the ad look like an invitation to the coronation of the new King of Country Music.

Mark Bates had really knocked himself out. But he called Fred a day before the deadline. The ad he had done for Lloyd was just fine, he said, and it would appear on schedule. But he'd had trouble with Dad's. The color was bleeding and it looked bad. And there was no way to correct it before the deadline. What should he do?

"Hold it 'til next week," Fred told him. "We aren't putting it in unless it's right."

Bates guaranteed that he'd have it by next week's deadline and hung up.

Fred immediately began trying to reach Dad to tell him of the change in plans.

But he never did reach him.

And that Monday, when Dad looked in the new issue of *Billboard,* there was a full-page ad for Lloyd Price and none for Willie Nelson.

Dad must have been sick. He would never let anyone know, of course. But he must have felt that he'd been let down and shoved aside one more time.

Dad never finished cutting the tracks to make up one complete album. And he signed with RCA Victor in November of 1964.

Fred was sick too. There went what he thought was going to be a twenty-year relationship.

Their friendship did continue, though. And Fred always tried to explain. Dad said, well, that was just one of those things.

Fred later said that RCA Victor made the same mistake with Dad that Liberty did. They tried to fit him into the Nashville formula, tried to make him sound like Jim Reeves or Eddy Arnold by laying string sections and vocal chorus tracks on top of Dad's basic cuts.

Now, of course, everybody knows that that was the wrong thing to do. "He didn't need a whole bed of strings," is the way Ray Pennington puts it.

Dad went along with it because he thought the record companies knew more than he did. "It turns out they didn't, but I didn't know that at the time."

Chet tells a story that kind of sums up the problem. Dad came in one day and told him that he wanted to record "with just my guitar."

"Man, he doesn't play good enough to accompany himself," Chet said to himself. Aloud, Chet said, "Why don't we record with just you, me, and Grady [Martin]?"

So Dad agreed, and they cut "I Just Can't Let You Say Good-bye," the song where you find out in the last verse that the man has been choking the woman to death the whole time.

I think that Dad plays well enough to accompany himself—and there are lots of folks who buy records who think so too.

☆ ☆ ☆ ☆

Dad was also working on being a performer.

When he got back to Nashville, just after buying the farm at Ridgetop, he met Hayes Jones, the booking agent who counted Ernest Tubb among his clients.

"Someone walked through the doorway and just stood there. After a bit, he said 'Hayes, I'm Willie Nelson.' And I started booking him."

As Hayes puts it, he represented Dad when he was Willie Who? everywhere but Texas. Even back then, Dad was pretty well known in Texas. He didn't really have a band in those days, although Johnny Bush and Wade Ray played with him quite a bit.

One of Dad's breaks came that year through the booking office at Pamper. They decided to put together a syndicated television show starring Ernest Tubb, with Dad as a co-host. The half-hour show ran on Saturday afternoons most places. It was in an alternating host kind of format, so every third week or so, Dad would be the host and the "star" for the show. He usually had the responsibility of singing the gospel number for each show.

These were the days when Dad was at the height of his "spic and span Willie" period. On the show, or whenever he performed, he always had a fresh haircut and was neatly dressed, usually in a conservative Sunday-go-to-meeting suit —at first. He was a picture of well-scrubbed clean living.

He did adjust to the styles. When Nehru jackets became the rage, Dad wore Nehru jackets when he performed. One time in 1973, after we had moved back to Austin and Dad had his earring and beard and his hair was starting to reach his shoulders, I got a bunch of his old publicity stills that were taken during the Nehru jacket era and sent them out to everybody in the area. They sure cracked up, because that picture didn't look anything like the Willie Nelson who was bringing the kickers and hippies together at the Armadillo World Headquarters.

The "Ernest Tubb Show" ran for about two years—until the end of 1965 or early 1966 — and Dad was a featured performer the whole time.

He got another break not long after he signed with RCA. He became a member of the Grand Ole Opry.

Being a member of the Grand Ole Opry had its good points and its bad points.

It was — and you could argue that it still is — the hub of country music. To be a member of the Grand Ole Opry meant that you were an important part of the country music scene. It gave you legitimacy. And that legitimacy helped your bookings. Hayes told me that Dad's being on the Grand Ole Opry and on Ernest Tubb's show really helped in getting him booked outside of Texas.

But being a member had its drawbacks too. One was money. Performers were paid scale, and scale back then was $35–$50 a show. They also had to appear a certain number of times — usually about thirty times — each year. Since the shows were broadcast live on Saturday nights, being a member meant that for thirty of the biggest honky-tonk nights of the year, you were going to be working for scale in Nashville.

When I talked to Ott Devine recently — he was the manager of the Opry for a long time, including the years when Dad was a member — he explained the difficulties to me. One drawback was that performing at the Opry cut into the number of big-dollar dates you could book. This became an even bigger problem for people who didn't live in Nashville — they would not only lose their Saturday dates but would also have to spend expense money just to get there to perform.

Another problem was that a new member would sing only three or four songs the whole night, and the songs would be spread throughout the show. The established stars like Roy Acuff or Hank Snow would do more, of course. After all, the people who tuned in expected to hear them. But even they would do a couple of numbers and then be off for an hour or so.

The scheduling was frustrating to new members, especially if they were like Dad and never wanted to stop once they picked up the guitar. It was that on-again, off-again pattern that made Tootsie's so important as a meeting place.

But Dad stayed a member in good standing of the Grand Ole Opry from late November 1964 until early 1970.

☆ ☆ ☆ ☆

Willie Nelson was becoming a fixture in the Nashville music scene. He was well respected as a songwriter who could produce hit material for other people, and he was building a solid reputation as a musician's musician. He had a distinctive voice, a voice "with an edge to it," like all the great country singers. Chet Atkins told me that what was needed was a voice that "sounds good on a bad jukebox," and he had that. He also had a unique style.

When you ask people in Nashville why Dad had so much trouble getting established as a recording artist and a performer, you get about as many different answers as the number of people you asked.

"He was ahead of his time," is one of the most common. But Ott Devine remembers that he was always well received by Opry audiences. And Wesley Rose of Acuff-Rose Publishing thinks Dad is so country that he makes everything he sings — even "Stardust"— a country song: "They'll buy him no matter what he does because he never changes his style."

Some people say that it was hard to dance to Dad's music and that hurt him, especially in terms of honky-tonk bookings. Others place the blame on record companies that covered his natural loose, spare style with strings and whatnot so that engineering slickness buried the real Willie Nelson. Still others blame the record companies for poor choices of material on the albums: "You're not going to sell an album with two good songs and six or eight bad ones on it."

And others blame luck, like the misunderstanding about Monument's ad in *Billboard*.

But whatever the reasons, there were a lot of people who were mystified because Dad's career hadn't taken off yet. They were sure he was going to be a major star, and they were waiting for it to happen.

Dad was waiting too. But he plugged away and kept his sense of humor while he was doing it.

When RCA opened up a big studio in Nashville, Ralph Emery decided to go over and tape all the artists under contract for his live morning television show. Actually, they were there in the afternoon but pretended it was morning. Ralph spotted Dad and said, "Well good morning, Willie. How are you?"

"I don't know," Dad answered, "I think I was up all night."

Another time, he and Mel Tillis were having a drink at Tootsie's when they got a phone call from Roger Miller. This was after Roger had his monster hits like "King of the Road," "Dang Me," and "Chug-A-Lug."

Roger was calling from his Lear jet. It seems he was flying to Florida to play at the Governor's Ball and he wanted Mel and Dad to come along. "Meet me at the airport and we'll have a good time."

Dad and Mel looked at each other. Why not?

So they flew down to Florida, dressed in the Levis and boots they had been wearing for an afternoon at Tootsie's.

The ball was formal, tuxedos and tails. And they didn't have any tickets or invitations.

"No problem," said Roger. "You're with me." He got them in and put them out by the lights off to one side of the stage.

Roger commenced to playing and he was feeling no pain. He had been imbibing pain killers during the flight just to make sure.

Evidently, the governor had been making sure of a painless evening too, because Roger had barely started when he began hollering for "King of the Road." Roger tried to ignore him, but he kept it up.

Finally, Roger stopped and said to the governor, "Please sir, let me set my own pace."

Dad and Mel knew Roger and what could happen when he gets like that. So Dad looked at Mel and said, "Let's get out of here."

"We went outside and caught a cab to the airport and were back at Tootsie's before closing time," Mel told me, "and I don't think anybody missed us."

☆ ☆ ☆ ☆

Even though Dad had royalty checks coming in and was working regularly on the Opry and the "Ernest Tubb Show," he would still run into what accountants call "cash flow" problems and what most folks call "getting broke."

Again he went to Faron Young for a loan. Faron gave him $240.

A few days later, Dad came back with the money, but Faron didn't want to be paid back in cash. What he wanted was for Dad to raise him some meat. Faron told Dad to pick out one of the heifers on the farm for him and to call him when it got to be about 300 pounds.

"You feed that cow to slaughter and I'll come pick it up and we'll call it even."

Dad said okay and put the money back in his pocket.

The years passed and no cow appeared.

Not long ago, a bunch of pickers and songwriters were taping a television salute to Sue Brewer. She was a lady who ran a place called the Boar's Nest, and she was always good for a cup of coffee and a kind word for all of the destitute songwriters who had frequented Nashville over the years.

Waylon Jennings was there. Hank Williams, Jr. was there. Dad was there. And Faron Young was there.

Faron was getting ready to sing, but he didn't have a guitar. He saw Dad and said, "Willie, get your ass up here and play a little rhythm for me."

Dad did. And then when the tape was off, Faron announced to the whole group in the room about the loan and that the "bull ain't showed up yet."

Somehow, he'd changed the heifer into a bull over the years.

Dad didn't say a thing.

About two weeks later, Dad called Billy Deaton, a booking agent who handled Faron.

"Billy, you know that thing that me and the Sheriff had going on all this time?" (Faron had been in a movie called *The Young Sheriff*.)

"Yep. Heard about it some fifteen years' worth."

"Well, that bull is gettin' ready to arrive. I'm going to have Mr. Polk call you because this bull eats special food."

Billy went up to Faron's office, which was on the second floor of his building, and told him that Dad had called and the bull was on its way.

"No it ain't."

"That's what he said. We'll see."

Ten days later, Mr. Polk called and gave Faron the feeding instructions for the bull.

By now Faron was beginning to believe that something might happen after all.

On the appointed day, a trailer pulled up in front of the building — and out stepped a bull that weighed 3,000 pounds if it weighed an ounce.

It was a registered Simmental bull that my brother Billy had bought at an auction for $30,000.

Faron found a place to pasture the bull before he went on Ralph Emery's "Nashville Now" television show and told the whole story.

I guess the moral is that when you're dealing with Dad, sometimes it's worth the wait.

☆ ☆ ☆ ☆

But back then, the wait was still on for Dad.

And for Lana and me, still living with Mama and Chuck out in Las Vegas, it was getting to where we couldn't wait any longer.

It was good that Billy had gotten away from Chuck and had gone to live with Dad and Shirley. But Mama was really under a lot of stress. And that meant that Lana and I were under a lot of stress.

By this time, both of my half-brothers, Charlie and David, had been born. So Mama had an eleven-year-old, an eight-year-old, and two babies less than a year apart. The house was full, and we still moved around a lot because of Chuck's job.

To top it off, Mama and Chuck weren't getting along. Mama was beginning to realize that she not only didn't love Chuck, she wasn't sure she could stand being in the same city with him.

And her drinking kept getting worse and worse.

When Mama was drunk and mad, she was hard to deal with. Lana knew how to stay out of the way and mind her own business. She'd be able to recognize one of Mama's bad moods and just kind of disappear.

But not me. I didn't have the sense to stay out of the way and keep quiet. For one thing, I wasn't as old as Lana, so I didn't know as much. Besides, that's just not my way. I was always the person who would speak up.

I was the one who would tell Dad all the bad things that Lana and Billy had done. And I was the one who would talk back and push things to the limit.

I remember times when I would get Mama so mad she'd pull me around the house by my hair.

If truth be known, I was a troublemaker. A snitch and a tattle-tale. Of course, I just thought I was doing the things that had to be done to get our lives back to normal, whatever that was.

And I'd do other things too — like skip school. I had just started school and already I was playing hooky. Of course, when you're six, seven, and eight years old and walking down the street during school hours, you're going to get caught. So I learned that if you plan to skip school, you have to hide out.

I'd also try to figure out ways to get Dad to fix everything.

Things got so bad one time that I went down to a phone booth and called Ridgetop. I told them all the bad things that Mama was doing and begged Dad to take me away from there.

That was a trip. I think Dad and Shirley came out to visit after that and words must have been said. Anyway, I got in real trouble for that. And what was funny about it was that nobody said anything about my phone call. Mama knew I'd called. I knew Mama knew. And Mama knew that I knew she knew. But we never said anything. I just kept catching more and more general hell from Mama.

Looking back, now that I'm a once-divorced, once-widowed mother of two, I have more sympathy about Mama's position. She must have really felt like a failure. She had five kids that she couldn't care for unless she stayed with this man she couldn't stand any more. She felt trapped. And now that I've been through a similar situation, I know just how awful it can be.

☆ ☆ ☆ ☆

But relief was on its way because it came time for us to spend our summer month with Dad and Shirley at Ridgetop.

Shirley tells me that Billy wasn't real happy to see us. He had gotten used to being the only child, and he would get Shirley off by herself and ask her if it wasn't time for me and Lana to go home yet.

But we didn't want to go. I talked with Dad about us staying, and he said, "We'll see."

Then one evening Dad and Shirley were talking and Shirley said, "Wouldn't it be nice if we could keep the girls too?"

"We will," said Dad. "We just won't send them back."

"We can't do that. Martha would have the law after us."

"You call her then, and see if we can't work something out."

Dad still couldn't bear to communicate with Mama in any way at all.

Fortunately, however, Mama and Shirley had gotten to where they could talk to each other. And the upshot of it was that Mama agreed. With one condition, and that was that Dad would still send her the $600-a-month child support.

I'm not sure why she agreed to let us go. But I'm sure glad she did, because some of the happiest memories I have of my childhood are from the years at Ridgetop.

THIRTEEN

Gentleman farmer of Ridgetop

"Our mailbox read: 'Willie Nelson and many others' "

When Lana and I went to live at Ridgetop, Dad had pretty much retired. Everybody who knew him in Nashville started calling him a "gentleman farmer."

There are probably people who would disagree with one or both of those terms. But he did retire from the road, just as Shirley had done before, and began to spend most of his time with us and the growing number of animals that were the reason the sign on our mailbox read: "Willie Nelson and Many Others."

☆ ☆ ☆ ☆

I don't mean that he stopped writing songs. Far from it.

And he still worked the Grand Ole Opry and the "Ernest Tubb Show."

He would still show up at a watering spot in Nashville now and then, and he would still play a weekend gig in the area every now and then.

But the main thing was that he wasn't on the road. He was home almost every day and almost every night. It was just like I'd wanted it to be. Just like a normal home. Of course, the only thing I knew about normal homes was what I saw on television.

I remember playing hide-and-seek with Dad, all over the house and the cow lot.

I remember family suppers around the dining room table, holding hands and saying grace.

I remember family singsongs after supper, with Shirley or Dad taking turns playing the guitar, teaching us the songs, and maybe showing us a chord on the guitar. I'll bet I could sing every verse of "The Red Headed Stranger" by the time I began the third grade.

That was a time of catching lightning bugs in jars at night. Of "camping out" on the front porch with our neighbor, Mike Mullin. We called him Moon. Naturally.

Moon was a red-headed, freckle-faced kid with the biggest jug ears you ever saw. He was three years older than I was, but he acted three years younger than Billy. Billy and I always hung around together. And Moon hung around with us. Being the age we were, Billy and I would fight to get Moon to be our friend for the night. One day he would be Billy's friend, with me mad and bothering them as much as I could. Then the next day he would be my friend, and Billy would be the odd man out.

Moon was also one of those kids who went everywhere at top speed. He would run at top speed. He rode his bicycle at top speed. When he was old enough for a driver's license, he drove his car at top speed. Sometimes I think it's a wonder he's still alive.

And Moon's mother was so good to us. She's one of those people who can't do enough to make you comfortable. Did you get enough to eat? Would you like some milk and cookies? How about a piece of pie or some of this chocolate cake?

And you know, she's still that way. I try to see the Mullins whenever I get back to Tennessee, and when I get into her kitchen it's almost like I stepped back in time to the good years of my childhood.

Billy thinks so too. He lives on the farm in a cabin Dad built and still sees the Mullins almost every day when he's not on the road.

It was Billy and Moon and me. And all the other neighborhood kids. In those days, Greer Road didn't have much traffic. It was nothing for us to walk or ride our bikes a mile or two up the road to see what the other kids were doing. Or head up into the hollers and swing on the grapevines like a pack of pint-sized Tarzans.

Not Lana though. She thought we were too young for her, and I guess we were. Not just in age, although I was three years younger, but mentally too. It always seemed to me that Lana was ready to be president when she was seven years old. She was smart and serious, and she preferred adults to us.

While Lana was an excellent student, I was just the opposite. It wasn't until I was an adult and went back to school to get my high school diploma that schoolwork began to make any sense to me.

I used to try to get Lana to help me with my homework. And she'd try. She'd show me how to do my math. Once. And then she'd get frustrated because I couldn't see it as fast as she could.

"I don't see why you don't understand this," she'd yell at me. "I showed you how to do it. If only you weren't so stupid." And she'd throw the paper at me.

Of course, I'd just get mad and frustrated and leave the room. As a result, I wouldn't do my homework. And I'd be in trouble in school the next day.

So Lana was the adult and I was exactly an eight-year-old little girl, who did little girl things.

But I wasn't a goody-two-shoes. I was rough. I was Billy's protector then. If any of the other kids did anything to Billy, they had to answer to me.

Which is funny in a way, because Billy and I would fight all the time. We were at each other's throats constantly. We'd fight about who got to ride which pony. We'd fight over toys, or cookies, or just about anything that would give us an excuse to pinch or poke each other.

Shirley got so sick of us fighting that she went out and bought two pairs of boxing gloves. She took us in the bedroom and made us put them on. Then she told us, "Now you two fight until you can't fight any more."

Shirley left the room and Billy and I just looked at each other.

"She can't be serious," I thought.

But she was. She came back in the room and said, "I don't hear any fighting. Now you two hit each other until you are all hit out. Until you can't do it any more."

So we fought. And when we stopped, Shirley would yell, "I don't hear any fighting in there." So we'd fight some more.

Finally, after what seemed like forever — it probably wasn't much more than a half hour but to us it seemed like all eternity — we timidly opened the door and called to her, "Can we come out now?"

I guess it worked. For a day. Then we were back at it.

I remember Dad tried it once. He made us put on the gloves and he'd say, "Okay Billy, you hit Susie. Now Susie, you hit Billy."

He didn't make us keep it up for long, though.

It's funny, but in my whole life, I can only remember Dad spanking me once and I can only remember him yelling at me once. That is over a thirty-year stretch.

The first time was when we were all living together in the little brick house in Goodlettsville.

There was a country Texaco station up the hill behind our house where we liked to go get sodas. One afternoon Billy had gone up for a soda. It was getting time for supper, so Dad sent me to get him. Instead of going back for supper, Billy and I ran into some other kids and stayed out and played until after dark.

When we got home, Dad took us by the hands and marched us to the bedroom.

"This is going to hurt me worse than it does you," he told us.

I remember thinking, "Now how can that be true?"

Anyway, he spanked me first. I didn't cry. Then he spanked Billy, who started crying. Then Dad started to cry. Billy looked up at him through his tears and said, "Don't cry, Dad. It didn't hurt very much."

The only other time was while we were living at Ridgetop. Dad was on the front porch talking with someone, I don't remember who. Anyway, I kept interrupting him. And he kept telling me not to.

Finally, I did it once too often. He picked me up and yelled, "Goddammit! I told you to stop interrupting me. I'll talk to you when I'm done. But right now I'm talking business."

I was crushed. That hurt me worse than any spanking. I went into the house and sat down in a rocking chair and pouted.

After a while, Dad came in and took me in his arms and said he was sorry. "Daddy loves you. I won't do that again."

When I was a kid, Dad could do no wrong.

☆ ☆ ☆ ☆

Those first years at Ridgetop when Dad was around most of the time were happy times.

I remember Mr. Hughes's wife Ruby baked Dad a cake with a big star on it for his thirty-second birthday. And he was sure pleased with it, although we kept teasing him that that was as close to a star as he would probably ever get.

That was also when he started playing golf. At least, that was the first time that I ever remember him playing. He'd get out in the cow pasture and practice his shots. If a ball landed in a cow patty, he didn't mind. He'd either move out and hit it again or he'd try to hit it right where it lay. Chipping out of a cow chip. If they ever held the Masters in a pasture, I'll bet Dad would place in the money.

We had just about every kind of animal there was.

But our favorites were the horses. We each had a pony and we wanted to ride every day. We used to pester poor Mr. Hughes all the time.

"Mr. Hughes! Mr. Hughes! Please saddle the horses."

After a bit it would be, "Mr. Hughes! Mr. Hughes! Please unsaddle the horses."

But just as soon as he had gotten back to work, we would be after him again to saddle up.

We used to enter little horse shows and rodeo events in the area. The first time I tried to run a barrel race on my pony Spot, we went around at a slow walk. Mr. Hughes wasn't sure I was ever going to finish.

And Dad liked the horses too. He still does. We had nine horses: three ponies, two palominos, a quarter horse named "Preacher" that was Dad's favorite, and three Tennessee Walking Horses.

Tennessee Walkers have a real high stepping action like they're picking up one foot at a time and reaching way forward with it. The breed was developed for overseers to ride while they watched the work in the cotton fields, and that high step was developed so they could step over rows of cotton without hurting the plants.

Today the gaits are exaggerated for the show ring. But to watch one in action is almost like watching Fred Astaire or Gene Kelly. It's hard to believe something of flesh and blood can move like that.

Mr. Hughes said that Dad was the best rider of Tennessee Walkers he ever saw. He could make them change gaits just as smoothly as a race car driver can shift gears.

Not bad for a poor boy from Abbott. I wonder if, when Dad was picking cotton and watching the cars go by on the highway, he ever thought he'd own horses bred for the men who bossed the cotton pickers?

☆ ☆ ☆ ☆

So we spent a lot of time pestering Mr. Hughes to let us ride the horses. Or pestering Mr. Hughes to let us go into town with him. Or to let us help him with his chores.

Chores.

You know, it's funny how you enjoy helping a grownup do his chores when you're a kid, but it isn't any fun to do your own chores.

But we all had chores.

We learned to keep up our rooms and help keep house. In fact, Shirley learned right along with us. She'd been a performer since she was fourteen, so when she and Dad married, she didn't know much about keeping a house, let alone taking care of animals or tending a garden. She could cook, though, and she was a willing, hard worker. And she and Dad made sure that we three kids put in our time too.

We learned about mowing the lawn, and bringing in firewood, and building fires (with the kindling first, then the bigger pieces, and finally the logs — hardwoods like hickory or oak so they would burn a long time).

And we learned about weeding the garden. About feeding the ducks and geese and hens and roosters. Not to mention the cows and pigs and horses.

All the animals had names. I can't remember them all now, but I know we had Lester Flatt and the Foggy Mountain Hogs. And we had a Bill Dudley rooster.

The chickens caused a fight between Ray Price and Dad. They had remained good friends after Dad and Shirley got off the bus for good that day at Goodlettsville. But chickens ended it between them for a while.

Ray kept fighting roosters. And he called one day and asked Dad if he could bring some up to the farm to exercise them. Dad said sure, as long as they wouldn't hurt any of the laying hens. Ray assured him that the hens were safe, and he brought up a rooster.

Two days later, Dad was out in the barnyard and found one of the hens dead.

"You better come get this rooster," Dad told Ray over the phone. "He's already killed one of Shirley's hens and she's got them all named."

Ray said he'd be right out to get the rooster and that he'd bring another laying hen. But three weeks went by and no Ray. Then Shirley found another dead hen. She was really mad and threatened to get the shotgun and finish that rooster off.

Dad didn't like the idea of Shirley running around with a loaded shotgun out near where the horses and cattle were. So he said he'd do it.

Dad shot the rooster and brought it in for Pearlie Mae, the house-keeper, to cook for dinner. Pearlie Mae was named after Pearl Harbor because that was the day she was born.

Anyway, Dad called Ray and told him what had happened.

"You just killed a thousand-dollar rooster."

"Ain't no fighting rooster in the world worth one good laying hen," said Dad.

Ray wouldn't speak to Dad for years.

☆ ☆ ☆ ☆

There was school, of course.

When Billy first went to Ridgetop, he attended a Seventh Day Adventist school down the hill from the farm. After Lana and I arrived, I went to the same school until the fifth grade, when I went to Watauga Elementary in Ridgetop. Lana went to junior high school in Greenbriar, about eight miles down the road.

I've never been too fond of school. I had trouble with the homework, and I had the bad luck to draw some of the worst teachers in the world—teachers who would try to make you mess up so they could embarrass you in front of the whole class. And I had already started the habit of skipping school when I lived in Las Vegas with Mama.

But during the first couple of years at Ridgetop, my third- and fourth-grade years, I even thought school was okay. I rode the school bus with Billy and all my friends, and we had fun.

Then I started having serious trouble again and went back to my old ways.

I remember one time I was sent home from school because my skirt was too short. Miniskirts were just coming in style, and I had gotten one from somewhere—maybe Mama sent it to me. I wore it to school to show it off, and the teacher couldn't stand it.

That made Dad mad. He got up and drove the pickup truck to school to talk to the teacher. I don't know what happened, but according to Mr. Hughes, one of the things he said was, "Don't you know I'll get out of this truck and wrap you around that telephone pole?"

When I did get back to skipping school, one of the ways I would do it was to leave the house dressed in my school clothes and then sneak up the road to Aunt Bobbie's house.

Aunt Bobbie always made me feel welcome. I'd tell her that I felt sick and didn't want to go to school. And she would hug me and say, "You poor baby" and fix me something to eat. Then she'd let me go to sleep in her big old bed. When it was time for the school bus to get back, I'd go home like nothing had happened.

But I'll bet you're wondering what Aunt Bobbie was doing in Tennessee.

☆ ☆ ☆ ☆

Living with us, is the answer. Or just down the street from us.

When she got divorced from her second husband Paul, the man who owned the used car lot in Fort Worth, Dad invited her and the three boys to stay at Ridgetop.

And they weren't the only ones.

Pop and Lorraine moved up from Fort Worth too, into a house not far from our farm.

And just to make it complete, Dad and Aunt Bobbie's real mother, Mother Harvey, and her husband Ken moved to a little red brick house about five miles up the road. And Wade Ray, who had played with Dad a lot, moved into a house a stone's throw away. Wade and his wife Grace were good friends of both Dad and Shirley.

So there was quite a family compound at Ridgetop when it really got going.

But I was happiest that Aunt Bobbie was there. Not just because her house was a good place to hide out, but also because of my cousins. Freddie was the youngest, about five years older than me, and I worshiped him like a big brother. When I stayed at Aunt Bobbie's, I loved to fix us egg salad sandwiches and listen to him talk. He always called me Susie Q.

When he'd leave, I'd run sleep in his bed and wait for him to come home. He'd come in and tackle me and say, "Susie Q, fix us something to eat." And I'd get up and wait on him and his friends.

Freddie fixed up this little basement house. It was all underground except for the roof—a dugout, really—and Freddie had his drums in there. He also had a bed and a place to keep his clothes.

One time he let me spend the night with him in his basement pad. Now that made me feel like one cool kid, to be invited to stay with Freddie in his hangout.

☆ ☆ ☆ ☆

Even Mama moved back to Tennessee.

She didn't stay at Ridgetop, of course, but she moved to the Nashville area so she could be near us.

Not long after Lana and I moved to Ridgetop, Mama divorced Chuck Andrews and married a man named Mickey Scott, whom she had known in high school back in Waco.

In fact, Mama took up with Mickey right after we moved to Ridge-top. We had gone to Waco to see Nannie and Pa before we went to Dad's, and I think I remember that she started seeing Mickey before we left.

At the time, Mickey was the manager of a TG&Y store in Houston. But not long after he and Mama got together, he lost that job. So he moved back to Waco and took up being a painting contractor.

Mama would get lonely and start missing us. So she would talk Mickey into moving to Tennessee so she could be near us. Then he would get dissatisfied with the way the painting business was going, and they'd move back to Waco.

☆ ☆ ☆ ☆

So that's the way things went.

Sometimes we'd go in to watch Dad tape his part for the "Ernest Tubb Show." Sometimes we'd go on a special trip, like the time we went to Atlanta to see *Snow White* because Dad had heard that the Disney studio was going to take it out of circulation for seven years.

But mostly we just had fun together as a family, the family that Dad announced to the world via the mailbox as "Willie Nelson and Many Others." The family of a picker who was trying to become a gentleman farmer.

FOURTEEN

The Willie Nelson Show

"This is the greatest singer I've ever heard."

T he life of a guitar picker turned gentleman farmer began to lose its appeal before too long.

It wasn't that Dad didn't like farming. It was just that he couldn't get performing out of his blood. Writing songs and cutting demos wasn't enough. Cutting records for Chet Atkins at RCA Victor wasn't enough, especially when he never knew what the finished product was going to sound like until it was released.

Singing three or four songs on the Grand Ole Opry thirty or so weekends a year wasn't enough. Neither was doing the "Ernest Tubb Show."

☆ ☆ ☆ ☆

So Dad started playing around the area. And getting a few gigs back in Texas.

Dad had always done pretty well in Texas. But one of the things that made this work so well was that Dad hooked up with one of the biggest Willie Nelson fans in the world, a man named Crash Stewart.

Crash owned a finance company in San Antonio and a ranch to the west, in Medina County. He also dabbled in booking country music shows.

In 1966 he was in Nashville discussing the details of a Texas tour with Ray Price. But while Crash and Ray were working out who would be on the tour, Ray got a call from another promoter to tour up north. The money was a whole lot better than the Texas tour, and Ray just couldn't turn it down.

Dad jumped in and told Crash he'd be happy to take Ray's place. Crash said he was willing, but pointed out that from a business point of view Dad was nowhere near the equal of Ray Price as a drawing card.

"I know that," said Dad. "What we'll do is hire another big star to replace Ray and we'll call it the Willie Nelson Show, starring the other names who are actually better known than I am."

And that is what happened. They hired Marty Robbins as the big name and added Stonewall Jackson, Jeanie Sealy, Hank Cochran, and Johnny Bush—the first Willie Nelson touring show.

They also hired an unknown singer out of Montana who had a record out called "Snakes Crawl at Night." He had a great voice, new and distinctive, and they hired him as the opening act for a couple of shows. Actually, a Texas promoter who knew Dad from his days with Ray Price hired this newcomer for five shows and sold two of the dates to Dad and Crash.

The singer's name was Charley Pride.

Now for those very few of you who don't know, Charley Pride is black. That is not very remarkable today. But in the mid-sixties, you didn't expect to see a black man singing country music. And if you did, given the way things were back then, the audience probably wasn't going to like it very much.

The first time anybody saw Charley Pride perform outside of Montana was on Crash and Dad's show in Fort Worth. And when Charley walked out, the crowd was quiet, staring in disbelief. But Dad fixed that. He introduced Charley, kissed him full on the mouth, and asked for a big hand.

And he did the same thing at the second show, in front of an even tougher audience in Shreveport.

Of course, the fact that Charley could sing his ass off and that his record had been getting air-play did a lot to defuse the situation. But Dad did his part.

☆ ☆ ☆ ☆

After the success of the first tour, Dad and Crash formed a partnership. They called it Alamo Talent and began booking out of Crash's finance company on Bandera Road in San Antonio.

Their first agreement was that Dad and the band would get $400 for a weeknight, $500 for a Friday night, and $600 for Saturday.

When he first started, Dad's band consisted of Johnny Bush on drums, Wade Ray on fiddle, and Jimmy Day on steel guitar. This was the group that did a four-hour show at Panther Hall in Fort Worth that was recorded live and issued first as *Country Music Concert* and then reissued not long ago as *Willie Nelson Live.*

The personnel changed a bit each time Dad went back to Texas to play. Late in 1966 or early in 1967, Dad came through Houston without a drummer. He looked up his old friend Paul English and asked him how to get in touch with a certain drummer from Fort Worth.

Paul said, "Shit, Willie! I'm better than him."

"Yeah, but would you work for $30 a night?" Paul was making about $500 a week working on a children's TV show in Houston. He owned about five rent houses and a couple of duplexes and had a few other sidelines going.

But Paul said "Damn right I would" to the $30-a-night offer and went straight to work. They did twenty-nine one-nighters in a row.

Over the years, Paul sold his rent property — one unit at a time — so he could keep on playing with Dad. He's really addicted to music.

It reminds me of the story about the independent trucker who inherited a million dollars. He spent about $100,000 on a brand-new, customized Peterbilt tractor — the Rolls Royce of trucks — and went through the rest of his inheritance trying to keep it on the road.

Paul's been with Dad ever since.

☆ ☆ ☆ ☆

Dad came out of retirement gradually.

At first, he would just get together a pickup band and they'd play a few dates in the area. Then they'd get maybe a long weekend — a Thursday through Sunday gig, or maybe a tour — in Texas.

But Dad was still trying to be a farmer.

The souvenir program he printed during this period had a four-page spread of the farm and Shirley and us kids. There was even a picture of Mr. Hughes in the cattle pen. And under the picture of Dad driving the Ford tractor, Dad was quoted as saying: "Farming is my business and songwriting is my hobby."

You know, Dad probably could have retired then and lived modestly but comfortably off his royalties from his songs. And he might have made the farm into a paying proposition too.

But he's just like most musicians. He's got to perform.

Besides, he was appreciated. Texas crowds wanted to hear Dad. And other musicians wanted to hear Dad.

Roger Miller and his wife Leah were two of the biggest Willie Nelson fans in the world. Leah was from a wealthy San Antonio family. Roger had met her when he and Dad were playing with Ray Price and the Cherokee Cowboys.

During those days, Roger was in a situation a lot like Dad's. He was getting royalties from his songs like "Imitation of the Blues" and "Summertime," but he wasn't a name that could draw. So he did his performing by pickin' and grinnin' with Ray Price.

Ray would leave Roger in San Antonio so he could romance Leah — the picker and the millionaire's daughter. Buddy Killen at Pamper would send him money, and after a bit Roger would take a plane and catch up with the band.

Leah and Roger got married. And Roger made it big with songs like "King of the Road," "Dang Me," and "Little Green Apples." He also had a prime-time TV show on a national network.

One time while Roger and Leah were flying to San Antonio in their Lear jet to visit her parents, they heard that Dad was playing in town. They called Billy Deaton, the promoter, and asked him to hold a table for them.

During the intermission, Dad came over and sat down with them. A guy named Ben Dorsey, who worked as the band boy or general gofer for the group, followed right behind Dad. Ben was known as a talkative kind of guy — a real motormouth. Dad, of course, wanted to talk with Roger and Leah, whom he hadn't seen for a long time, and he didn't have much time between sets. So he pulled out a $10 bill and said, "Ben, sit down. I'm gonna hold this $10, and for every minute that you do not talk, I'm gonna give you a dollar."

Ben sat there, squirming like a little boy who had to go to the bathroom. But he kept his mouth shut ten dollars' worth.

Another big fan of Dad's was Jimmy Dean.

Dad was playing at Randy's Rodeo in San Antonio one year when the San Antonio Fat Stock Show and Rodeo was going on. Jimmy, who was a major star at this time with his own national TV show, had been booked by Billy Deaton to do a night at the rodeo.

After his performance at the rodeo, Billy told him that Dad was playing in town.

"Let's go. Where's your car?"

Billy had arranged for a special table for Jimmy, which was a good thing, because the place was packed. Billy told me there must have been a thousand people there.

Jimmy made quite a stir when he arrived, and a lot of people came over to get his autograph. They were disturbing Dad's set.

Billy suggested that Jimmy go and interrupt Dad on stage and tell the crowd that he was there to hear Dad but would be happy to sign autographs during the intermission.

And that's just what Jimmy Dean did. He got up on the stage and announced that "this is the greatest singer I've ever heard and I'm here to hear to him." He would be happy to sign autographs later, but right now he wanted to listen. And it worked.

☆ ☆ ☆ ☆

By 1967, Dad was going out for two or three weeks at a time. He had bought an old school bus to carry the band (it looked a lot like the bus that the band rode in the movie *Honeysuckle Rose*, except that it didn't look that good). They'd all get on, and the driver would put it in gear, and you wondered how in the world it was going to make it around the bend.

And there were more than a few times when it didn't make it.

Dad had become known well enough to cut a commercial for Rainbo Bread in Texas. Rainbo paid Dad and the band $900 for the spot. About four months went by after they cut the jingle, and finally the money came in. Dad was playing in San Antonio and the bus had broken down. It just so happened that he needed exactly $900 to get the bus out of the repair shop.

Life on the road was not all hard traveling and broken buses. They also managed to have a pretty good time.

Make-believe fights were one way they amused themselves.

David Zentner, who played bass and steel guitar with Dad during those years, told me about a fight they staged in a Houston motel to get Dad away from a bunch of folks who were partying in his room. The visitors kept asking him to sing another song, or have another drink, or take another toke. And Dad did. Because he can't say no.

So the band members gathered up a bunch of little plastic containers of ketchup and hid them down their shirts and in their pockets and wherever. Then they went to Dad's room, with all the people in it, and told him they were going to go over the dailies.

The dailies listed all the band's expenses, to see who had been spending money on what. Johnny Bush was the bookkeeper, so the band set it up where he would accuse Jimmy Day, the steel guitar player, of spending too much money. Jimmy was to deny it, and their argument was supposed to escalate into a free-for-all.

Everything went off like clockwork, with Jimmy bouncing off the TV and getting covered in ketchup. Everybody got into it, spreading their ketchup/blood all over the place.

Dad, not knowing what was going on, jumped to his feet. The band got up and split down the hall to another room.

Dad went down to the room and wanted to know what was going on. They told him, and he just stood there looking at them like they were a bunch of kids.

"Well, you took a good shot at it," he told them as he left. They never did know whether he was mad at them or not.

Another way they would try to get Dad away from people was to work a deal with the motel or hotel security guards. Usually, Johnny Bush or Paul English would explain the deal to the guards and they would show up in Dad's room and pretend to arrest him for being too noisy.

Paul and Johnny served as the business managers in those days, at least as far as making sure the band got paid. "They were into the numbers," is the way David Zentner put it to me.

Both knew the club owners — and how to get into the clubs to get the band's money. Because getting paid wasn't always the easiest thing to do, considering some of the clubs where they played. Upon occasion Paul or Johnny, even Dad sometimes, had to use a little of Colonel Colt's contract enforcement technique to collect their fee. Of course, that's just part of the traditional way of doing things in some Texas circles.

It was during this period that Dad became good friends with Darrell Royal, the University of Texas football coach.

Coach Royal was a country music fan of the first order. When he first went to the university, he used to catch the package shows that played the old City Coliseum. As his teams started winning and he became better known, he would get invited backstage.

He figures he probably met Dad when he was playing on those package shows, either with Ray Price or on his own. But the time he remembers best happened in 1967.

Coach Royal had the habit of having the football team stay together at the Holiday Inn the night before home games. It happened that Dad was staying at the same motel one night. He left some of his albums for Coach Royal, who took them home, listened to them, and has been a "kicked in the head Willie Nelson fan" ever since.

☆ ☆ ☆ ☆

Dad's touring gradually increased until it was nothing for him to be gone for thirty days at a stretch.

The bus wore out, never to run again, so Dad bought a station wagon and a trailer to carry the band and all the equipment. There were five people, plus the instruments, amps, P.A. system, one microphone, and one microphone stand. They would set everything up themselves.

The tours could be monumental. Paul likes to describe the longest route they did during those years. It lasted eighteen days, they played nine dates, and they covered 15,000 miles.

That is not a typo. Fifteen thousand miles in eighteen days.

They began in San Antonio, went to New Jersey, and then to Los Angeles. From L.A. they went to San Francisco, then San Diego and *back* to Los Angeles for the American Association of Country Music (AACM) awards. The last stop was Stamford, Connecticut — 3,280 miles away. They had sixty-nine hours to make it.

That kind of schedule can wear you down in a hurry.

Luckily, there were times when they could afford to fly. But flying wasn't all that convenient either. Dad made one airplane incident famous in his song "Me and Paul":

> And at the airport in Milwaukee
> They refused to let us board the plane at all
> They said we looked suspicious
> But I believe they like to pick on
> Me and Paul

What happened was that they were late trying to catch a plane and Paul left his briefcase in the cab. Dad went back to get it while Paul tried to buy the tickets. An airline employee was talking on the phone while Paul waited impatiently, and in the meantime he became engrossed in looking at the employee's twenty-year service pin on his lapel.

When he hung up, Paul told him, "You must have to take that pin on and off every day." That made the guy mad, for some reason or other. He told Paul that it was impossible for the band to catch the plane because it was about to depart.

"Can't you sabotage one of the engines for about four or five minutes?" Paul asked.

That did it. The employee shouted for the security men, claiming that Paul had threatened to blow up the plane.

As soon as they heard the story, the security guards relaxed. But Paul and Dad had missed the plane.

Not all the hassles of the road came from the unpredictable actions of airline employees or screwed-up schedules. Indian-giving club owners and the monotony of traveling weren't the only problems either.

Drug laws also posed a problem.

The incident in Laredo, when a maid found a roach in the motel room and called the cops, was part of "Me and Paul." Another close call happened in El Paso during a local drug crackdown. The police brought some trained dogs down to the bus to sniff around. Luckily, the band had just gotten a bunch of hamburgers to fortify them before going on that night, and the dogs were more interested in grease than grass.

Getting to play could be a problem too. The verse in "Me and Paul" about the package show in Buffalo really happened. Kitty Wells hogged the show, according to Paul. They had driven a long way in the station wagon and wanted to perform. But every time they looked up, there was Kitty Wells selling cookbooks, or introducing members of her family.

Dad had already found the bar downstairs and was holding court. Paul finally gave up when he was told that their part was going to be cut down to eleven minutes. He joined Dad in the bar.

"You're behind," Dad told him.

So Paul ordered four doubles at one time and fixed that problem in a hurry.

☆ ☆ ☆ ☆

The thing that made everything so frustrating was that Dad was drawing well, especially in Texas. But his albums weren't selling— maybe 20,000 copies of each a year.

One of the problems was that they'd go into the studio, lay down a voice track, and then the album would be released with a thirty-seven-piece orchestra. No matter how fantastic the arrangement was, it just wasn't Dad. It didn't fit his relaxed, picking-on-the-front-porch kind of style. And it sure wasn't a sound that Dad and the band could duplicate on stage.

They knew there was an audience for the sound they did produce on stage. For one thing, people came, especially in Texas. And they would come up after a show and say, "We like to hear you in person, but we just don't like your records."

So Dad's frustration level was growing. And part of the problem was the money.

During this period, Dad was probably getting anywhere from $60,000 to $100,000 a year from his song royalties. But most of that was going into paying for the farm and supporting us kids, not to mention Aunt Bobbie and her children, and Pop and Lorraine and Ken and Mother Harvey. There was hardly anything coming in from Dad's own records, and the band was barely breaking even, if that.

And, of course, Dad has never paid much attention to money anyway. He built us a swimming pool at Ridgetop. When Shirley wanted a Corvette, he had her fly down to San Antonio on her birthday and surprised her with one. They drove it back to Ridgetop together. He even bought Paul a car. But since Paul handled the money, he knew they couldn't afford it and took it back.

The band sometimes would go a couple of months without getting paid. Of course, when they were on the road, where they slept and what they ate came out of expense money. But that wasn't much help for the people at home. It was during these lean times that Paul would sell off a piece of property to keep things going.

Why was the band willing to do that?

They liked Dad, for one thing. And they were musicians. Like Paul says, if you want to make big money, go into plumbing. He advises young musicians that "if you think you ought to quit, and you can, then you should."

But the band couldn't quit. And neither could Dad. He'd tried that.

It was sure starting to play hell with our happy home at Ridgetop.

FIFTEEN

Falling to pieces again

"Lady, you hit everything in sight."

D ad's return to life on the road started to eat away at the idyllic life we had at Ridgetop.

It probably was the result of a combination of things that none of us understands fully yet. Maybe things would have fallen apart even if Dad had stayed retired and tried to make it as a hog farmer who happened to have a talent for songwriting. In some ways, those early years at Ridgetop were too good to be true—or too good to last, anyway.

☆ ☆ ☆ ☆

At first, it didn't seem as though anything had changed.

Of course, Dad wasn't there all the time, but he wasn't gone very often and not for very long at a time. And he would call us every night. He'd usually call after supper, and we would each talk to him and fill him in on what we'd been doing.

Shirley would talk, then Lana, and then Billy. Then it would be my turn. And I was the little reporter—or tattletale.

"Dad, there's something I think you ought to know," I'd begin, and then I'd tell him how Lana and Billy had screwed up.

Lana wouldn't help me with my homework. Or Billy tried to ride my pony Spot. Things like that.

Looking back on it, I'd have to say that I was a little bitch. Sometimes I wonder how anybody put up with me then.

"Well, Daddy loves you," I'd hear over the phone, and then Dad would ask to speak with Shirley.

One of the ways Dad coped with not being there was to set up projects for us to do before he got back. If we did them, then something would happen when he returned.

For instance, when he built the swimming pool, none of us could swim at all. We all had to wear life jackets when we went in the pool. Dad told us if we wore our life jackets whenever we swam, we would be able to swim without them when he got back. Guess what? He was right.

Or if Billy and I could learn to ride without fighting over Spot, then we could ride in the parade when the rodeo came to Springfield, Tennessee.

It was a good idea, and it made us eager for Dad to come home. It made homecoming an event. And now that I am a mother of two myself—and a single parent—I can appreciate the amount of effort Dad put into staying in touch with us and trying to be an everyday part of our lives even while he was touring.

But he still wasn't there.

And when he would leave, it would bring back the feelings I had had when we'd say goodbye to him in Goodlettsville. It was back to "you dream about me and I'll dream about you." And part of those memories involved the trouble and the fights that Mama and Dad had had, and how our home had broken up, and how everything was scary and unhappy for years.

I don't mean to say that I consciously thought all of this. But we kids had missed Dad so much and were so happy when we got to live with him that when he started to be gone a lot of the time, the old feelings started to resurface.

We were so hungry for attention that we each wanted to be the only child. We were all jealous of each other.

I remember that I stayed mad and hurt for a long time because Billy and Lana got to have their tonsils taken out and I didn't. They got to stay home from school, but I had to go. They got to stay in bed and have cool cloths on their foreheads, but I had to stay up and help out. They didn't have to eat anything but ice cream, but I had to eat everything on my plate before I could have any dessert.

Since I didn't understand about tonsils or infections or anything, I assumed that they got special treatment because Dad and Shirley loved them more than they loved me.

☆ ☆ ☆ ☆

Looking back on it after all these years, I wonder whether Shirley felt the same jealousy of Dad and the band.

After all, she had been successful in her own right. If she wasn't exactly a star, she was known by most everyone in the business and had a solid performing and recording career before she and Dad got together.

David Zentner told me that Shirley was a real good bass player and that she put the comedy into the show when she and Dad played together. According to David, it was like a Las Vegas act. Or like Johnny Carson and Ed McMahon, with Dad as the straight man and Shirley delivering the funny lines.

And of course there was Shirley's yodeling. She would open up and finish her set with yodeling that would leave everybody standing and calling for more. Then she would bring on Dad. And a lot of people suspect that Dad was jealous of her yodeling. I don't know about that because all Dad has ever said was, "How'd you like to have to follow that . . . a standing ovation before you even get on stage?"

Shirley also says that Dad asked her to stop writing songs.

So when you add everything together, you have to figure that Shirley was jealous of Dad's career.

She didn't show it. Not at first.

A lot of the band moved to the area, and she would cook these enormous meals for everybody. David always remembers her as the cheerful one who kept everyone going. She taught David a lot about playing bass — "She was an ungodly good bass player."

But as Dad began to tour more and more, it became obvious that there were problems.

☆ ☆ ☆ ☆

And the reason was that Dad was staying away for thirty days at a time. When he did get home, he would bring a lot of people with him to stay with us.

It was driving Shirley crazy. Her home wasn't her home any more.

Dad wasn't there a lot of the time. And so when we would sit around the supper table and say grace holding hands, we all felt that something was missing. Shirley would try to keep us on the routine of school and chores and bedtimes that she and Dad had worked out earlier, but it kept getting harder and harder.

And when Dad was home it was even worse. We wouldn't go to bed on time, we wouldn't do our chores, the whole routine would fall apart because we were so excited to see Dad. Instead of being a regular, everyday part of our lives, he was back to being a special event.

When Dad was back, the house became a hotel. Shirley had to step over sleeping or passed-out people to get to her own bedroom.

From her point of view, she had given up everything that she had — a career, a marriage, even her reputation as far as some folks were concerned — in order to make a home and have a family with Dad. She had spent the money she had earned from her career, money that meant security in a way that only people raised during the Depression can understand, to make a home for us — her family.

And now she could see it all crumbling down around her.

She didn't know what to do.

☆ ☆ ☆ ☆

And I started skipping school. I developed several new techniques for playing hooky. Sometimes I wouldn't leave the house. I'd stay in my room in the basement and pull the two beds together to make my own little safe, secure den. Then I'd crawl in and spend the day sleeping. When 3:30 rolled around, I'd get up, get dressed, and go upstairs like I'd been at school all day.

And I'd steal pills from Shirley. Or I'd get some acid from the kids in the neighborhood. Yes. Acid had reached the mountain town of Ridgetop.

It took a couple of years for things to get the way they were. But I remember at my worst, I had skipped school for twenty-eight days. That was in the fifth grade at Watauga Elementary. I couldn't handle the Seventh Day Adventist school any longer. They couldn't handle me, either. We agreed to disagree. (But now, when I go back to Ridgetop for a visit, I always stop in at that school.)

At first, I skipped a day or two at a time. Then four days, then a week. And I was able to get some sympathy from the people at school by explaining how bad things were at home. In a community like Ridgetop, the teachers and the principal knew something about what was going on.

I had worked out my way of dealing with things. I wouldn't call it a con, exactly. But it was close.

Twenty-eight days was a record. I was able to get away with it because Dad was on the road and Shirley was running around all the time. When Dad left, so did Shirley, for all practical purposes.

The notification came from the school the same day that Dad got in off the road. It started a real fight between Dad and Shirley, with Shirley using my behavior as an example of what all was going wrong and with Dad wanting to know just what in the hell Shirley was doing while he was away.

They were arguing in the kitchen when I came up the stairs from my room in the basement — right into the middle of it.

Shirley turned and confronted me.

And I lied.

In fact, I called her a liar. Which wasn't too bright, since she had the letter from the school right there in her hand.

Shirley slapped me. It was the only time she had ever hit me.

That made me really mad. I went to my room, shut the door, and started trying to figure out how to get rid of her.

That was always my way. What I wanted was to be with Dad. My daddy could do no wrong. When we were living with Mama and Chuck, I figured everything would be all right if we lived with Dad. So I wrote letters and made the phone call to try to get that to happen. In the same way, I now blamed Shirley as the cause for all the problems. If I could get rid of Shirley, then we could have Dad all to ourselves and everything would be back to normal.

Scheming was my way of trying to fix things.

Lana's way was to get away herself.

In a lot of ways, Lana is like Dad. She and Dad have this way of communicating through looks and expressions. It's like they're on the same mental wavelength and don't need words. Anyway, one of Dad's ways of coping with difficult situations is to leave — I think that's one reason he likes the road so much. So Lana was planning on leaving too.

She was fourteen at the time and had been dating Mickey Newberry, a songwriter who was twenty-seven. They were going to run away and get married.

The plan was for Mickey to pick her up after school. How do I know? I listened in on their phone conversation when they made the plans, that's how.

And I'm the one who blew the whistle on them too.

"There's something I think you ought to know," I told Shirley. And Shirley told Dad. And Dad got his pistol and the two of them drove down to the high school in Greenbriar. There was Mickey sitting in his big Cadillac waiting for Lana to get out of school.

Dad pulled up and signaled Mickey to get out of the Caddy and get in his car. Dad proceeded to explain to the young Mr. Newberry that not only was he not getting married that day, he was never going to see Lana again. And if he tried to, Dad was going to fix it so he wouldn't need a woman ever again.

Then they waited for Lana to get out of school and told the two of them together just how it was going to be.

Lana was mad. But she blamed Shirley for ruining her life, for making her lose her one true love. I was really the reason for it, but I didn't volunteer that bit of information. I was perfectly happy to let Shirley take the blame.

Lana coped by trying to leave, and I coped by scheming to get rid of Shirley. Billy didn't cope.

All Billy knew was that something was terribly wrong. He would look at Shirley and ask her, "When you leave, will you take me with you?"

"Of course I will," Shirley would tell him, knowing full well that there was no way in the world she could do that.

And, of course, when she did leave, she didn't take Billy. And Billy hasn't talked to Shirley, or even mentioned her name, to this day.

☆ ☆ ☆ ☆

So things kept building and building toward an explosion.

Including our cars. The Corvette that Dad had bought Shirley for her birthday was one of the first. It had developed a problem in the carburetor or throttle linkage, which was pretty exciting. It would lock wide-open.

I remember one time I was riding with Shirley in that car when it happened. I think we were going to the airport. We were just coming to an intersection with a major highway and a big semi was coming down, doing seventy or eighty miles an hour. Our throttle stuck. Shirley thought quickly and did the only thing she could do: she forced the gearshift into park and turned off the key. So much for the Corvette. It got traded in for a Mercury Cougar.

But with her pills, drinking, and running around, that Cougar didn't last too long. Coming home one night and feeling no pain, Shirley got into a skid that lasted some 180 to 200 feet. Mailboxes, fence posts—you name it, Shirley hit it.

She finally ran into a little telephone pole that was leaning at better than a forty-five-degree angle. That stopped her, mainly because the pole went in the right front window and out the left rear.

"What did I hit?" Shirley asked the policeman who arrived shortly thereafter.

"Everything in sight, lady. Everything in sight."

Dad wasn't having much luck with the station wagon they used to pull the equipment trailer. They had just bought it from Lucky Moler, who was managing the group at the time. It was parked facing the swimming pool, and the trailer was full of equipment and clothes and everything. And the car caught on fire.

A couple of band members went into the house to tell Dad: "Will, we got to get us another car, that one just burned up."

So they went over to the Mercury dealer and got a brand new Marquis. The first or second night out, Dad called to talk to Shirley and when he hung up he told the band: "She just rolled the car off the cliff."

"We practically lived over at that Mercury place. We bought a new car every month," says David Zentner.

The cars even became a part of the fights between Dad and Shirley. I remember us kids watching from the house while Dad and Shirley sat in the car and argued. Dad got so mad he broke the windshield with his hand. Then he saw us watching and he calmly said that it was time for us to get ready for bed.

"Okay, Daddy," we said, "We'll go take our baths now."

Our house wasn't protected from their fights either. One time Shirley threw Dad through the sliding glass door. Dad was a karate black belt and had taught Shirley a bit about it.

"He taught me just enough karate to make me dangerous," Shirley says.

On this night they were having an argument. Dad wanted to camp out in the holler behind the house—he did that all the time—and Shirley wanted no part of it. Both of them had been drinking. When Dad made a gesture and a move toward her, Shirley got hold of him and threw him through the door. She says that he actually stumbled and fell, doing most of it on his own. But now when Shirley identifies herself as the second Mrs. Nelson, she can say that no, she wasn't the wife who sewed him up in a sheet, she was the wife who threw him through the window.

☆ ☆ ☆ ☆

Some of the things that happened during that time were funny, but mostly they were bad times.

Things just kept getting worse and worse.

Mr. and Mrs. Hughes couldn't stand it any more. They loved both Shirley and Dad and they couldn't bear to watch what was going on between them. One day Mr. Hughes just parked the pickup by the barn and walked away for good.

Neither Dad nor Shirley would talk about divorce. I don't know what either one was thinking, but according to Shirley, the subject of divorce never came up between them. They were trying to resolve their problems, trying to get things back together the way they used to be.

But the divorce happened anyway. We kids were hustled up and moved to the apartment complex in Madison where Paul and Carlene English lived.

And Dad and Shirley didn't speak to each other for almost ten years.

☆ ─────────────────────────────────────

SIXTEEN

Another New Mother

"What can you do to me now?"

After we left the farm, we never saw Shirley again. Nobody told us anything about how she was doing or what she was doing. Nobody even spoke her name. Not Paul or Carlene. Not Pop or Lorraine. Not Mother Harvey or Ken. Not Dad.

It was like she died.

☆ ☆ ☆ ☆

I recently got in touch with Shirley as part of doing research for this book, and I learned a bit about what happened.

For one thing, she had been sick with pneumonia. For two or three winters before the breakup, Shirley came down with pneumonia almost like clockwork. It was probably a result of the pills and the alcohol weakening her resistance, but you could count on Shirley being in the hospital for at least a week every year. Mr. Hughes would go visit her and take her bananas and baloney. They weren't on the hospital menu, and for some reason that's what Shirley always wanted.

After the last fight, Shirley stayed alone at the house for a couple of days, too sick to move or even know much about what was going on. The only contact she had with the family was with Lana and cousin Freddie, who showed up a couple of days after we moved to Madison to ask if they could get some things to furnish the apartment.

She said yes, and they collected a load of dishes and pots and pans, sheets and towels, and things of that nature.

She did drive down to Madison to see us. Or try to. When she got there, she asked Carlene, who was one of her closest friends, if she could talk to us. Carlene had to tell her no, that we couldn't talk with Shirley and that Shirley was not allowed to see us or communicate with us in any way.

A day or so later, Shirley went to see Dr. Bottsford. He told her that if she didn't go home, get to some people she loved who would take care of her, she would be dead within two weeks.

She called up her family in Chillicothe, Missouri, where she hadn't lived since she was fourteen, and asked one question: "Can I come home?"

She was thirty-nine years old, and for the first time in her life she asked if she could come home.

The answer was yes. So she called an old friend and asked him if he would drive her the 600 miles. He would, if she paid him.

So Shirley packed a few pairs of blue jeans and her guitar and paid her former boyfriend to take her home. When she got there, she got out of the car, walked to the door, and collapsed in her mother's arms.

She never saw the guy who drove her again.

It took her a year to recover from the pneumonia and the drug and alcohol abuse.

"My parent's house in Chillicothe? That's cold turkey."

☆ ☆ ☆ ☆

Things weren't going very well for us either.

For one thing, the apartment was tiny. I used a double closet for my room. I laid a mattress down on the floor, put in blacklight posters, had a phone put in, and hooked up my stereo on headphones.

I called it my psychedelic closet. I'd smoke a little dope, turn on some Jimi Hendrix or Janis Joplin, and I was home.

Dad used to visit me in the closet. We'd smoke a number and I'd turn him on to my music. Or we'd talk about what we wanted to be when we grew up. I'd tell him "a receptionist." I don't know why. It was just the first thing that popped into my head. And I'd ask him what he wanted to be when he grew up and he'd always say "a farmer." I guess Ridgetop was still in his system.

But then Dad would try to get inside my head. He'd try to find out what I was thinking, where I was as a person. And that would make me mad.

"Dad, I know what you're doing." He'd smile at me with those big, brown eyes. He'd even look a little guilty, like he had been caught red-handed.

So I would smile back and give him a kiss. "I love you, Dad. But don't you try to get inside my head, okay?"

"Okay," he'd say. And he'd take another hit or two and listen to another Jimi Hendrix track and hold my hand a few minutes more. Then he'd leave. "Daddy loves you," he'd say. And off he'd go.

It was strange to be jerked out of our home and now living in that tiny apartment. Of course, I pretty much stopped going to school. Dad was still going on the road. And the question was, who was going to look after us while he was gone?

He solved that problem, or tried to, as only Willie Nelson would. He came back from a road trip with a dancer from Atlanta.

"This is Helen," he told us, "and she's going to stay with you awhile."

Helen was a short, beautiful twenty-four-year-old with all the physical equipment you would expect a dancer to have. She was a sweet person, really, but she had no more idea of taking care of a house full of halfway grown kids than the man in the moon. She was a party girl, which is all right. But here she was with two girls, ages fifteen and twelve, and an eleven-year-old boy that she was supposed to take care of.

She was out of her league, to put it mildly.

I looked at her and thought, "Boy, it's sure getting weird around here."

And on top of everything, I was mad. I had done everything I could to get rid of Shirley so it could be just us and Dad. And as soon as I succeeded in driving Shirley away — at least, that's what I thought I had done — then in comes another woman.

And it proceeded to get even more weird.

One night when Dad was off the road, we were sharing a joint in my closet and he told me about Connie. He had met her at a club in Cut 'n Shoot, Texas, not far from Houston. He told me about how nice she was, and we telephoned her right from the closet. And that's how I met my second stepmother-to-be.

But Helen was still there. Dad went on the road again and while he was gone, Lana fixed it so she could get away.

She came in one day and told Helen that she was pregnant and that she had to get married. The father was another twenty-seven-year-old man named Steve Warren, who lived not far from Ridgetop. He was a real hillbilly.

What had happened was that one of the last things Shirley had done before she left was answer a phone call from Mickey Newberry.

Apparently, she told Mickey that Lana was married. Shirley was so strung out at this time she doesn't remember whether that's what she said or not. But she must have told him something, because Mickey was heartbroken. And he got married just to show the world in general and Lana in particular.

Now Lana was heartbroken and she was going to get married to show the world and Mickey. Not to mention get away from the family situation, which was getting crazier every day.

Poor Helen. There wasn't anything she could do, but she sure knew that Dad wasn't going to be happy.

☆ ☆ ☆ ☆

We didn't stay at the Madison apartment too long. After Shirley left, Dad had the farmhouse remodeled and we moved back in. Me and Billy and Helen—and, as soon as Dad went on the road again, Helen's two kids. She had two daughters, ages three and two, and they came to stay with us.

Then Helen began messing up.

When Dad left on a tour, he would leave her with plenty of money to run the house. But she'd spend it on clothes and rock concert tickets. She would hardly keep any food in the house, and she expected me to babysit her kids while she went out partying.

I didn't say anything. But I'd think, "You just keep it up darlin'. Because you are messing up and it won't be long before your ass is out of here."

And it didn't take too long for the stuff to hit the fan. She had gone out to a Tom Jones concert one night when Dad called to see how things were going.

"Not good, Dad," I told him. "There isn't hardly any food in the house. Helen's gone off to hear Tom Jones, and I'm stuck home babysitting Michelle and Susie."

"Okay. Daddy loves you. You just sit tight and we'll get everything straightened out."

An hour later, Paul's wife Carlene showed up at the house. She threw all of Helen's things into a suitcase and did the same with the kids' stuff.

About eleven, at intermission, Helen called to see how the kids were doing. Carlene took the phone and told her to go to the bus station right then.

Carlene drove the kids to the Greyhound station and handed them to their mother, along with a one-way ticket southbound out of town.

That took care of Helen.

But it still wasn't going to be just Dad and us.

When the bus pulled in off the road from this trip, Connie was with Dad.

☆ ☆ ☆ ☆

"Here's your new mother," Dad told us.

I got along all right with Connie. At least I did at first.

But not Billy. He had had more than he could stand. He took one look at Connie and went straight to his room.

"He'll get over it," Dad told her. "Just give him time to get used to the idea."

I followed Billy and started telling him he was being a brat, that he shouldn't have acted that way. He just looked at me with tears in his eyes and didn't say a word. Just like he did at the old lady's house where he was force-fed oatmeal.

So we were back at Ridgetop. The house was remodeled. We were trying to get life back to normal.

But it was hard. Connie tried with Billy, but it never worked.

There were still a lot of tensions in the air. Connie was twenty-seven and hadn't had much experience with running a house. And even though it was remodeled, it was still another woman's house.

And she had acquired three children. Billy was eleven and openly hostile. I was twelve, and while I was trying to get along with her, I was doing drugs and going through my own problems. Dad was still on the road a lot. Connie couldn't have had an easy time of it.

And then there was Lana.

Lana had made a big mistake. She had married a real turkey, which, as I was to find out later, is real easy to do when you marry for the wrong reasons — such as, to get out of what you think is a bad situation. A lot of the time you find that the fire you jump into is a whole lot hotter than the frying pan that was scorching your feet.

Anyway, that's what happened to Lana.

Steve Warren turned out to be one of those macho country kind of guys who think it is their God-given right to beat up on their wives.

One day Steve and Lana came by the house for something. Steve came in, but Lana wouldn't get out of the car.

I went down to visit with her and asked her why she wouldn't come in for a drink or something. She didn't say much, and when I got closer I could see why. Both her eyes were black and she had bruises all over her face.

"What happened?" I asked.

"Steve hit me."

About that time, Steve came back to the car and they drove off.

I went straight to Dad and told him that Lana was all beat up.

"She's got two black eyes and her face is all swollen. Dad you've got to do something."

I don't think I've ever seen him so mad. Not even when he told Mickey Newberry to stay away from Lana. Not in any of the fights he and Shirley had.

He jumped in the truck and drove down to Steve and Lana's. And from what I understand, Dad grabbed Steve by the neck and beat his face into the wall.

Steve may not have been smart, but he was persistent.

He took it out on Lana, and she got out of the house and went racing back to the farm. Her main concern was that she hadn't been able to get Nelson, the baby, out.

But Steve wasn't far behind. He came roaring up and started shooting at the house.

Mama was in town, visiting, and just happened to be at the house with her husband, Mickey. So Dad, Paul, and Mickey all grabbed guns and headed outside.

"You all go to the back and stay on the floor," Dad told us.

That started the great shootout at Ridgetop. Dad got up in the hayloft and Paul found some cover somewhere and they began shooting back. Poor Wade Ray, the fiddle player, was out mowing his lawn across the street a ways when bullets started tearing up his yard. He ran for cover and must have wondered why World War III was starting in Ridgetop.

It didn't take Steve too long to figure out that he was on the short end of the deal, so he hightailed it out of there. But the fool went to the police, and before long a cop showed up and wanted to talk to Dad about a complaint that had been received from a Mr. Steve Warren that a Willie Nelson had shot up his car.

This cop was not the brightest light in the county. Dad looked at him and said that maybe Mr. Warren had run over a bullet.

"Run over a bullet. I see. Well, thank you Mr. Nelson for explaining this to me."

The whole thing finally blew over, but it sure was exciting there for a while.

☆ ☆ ☆ ☆

Dad sure had a lot of things going on. He and Shirley had split. Connie was now in the house at Ridgetop. His oldest daughter was married to a wifebeater. I was running around stoned or tripping all the time. And his only son was in a perpetual state of shock and wouldn't talk to Connie.

On top of that, his records weren't selling that well.

But he was still working on the road and he was still writing songs.

Whenever he and the band would come off the road, they would work on songs. Sometimes Hank Cochran would come out, sometimes Roger Miller would drop by, and they would have songwriting sessions.

David Zentner had an old tape recorder that they would set up in the basement sometimes. He remembers once when Roger and Hank and Dad all got crazy drunk. Dad gave him something like three or four hundred dollars and told him to drive to town and get some tapes. David went to Nashville and bought all the tapes he could find. When he got back, they were into scotch and beer and songwriting.

"Can you just run the machine and keep it going?"

That's what David did. He worked the machine. Roger Miller would go out and walk around the bottom of the hill and come back and sing a song or a piece of one. Whenever anyone had a song worked out, or an idea for one, they would sing it into the tape recorder and write it down. David finally got to where he wouldn't do anything until the beeper signaled the time to change tapes.

You make it a habit to work like that and after awhile you can build up a lot of material. Dad estimates that there were probably tapes and charts for four or five hundred songs down in the basement.

One of the last ones that he wrote down there was one he did with Hank Cochran called "What Can You Do To Me Now?" It kind of summed up the last year or so. Four or five wrecked cars. Shirley gone. The whole thing.

They wrote that song not long before Christmas of 1969.

A few days later, the farmhouse at Ridgetop burned down.

There are a lot of versions about what happened then.

I wasn't home the day it happened. I was at a friend's house.

Waylon Jennings says that Dad was in Nashville when he got the news, and it was the only time he ever saw him rattled. "Willie walked past me and said, 'Can't talk now, man. My house is burning down.'"

The story also goes that Dad raced home and tried to save the songs and his marijuana stash. He saved the prime Columbian that was in a guitar case, he saved his guitar, but he lost the songs.

David Zentner had gone home to visit his parents in San Antonio for the holidays. He called to wish us a Merry Christmas but couldn't get an answer at the house. He finally reached Dad at Mother Harvey's house.

"You're not home and the phone isn't working."

"Yes," said Dad. "Merry Christmas."

"I'll be back up there real soon and I'll be bringing all you guys Christmas presents and everything."

"No. I'll tell you what. Why don't we just meet in Fort Worth? There's no reason for you to come all the way up here."

Dad finally handed the phone over to Mother Harvey and she told David that the house was gone. He just couldn't bear to tell the bad news himself.

☆ ☆ ☆ ☆

It's funny, but that was just about the best Christmas we ever had.

We moved into the trailer up behind where the house had been. Moon and Billy and I went out about midnight and cut a tree—a scrawny, pitiful little tree. We waited until everyone was asleep, and Moon and I dragged the tree behind his bicycle. I remember it was so cold and clear, with snow on the ground. We used one of Dad's cowboy boots for the Christmas tree stand, and we decorated it with Dad's socks and with ribbons from the presents.

We finally finished around three in the morning. I went outside with Moon and hugged him goodnight. He wished me a Merry Christmas and I stood there for a while listening to him whistle as his bike crunched through the snow toward his house.

That morning Connie woke me. And there was everybody, surprised and happy to see the tree. Dad was standing there in his blue jeans, flannel shirt, and stocking feet just smiling and looking proud.

But it was time for a change of scenery. So we moved to Bandera, Texas.

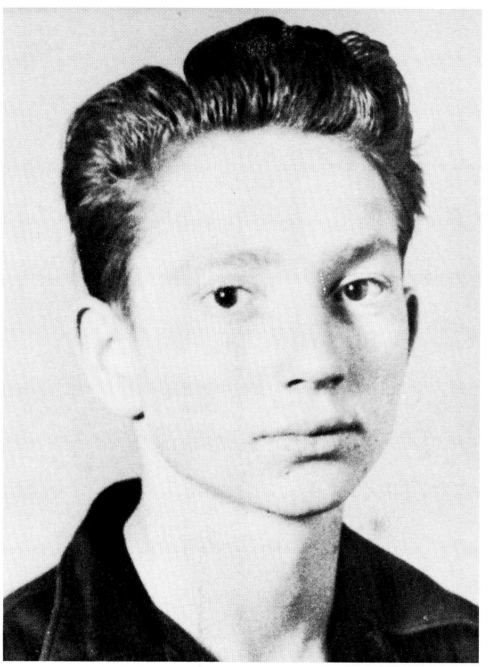

The young Willie Nelson.

Dad as a member of the Abbott High School football team.

Airman Willie Nelson.

"Mama and Daddy Nelson."

— Lana Nelson Collection

Dad's parents, Ira and Lorraine.

My mother, Martha Matthews.
— *Lana Nelson Collection*

Spic and Span Willie.
— *Lana Nelson Collection*

Dad and Bobbie (left) played and sang in a band organized by Bobbie's husband, Bud Fletcher, shown playing the fiddle. Dad's father, Ira "Pop" Nelson, is at right with a guitar.

— *Lana Nelson Collection*

Willie (fourth from left) sang with this early-day western band, Joe Massey and the Frontiersmen.

— *Lana Nelson Collection*

Performing on the Grand Ole Opry.

— Photo by Alan L. Mayor

Dad with me, Lana, and Billy.

Aunt Bobbie.

— Photo by Rick Hensen

"Nannie and Pa" Matthews, Martha's parents.

— Author's Collection

Martha and Willie, from an early photo taken shortly after they were married.
— *Lana Nelson Collection*

Lana, me, and Billy in the early 1960s, soon after Mama and Dad's divorce.
— *Author's Collection*

Dad holds a birthday cake with a star in the center made by Ruby Hughes in 1965 and delivered early in the morning, while Dad was still in his bathrobe.

— *Photo by Alan L. Mayor*

As a disc jockey at KVAN in Vancouver, Washington, 1957.

— *Author's Collection*

Performing at "Big G's," Round Rock, Texas, 1970.

— *Author's Collection*

In the sixties.
— *Photo by Alan L. Mayor*

Dad at twenty-three.
— *Author's Collection*

Willie "and many others" including Lana, Billy, and Susie.
— *Photo by Alan L. Mayor*

Dad and actor James Garner on stage.
— *Photo by Rick Hensen*

With friends in the early 1960s.

Dad with his first airplane and pilot Glenn Jones. Mr. Hughes is at far right.

Dad and Ernest Tubb.

— Photo by Rick Hensen

Dad and Waylon Jennings.

— Photo by Rick Hensen

Dad accepting an award from former Longhorn coach Darrell Royal.
— *Photo by Rick Hensen*

Dad and his gray Mercedes after a concert.
— *Photo by Rick Hensen*

With Buddy Lee, owner of Buddy Lee Attractions of Nashville, who has booked Dad since 1972.

Posing for Farm Aid video promotion.

Recording session.

— Photo by Alan L. Mayor

Relaxing between takes for *Honeysuckle Rose.*

— Photo by Rick Hensen

With Dyan Cannon during filming of
Honeysuckle Rose.
— *Photo by Daniel J. Schaefer*

With country music's legendary Mae
Axton ("best friends forever").
— *Photo by Alan L. Mayor*

With Francis Preston at Country Music Hall of Fame in Nashville for the opening of the Willie Nelson exhibit.

— Author's Collection

Dad and Kris Kristofferson at a press conference for the movie *Songwriter*.

— Photo by Alan L. Mayor

A Willie Nelson Christmas.

— Photo by Rick Hensen

Willie going electric.
— *Photo by Daniel L. Schaefer*

Dad in the early 1960s.
— *Photo by Alan L. Mayor*

Shirley Nelson in the mid-1960s.
— *Photo by Alan L. Mayor*

Shirley Nelson and I sing a duet on the front porch of George Hughes's home.
— *Photo by Alan L. Mayor*

Dad and Connie (right) with Billy and his wife Janet.

Connie, Paula Carlene, and Amy with the 1979 Country Music Entertainer of the Year.

Me and my children in 1981, shortly after my husband Tony was killed.
— *Author's Collection*

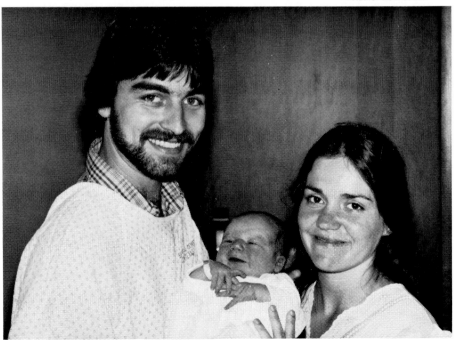

Me and second husband Tony with son Anthony, three days after his birth on August 22, 1980.
— *Author's Collection*

Me and husband Roy in 1974.

Dad and me at my wedding to Roy Owen, September 7, 1973.

My sister and brother, Lana and Billy, and mother, Martha, in 1985.
— *Lana Nelson Collection*

Billy Nelson as stand-in for Merle Haggard in the "Poncho and Lefty" video.
— *Photo by Rick Hensen*

Daughter Lana with Willie.

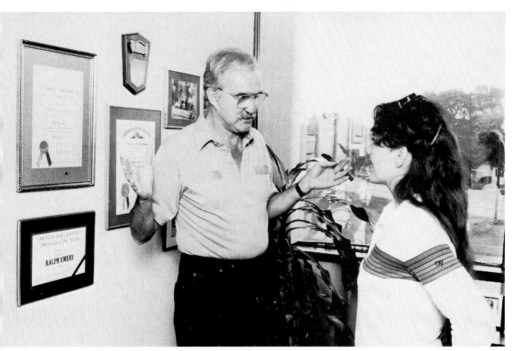

Ralph Emery and I reminisce about his recording of "Hello Fool," a takeoff on "Hello Walls."

— *Photo by Alan L. Mayor*

With Ott Devine, who signed Willie on to the Grand Ole Opry.

— *Photo by Alan L. Mayor*

Interviewing Faron Young, Charlie Williams, and Bobby Bare.
— *Photo by Alan L. Mayor*

Hayes Jones and I looking over old photos of Dad.
— *Photo by Alan L. Mayor*

Me in 1981 while a dancing instructor at Lillian Coltzer's Dance Studio.
— Author's Collection

At his golf course in Austin, Texas.

— Photo by Rick Hensen

A session of Kung Fu Karate.
— *Photo by Alan L. Mayor*

"It's a hard job but someone has to do it." Dad in Japan in the early 1980s.
— *Author's Collection*

Keeping the dream alive in Big Spring, Texas, 1970s.
— *Author's Collection*

Dad is a great believer in keeping fit.
— *Photo by Rick Hensen*

Dad dresses for every occasion.
— *Photo by Rick Hensen*

Doing what Dad loves to do most —
perform for an appreciative audience.
— *Photo by Rick Hensen*

Taking a day off at the golf course.
— *Photo by Rick Hensen*

Dad's smile can be disarming.
— *Photo by Rick Hensen*

"Poncho and Lefty" music video, written, produced, and directed by Lana.
— *Photo by Daniel J. Schaefer*

Faron Young with bull that paid the debt.
— *Photo by Alan L. Mayor*

Triple-platinum album award for *Always On My Mind*.
— Photo by CBS Records

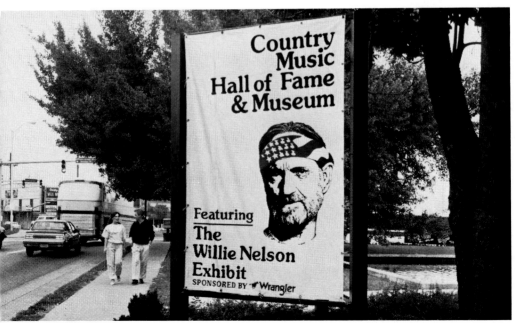
Country Music Hall of Fame sign featuring the Willie Nelson exhibit.
— Photo by Alan L. Mayor

Hal Smith, Hank Cochran, and Francis Preston in the early 1960s.

Chet Atkins, who signed Dad with RCA Victor.

Wade Ray, Dad's fiddle player in the 1960s.

Bee Spears and Mickey Raphael, Dad's bass and harmonica players.
— *Photo by Rick Hensen*

Paul English, longtime drummer in Dad's band.
— *Photo by Rick Hensen*

Johnny Bush, a member of Dad's group in the early years and author of "Whiskey River."
— *Photo by Alan L. Mayor*

Jody Payne, Dad's guitar player.
— *Photo by Rick Hensen*

Dad took part in the making of the album called *We Are The World* with proceeds supporting the people of Africa. Shown with him here are Lionel Ritchie, Bob Dylan, Michael Jackson, Cyndi Lauper, Tina Turner, and Bruce Springsteen.

Farm Aid I, September 25, 1985, at Memorial Stadium, University of Illinois at Champaign.

— *Photo by Earl Miller*

Dad's 1986 July 4th Picnic was also Farm Aid II which benefitted a fund for the American farmer. The thousands who attended came early and stayed late under a warm Texas sun and star-filled night. The location for this picnic was Manor Downs just east of Austin.

— Photo by Tom Lankes, Austin American-Statesman

Poster advertising Dad's Fourth of July Picnic on July 4, 1979.
— Lana Nelson Collection

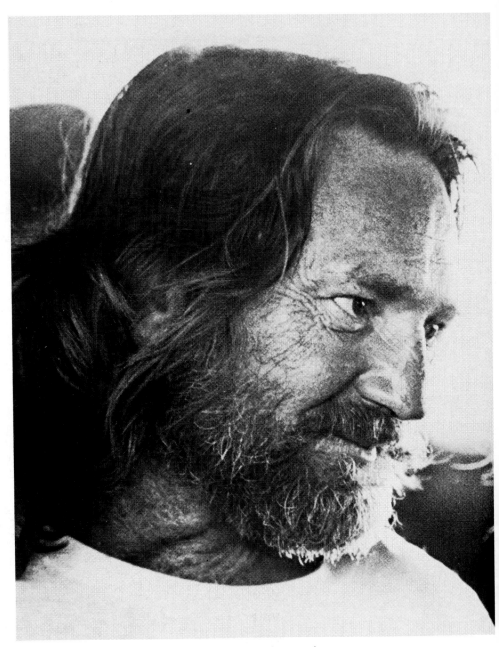

Caught in a pensive mood.

— Lana Nelson Collection

Bandera

"Always let wisdom, strength, and love be your guide."

verything was in a shambles after the house burned down. We moved into some apartment, in Madison again, I think, while Dad and the band tried to get things sorted out. But since they did most of their playing in Texas—and because of disagreements with Lucky Moler and the fact that things weren't going well with RCA Victor—there didn't seem to be much point in staying in Tennessee.

So Dad called up Crash Stewart and asked him to find the band and the family a place near a golf course.

Crash learned that the Lost Valley Ranch in Bandera was closed for the season. So that's where we went.

☆ ☆ ☆ ☆

The Lost Valley Ranch was a run-down resort on the eastern edge of the Texas Hill Country, about thirty-five or forty miles from downtown San Antonio. It had kind of a main lodge and half a dozen or so guesthouses, and we all moved in for a while.

Billy and I lived in the main lodge with Dad and Connie and their baby, Paula Carlene. Aunt Bobbie had moved back to Austin by this time, but good old cousin Freddie was being a rebellious teenager, so he came to live with us in Bandera too. Paul and Carlene lived in one of the guesthouses, and the other band members and various friends and people passing through occupied the rest of the buildings.

It was a great place to get away from it all for a while, and there were a lot of good times and crazy things going on.

But for me, it wasn't so hot. Not that any other place necessarily would have been better. I was going through a difficult time.

151

Part of it, of course, was that I was thirteen and in the middle of adolescent changes. Another part had to do with the fact that I really didn't have a grown woman to talk with or even to look to as an example. Connie had an infant to care for, and she was trying to get used to the wild and crazy new world she had gotten herself into. Aunt Bobbie was in Austin, and Lana was still living in Tennessee with Steve and their children.

There had been constant turmoil for the last couple of years. Home life had been anything but settled. And to top everything off, I had done everything I could think of to get rid of the problems—at least, what I thought were the problems—so we could have Dad to ourselves. But now Billy and I had to share Dad with more people than ever. And you would hardly call living on a closed resort normal— even if it did have a golf course.

So I turned into a quiet kid. I retreated into myself and wouldn't let anybody in. I wouldn't tell them what I was thinking or feeling. I'd just put on my tie-dyed T-shirt and a pair of jeans and head out with Freddie or Billy. We'd smoke some dope and go down by the river or mess around in the hills. Or maybe I'd just go into my room by myself and listen to Chicago or Jimi Hendrix or Neil Young—he was my favorite at the time.

What I didn't do was go to school.

As I've made clear by now, skipping school was what I did when things weren't going well. I'd started it in the first grade and kept it up all the way through the normal school years. It wasn't until I was twenty-seven and went back to school to get my high school diploma that I realized that I could be a good student.

I have to thank Connie for that. In 1984 we were in the ladies room together and out of the clear blue she said, "Susie, why don't you go back to school, if for no other reason than for yourself?" I thought that was going to be the start of our being close, like we had been when she first came, but she never said a word after I did graduate. And I was hurt.

The twenty-eight days in a row I had missed during the real bad times at Ridgetop were nothing compared to how much I skipped school when we lived at Bandera.

☆ ☆ ☆ ☆

In some ways, though, the time we spent at Bandera was better.

For one thing, Dad was there a lot more. Billy and I may have had to share him with Connie and Paula Carlene, not to mention the band, but he was there.

I remember he used to come down to my bedroom in the lodge to talk. This usually happened at night. We would share a joint and listen to music, just like we did in my psychedelic closet in Madison.

Of course, one of the things he was trying to do was find out how I was doing, what I was feeling, where my head was. He'd try to talk to me about how I needed to go to school, that I had to quit skipping. But then he'd see that he wasn't getting anywhere, that I refused to listen, that I wasn't going to let him inside. I wasn't going to let anybody get close to me.

I was pissed off and confused. I wasn't sure if we knew each other any more. "Do you say I can trust you because you love me, or are those just words to say at times like this? Do you care?" was what I thought. But I didn't say anything.

So he'd change the subject. We'd listen to records, and I'd tell him he ought to play like that.

Then I'd relax a bit and ask him questions.

We'd discuss abortion, or what happened when you died, or what life was all about.

Sometimes he would ask out of the clear blue, "Susie, what do you think of me? Do you think I'm a good father?"

Of course, I'd hug him and give him a kiss.

"Oh, Dad. You're the greatest."

But if I thought he was messing up, I would tell him.

When he'd leave, he'd tell me things like "Susie, always let love and strength and wisdom be your guide. Don't forget to say your prayers. And remember, Daddy loves you."

I was a thirteen-year-old kid preoccupied with trying to figure things out for myself and not having too much success. I didn't know what he meant by all this strength and wisdom stuff. I'd think, "Poor Dad. He's had too much smoke today," and left it at that.

But I did know that Dad loved me. He never put me down and he always tried to let me know that he was there for me. If not physically, at least in spirit.

When I look back on it now, I think that Dad and I were trying to do the same thing during that time we spent in Bandera. He was trying to figure things out too. He was trying to get his career and his life in order.

I don't know when Dad first got interested in *The Prophet* by Kahlil Gibran, or in the books about reincarnation by Edgar Cayce. But I do know that he had a lot of time to read and think while we were in Bandera.

One of the things almost everyone I interviewed for this book mentioned is Dad's serenity. That and his eyes.

"When Willie looks at you, his eyes bore right through you. It's like he can see right into your soul. I'd rather do anything else on this green planet than lie to Willie Nelson."

That's what Charlie Williams told me.

Along with the direct, penetrating way he looks at you, Dad projects an aura of serenity and spirituality. Nothing ever seems to upset him, nothing ever seems to ruffle his feathers.

"Willie was laid back before it was the in thing," Waylon once told an interviewer. "We all thought he was just lazy."

It's the calm, genuine love of his music and the audience he is playing it for that people talk about over and over again. And his sincerity. His eyes play a part in communicating that sincerity because Dad always makes direct eye contact with people in the audience. That's something even people who don't care for country music always comment on.

One guy who met Dad only once when they were in a bar told me about his eyes: "They look right at you, and you can see a profound love for you in them just because you are part of the human race."

Maybe Dad is the first Zen country star.

But Dad wasn't always that calm. He has a temper, and he had been losing it with more and more regularity.

So Bandera became a place to get his spiritual life back on track. He was able to meditate, to return to a balanced perspective about who he was, what he was trying to do, and what the really important things were in his life.

That doesn't mean he didn't have some wild times too.

☆ ☆ ☆ ☆

There was a lot of drinking and drugs going on during this time.

I remember one time somebody brought out a lot of acid, bowls of it, and ate those little things like candy. They chased some cattle through the brush down toward the river — on foot, thank God. Then they all tried playing golf. David Zentner claims they took so much acid they finally all got straight.

Of course, you can't assume that David has a photographic memory about everything during this period because, as he says, "I turned into a stoned alcoholic during all of this."

But there were lively times all right.

For instance, there was the great Halloween shootout. A bunch of high school kids had come down from town to throw a Halloween party in one of the vacant buildings. They set up a bunch of *luminarios* — candles inside of paper bags with about an inch or two of sand in the bottom — and were having a good old time.

They weren't bothering anyone, but the old Mexican caretaker of the place, Alonzo was his name, heard the noise and thought somebody was trying to vandalize the place. He got his .22 pistol and went down there to see what was going on. One of the kids scared him in some way, scared him or startled him, and Alonzo wounded him.

I remember that another of the caretakers, an ex-pro golfer, came up and got Dad and a lot of the band to drive down there.

One of Dad's closest contacts then was a man named John T. Floores. John T. owned a general store in Helotes, a town about midway between Bandera and San Antonio. The signs outside advertised sausage, insurance, and real estate for sale — and that's pretty general.

But inside, it was really a country music dance hall.

Dad had been playing at John T.'s store for years, and the fact that the Lost Valley Ranch was close to it was undoubtedly one of the attractions of moving to Bandera. Dad and the band played at John T.'s quite a lot then. In fact, after we moved back to Texas to stay, Dad made a point of playing there one Saturday night a month until he just got too big and too busy.

But they played around the Texas circuit too. As Dad explained, "I knew we could make a living just playing Texas because we had been doing it for years."

Mel Tillis told me a story about Dad from this period.

Mel was real big at that time, selling a lot of records and doing the road in one of the first big customized Silver Eagle buses any country star used. Mel stutters except when he's singing, but you should know that, unless you are one of the few people in America who hasn't seen one of his commercials for Burger King. Mel needed a big bus because he was traveling with a twelve-piece band, and on the back of the bus was written "M-M-M-Mel."

He had a date at Panther Hall in Fort Worth one night, and after the show they all went to an afterhours place where Dad was playing. Dad was glad to see them because he'd been away from Nashville for a while.

So they spent as much time with Dad as they could, listening to him play and talking with him during the breaks. But Mel had a gig in Shreveport at 8:00 that night.

It soon came time to get in the bus and go.

But the piano player, a man named Ronnie McCowan, didn't want to go.

"I want to stay with Willie for a while," said Ronnie Mac (that's what they called him, Ronnie Mac, or Whipple). "You guys go on and I'll catch a plane to Shreveport."

Mel told him okay, but he'd better not be late.

Fifteen minutes to airtime, old Ronnie finally showed up. He was a big man, weighing in the neighborhood of 350 pounds, and he was still wearing the maroon western suit that Mel made his band wear —and they were ugly, according to Mel. He had been up all night with Dad, and both he and the suit were somewhat the worse for wear. The big old pat of butter on his tie didn't do anything to improve his appearance.

"Where in the hell have you been?"

"I've been with Willie."

"Well, you can just go back with Willie. You ain't going on this stage with us. Get on that plane and get out of here and go."

"Okay chiefie-wiefie," said Ronnie in his duck voice.

Ronnie went. Later, he reported that that was the stormiest ride he had ever been on. He thought the Lord had hit the plane with lightning four times—he stopped counting after four.

He got back to Fort Worth before Dad had finished his show that night. Dad was singing when Ronnie came in and walked by the stage.

"What are you doing here, Whipple?" Dad asked. "I thought you were supposed to be with Mel in Shreveport."

"He fired me."

He still had the maroon suit on, pat of butter on his tie and all.

And without missing a beat, Dad said, "Well, maybe he didn't fire you. He stutters so bad maybe he's still stuttering from the last time he fired you."

☆ ☆ ☆ ☆

Dad even got involved in politics during our Bandera interlude.

For years, Johnny Bush had been introducing Dad at shows as a future governor of Texas: "I now give you the next governor of the State of Texas—Willie Nelson."

He never ran for governor. But when U.S. Senator Ralph Yarborough ran for reelection in the Democratic primary against Lloyd Bentsen, Dad did a song on a half-hour television spot for him.

The spot wasn't enough. I don't know if Dad helped or hurt.

He supported Sissy Farenthold for governor and Jimmy Carter for president in 1980, and they didn't win either. So you can't say that he's backed a lot of winners.

Then too, Dad helps politicians he likes and those he thinks would be good officeholders. He picks politicians to support in the same way he decided what to do in his own career—by what he thinks is right. Of course, he's had more success in his career. But then again, he had more than twenty years of trying before he started to make it in a big way, so maybe by 1990 he'll support a winner.

Between meditating, partying, and picking on the Texas circuit, Dad managed to keep pretty busy.

But he was still under contract to RCA Victor, and they wanted to cut another album.

Dad asked David Zentner if he wanted to go to Nashville with him.

"Sure," said David.

So they booked a flight out of San Antonio and after they got on the plane, David asked Dad what was going on.

"Got to cut an album and I'm behind schedule. I really don't know what I'm going to cut."

"You mean you don't have any material?" asked David.

"You got it."

"What do you want me to do?"

"I don't know, but we're going to have to come up with something. Maybe you can think of some tunes."

David told me this story. "Now Susie," he said, "this is on the airplane when he was telling me this stuff. That's when I got scared. I thought, 'Man, you can't fall apart on me now.'"

They got a motel room at the old Holiday Inn on Church Street. Larry Moler had met them at the airport, and they sat around batting the breeze for a bit. Then David and Larry decided they would catch Aretha Franklin that night and, wanting to get an early start on things, they left Dad at about three in the afternoon.

Larry brought David back to the motel around four or five in the morning. The room had a "Do Not Disturb" sign on it, but since it was David's room too, he had a key.

When the door opened, they saw pink wallpaper everywhere. Dad was sprawled out, asleep on the bed, and the room was full of pieces of paper.

They didn't wake him. They flashed the light on and off and Dad didn't even wiggle. So they shut the door and went downstairs.

"What do you think?" asked David.

"Apparently, he's been working," answered Larry. "We better call him up pretty quick, because he's got a session today."

So they did.

"How's it going, Will?"

"Come on up. Just give me a minute to clear the path."

They got up there and started looking through all the pieces of paper Dad had gathered up. There must have been 200.

Every one was a song.

And every one was good.

David told me that that was when he saw Dad's genius. He asked him how he did it.

"I've got a rule that if something comes across and it's real good, it will come back," Dad told him. "I may have it down on paper, but then I'll dismiss it from my mind. If it comes back by itself, I'll pursue it."

What had happened is that all these songs came back by themselves — with a little pharmaceutical encouragement from a black mollie.

The album was *Yesterday's Wine,* and it is viewed by Dad's fans as one of his best. It is also regarded as the first of the concept albums, the most famous of which is, of course, *Red Headed Stranger.*

"Family Bible" is on the album. So is "It's Not For Me To Understand," and "December Day." But the two most significant songs on it are "Yesterday's Wine" and "Me and Paul," because they are statements of where Dad had been and where he was going.

"Yesterday's Wine" is a song of bittersweet acceptance:

> Yesterday's wine, I'm yesterday's wine,
> Aging with time, like yesterday's wine;
> Yesterday's wine, we're yesterday's wine,
> Aging with time, like yesterday's wine.

And "Me and Paul" is autobiographical, but with the same reflective tone:

> It's been rough and rocky travelin', but I'm finally standin'
>   upright on the ground;
> After takin' several readings,
> I'm surprised to find my mind still fairly sound;
> I guess Nashville was the roughest, but I know I said
>   the same about them all;
> We received our education,
> In the cities of the nation, me and Paul.

They were brilliant.
But they didn't sell.

☆ ☆ ☆ ☆

Not too long after Dad cut the *Yesterday's Wine* album, we went back to Tennessee.

The house had been rebuilt, and Dad was going to redirect his efforts along the lines that began to take shape at Bandera.

For one thing, his contract was up and he was going to try to find a label that would let him record things his way and that would put more into promoting them.

For another, he was going to try to find someone who could deal with record companies and promoters in their own terms, who knew their language and their tricks and could get him the deals he deserved.

So we all went back to Ridgetop. I was in the ninth grade, Billy was in the eighth, Lana was still there, with two children by now, and Paula Carlene was going on two.

Dad had hopes of really turning things around. And I ran into someone who started turning me around.

EIGHTEEN

The Armadillo

"I think we found something."

S o we went back to the rebuilt house at Ridgetop. Billy and me, Connie and Paula Carlene, and Dad.

And I changed my ways completely. I quit drugs, and I started going to school. I not only went, but I started making good grades — A's and B's.

☆ ☆ ☆ ☆

The reason was a boy. Donnie Killom. He was a senior and the Big Man On Campus, the star of the football team, the president of the student body, and he was good looking.

Every girl in school wanted him, and I got him.

Don was also an honors student and a straight arrow. And I quickly realized that if I wanted to attract him, if I wanted to fit into his world, I was going to have to clean up my act.

So I quit skipping school and began to concentrate on the books. I stopped doing drugs and smoking dope. I went out for cheerleader and made the squad. I joined the drama club and got a leading part in one of the school plays.

When I look back on it, I have to marvel at the powers of teenage love.

Here I was, just back from Bandera, which had been like a hippie commune with guitars and cowboy boots. Now I was acting like I had just stepped off the set of "The Donna Reed Show" or "Life With Father."

Things weren't perfect, however.

For one thing, Dad was on the road a lot. And Connie wouldn't come to my plays. I was the only kid in school who didn't have a family member there to watch me. And that hurt my feelings.

But Connie and I were getting along fairly well at this point. She was putting a lot of effort into learning how to run a house, how to put good meals on the table, and so on. She had lived alone in small apartments, working in a glass factory and then as a keypunch operator until she was twenty-seven. And now here she was, having to keep a big house with two teenagers and a baby. Not to mention all the other turmoil.

So now I can kind of understand why she was reluctant to come down to the school with all the other parents and act as the mother to a stepdaughter she didn't know very well. I suppose I'd feel the same way myself.

But it bothered me at the time. And to be honest, the feelings of abandonment, of feeling shut out, can still come back to me.

Dad seemed happy then. Connie sure wasn't doing speed and downers the way Shirley had (in fact, Shirley came close to overdosing several times during that period and had to go into the hospital to detox). And Dad and Connie weren't fighting all the time whenever he came in off the road.

And then there was Paula Carlene. I liked babies. I took care of my half-brothers Charlie and David—the children Mama had had when she was married to Chuck Andrews—when I was only seven and eight. They used to call me Mama, in fact. I didn't even mind taking care of Helen the topless dancer's two children. So I enjoyed taking care of my new stepsister.

Things were better at home than they had been. But I was also learning to make a life for myself out of the house. With Donnie and my new enthusiasm for studies and school activities, I was starting to make my own way, independent of what was going on with the family.

☆ ☆ ☆ ☆

And Dad was starting to make some major changes in his career.

One of the most obvious was the clothes that he and the band wore.

When Dad was a guest on Ralph Emery's show late in 1975, Ralph had gone back and collected a bunch of Dad's album covers to show his changes through the years. "They do look kind of like a movie," said Dad.

While Dad hadn't worn a Nudie suit since he had played with Ray Price and the Cherokee Cowboys—Nudie was a Hollywood tailor who made the fancy, fringed Western suits that a lot of the stars wore back then—he had gone through a range of fashion changes. His covers showed him over the course of several years in a dark suit, the epitome of "spic and span Willie," in a Nehru jacket, and wearing polyester bell-bottom trousers with a cowboy hat and sunglasses. With all the touring, Dad began to pick up on the fact that the audience was changing with the times.

But I really don't think Dad ever worried too much about clothes in the first place. He probably just wore what other people thought was the "in" thing.

David Zentner told me that he always figured Dad was color-blind. When they left on a tour, Shirley would have four sets of performing costumes all racked together—each color coordinated with pants, coats, shirts, and ties. David had the job of keeping the bus neat and clean, and one of his chores would be to get Dad's dry cleaning and laundry done.

But Dad would go into his closet and take off all the cleaners' wrappers and come out wearing the worst pair of pants possible to wear with the coat he had chosen.

"How do I look?" Dad would ask.

"Real good," David would say, all the while thinking, "Is he doing this on purpose?"

So David would go to Paul and ask, "Doesn't he know that it doesn't go together?"

And Paul would go talk to Dad.

What they had to do was hand him the clothes. "Willie, here's something nice for you. Put this on."

And Dad would say, "Thank you guys." That would do it.

But if they let Dad go into the closet by himself, like when they were setting up or something, when he came out he would look like he'd dressed by Braille.

But that started to change when they were going to play the Country Music Association award show one year.

Dad told Paul they were going to change their image. No more suits. Then he told the band, "Everyone go out and find you something you really like. Just make sure it's neat and we'll go from there."

Paul handed out $300 each, and the band went shopping for clothes in Hollywood.

Jimmy Day and David went to the first shop in Hollywood that looked good. It turned out to be a store that was owned by and catered to the gay crowd, and a couple of salesmen latched onto them.

"We came out of there looking like Easter eggs. Pink shirts and lavender scarves, buckskin jackets and beads, the whole number."

That's the time when Paul bought his cape. "He came back looking like Batman."

And Dad came in looking like he had taken the center out of a volleyball net and used it for his shirt. David thought it looked weird, but he didn't worry about it because they were in California.

"But what's he going to do when we play Fort Worth?" he wondered. "There's still a lot of rednecks out there."

One time they opened at Mr. Lucky's in Phoenix. It was a big club with two dance floors: upstairs was for country and western and downstairs was for English-style hot rock and roll.

Dad, of course, was working the big country and western ballroom upstairs. He had just seen *The Good, The Bad, and The Ugly,* and he came in wearing a poncho and sporting about a four-day beard.

Since it was a ballroom, the lights would be low for three numbers or so and then Dad, or Johnny Bush, would turn up the lights and welcome any of the new folks who had come in. Then the lights would go back down and they'd play some more.

During one of the breaks, some guy wearing a flat-topped straw hat — what they used to call a boater or a skimmer — and a red and white candy-striped shirt, white pants, and red shoes, came across the floor to the bandstand.

"Watch this one," said Jimmy Day.

He looked like he'd come straight from work at a pizza parlor.

He went up to Dad and said, "I just want you to know that I paid good money to come in here because I always liked your music. But you look like hell in that."

Dad had held the microphone so the guy could be heard all over the club. And everybody in the joint cracked up because this guy who looked like he had escaped from a circus was telling Dad how bad he looked.

☆ ☆ ☆ ☆

Dad was still keeping in touch with his friends in Nashville, particularly those guys who were dissatisfied with the way the record companies were handling their releases.

One of them was Waylon Jennings.

Waylon was different than Dad because he was a solid commercial success. But he was taking a lot of heat because the record company executives had a hard time pigeon-holing his music. Was it rock? Was it country? Just what was it, anyway?

Waylon didn't conform to the image laid down by the country mainstream; that is, decked out in western suits (tuxedos for special occasions like award ceremonies), and always polite and law-abiding — at least in public. In a word, noncontroversial. But Waylon made no secret of the fact that he did a lot of drugs, and he went around in Levis and wearing a lot of silver and turquoise.

Like Dad, Waylon was increasingly frustrated by the way his albums sounded when they left the studio. He wanted to record with his road band so they could use all of the things they had learned playing together for 300 one-night stands every year.

Dad had met Waylon years before when he played once in Phoenix. Waylon had quite a local reputation, but he asked Dad whether he should move to Nashville or stay in Phoenix. Dad's advice was to stay.

But Waylon went to Nashville anyway.

One night Dad dropped by his house for a poker game. Waylon had a recording session the next day and mentioned that he was stalled on a song he wanted to record. He read Dad the first verse and chorus and told him that if he could finish it, he could have half the song. Dad stayed the night and finished it right after breakfast. The song was "Good-Hearted Woman."

Dad was shopping for a new label since he hadn't renewed his contract with RCA Victor. He had also acquired a new manager, Neil Reshen, who was a show business lawyer from New York. Neil kept urging Dad to sign with a New York label, and Paul agreed with him.

At the same time, Atlantic was wanting to move into country. Atlantic was the premier "respectable" rhythm and blues label. The vice-president was a man named Jerry Wexler, and he was a genius at recognizing outstanding talent before anyone else. He had signed groups like the Coasters and the Drifters. And he had signed Wilson Pickett and the king and queen of soul, Ray Charles and Aretha Franklin. You couldn't say he discovered these stars, but he did realize their appeal to a wide, if not mass, market while others were dismissing them as interesting talents but not "commercial." Now he sensed that country music was the way to go.

He was familiar with Dad both as a singer and songwriter, but he had never heard Dad until he went to Harlan Howard's big bash in 1971. Harlan always held a big party during the country music convention, and he would invite a lot of producers and company executives as much to help his writing career as anything else.

Harlan knew Dad from the early days of hanging around Tootsie's. He was from California and had come to Nashville a couple of months earlier than Dad. He met Dad sometime around August of 1960. Harlan's early songs included "Heartaches By the Number" and "Pick Me Up On Your Way Down," and he went on from there to be one of the handful of writers, along with Dad, who dominated the Nashville songwriting scene in the sixties.

Harlan had invited Dad to his party and Dad said he'd come. Hank Cochran was going to be there and told Harlan to make Dad promise to come. Hank knew that to Dad, a promise was like a written contract. He never breaks a promise.

Dad promised. But he got there late.

Harlan had it set up as a songwriter's showcase, he explained to me. "Nobody else could sing. No stars. No nothing. It was just a songwriter getting up on a stool in front of a gas log in a big old room and it was neat."

The evening was half gone when it was Dad's turn to sing. He got on the stool about one or two in the morning, after everyone had been listening and having a real good go at Harlan's free food and free booze. And he sang just about the whole *Phases and Stages* album.

I don't mean that it was recorded yet. He hadn't yet written all the songs that were on the album when it came out. But according to Harlan, Dad had it all memorized: "He got on the stool late at night when the party had halfway thinned out, and he sang like a total album with a gut string and a stool. He just went from one song to the other and then this guy from New York, I can't remember his name any more, he flipped out."

Jerry Wexler was the guy from New York. He went up to Dad when he was done and he said, "I've been looking forward to meeting you for a long time."

And Dad's answer? "Have I been looking for you for a long time."

So Jerry let Dad record with his road band. They recorded three albums on Atlantic, *Shotgun Willie, Phases and Stages* and *The Troublemaker. Shotgun Willie* and *Phases and Stages* sold far, far better than any of Dad's earlier albums. *The Troublemaker*, which was almost all gospel songs, was released on CBS because Atlantic had some business setbacks and had to dismantle their country music operation.

But before all this happened, we moved back to Texas.

☆ ☆ ☆ ☆

I was mad, really upset, when I found out we were going back to Texas. I had a boyfriend and I was finally doing well in school. I had even gone to summer school to improve a bad math grade so I could be a cheerleader my tenth-grade year.

And now the turmoil was back.

Dad's reason, of course, is that he just wasn't getting anywhere with the Nashville record companies, so he figured he couldn't do any worse from Texas than he had been. At least he could make a living playing the Texas circuit, just as he always had. In fact, the crowds were getting bigger and bigger.

We moved to Houston first. I don't know why. Maybe it was to be near Connie's folks. We didn't stay there long, though. Just long enough for Dad to buy me a car, a green Datsun 210.

I was only fifteen, so I couldn't get a license. Dad told me I could just drive around the block. When he gave me the keys, he said, "Now I've driven this car as fast as it will go. It will go eighty. So there's no need in you finding out for yourself."

I drove around and around the block until I wore a groove in the pavement. All the folks that lived in the neighborhood must have really wondered about the freaky girl who didn't go anywhere except in circles.

But before long, we moved to Austin.

First we got an apartment on East Riverside Drive and I went to Travis High School—when I went. I was still so mad about moving that I went back to my skipping school ways. And after we moved to Austin, Dad didn't limit my driving to only around the block, so with a car I could really cover some ground. Without a license.

Later we moved to Lake Austin Estates and I went to West Lake High School—infrequently.

We wound up in Austin for a number of reasons. Aunt Bobbie lived there. And Coach Royal was there. In fact, he organized some private parties at a room over Cisco's Bakery and charged people $25 a head. Dad didn't think anyone would pay that much to hear him. But they did. "Those were big paydays for Willie back then," says Coach Royal.

It was a nice, laid-back town right on the edge of the beautiful Hill Country.

But the most important feature was that Austin had a music scene.

☆ ☆ ☆ ☆

Austin had been the home of oldtime musicians like barrelhouse piano player Robert Shaw, who ran a grocery store and barbecue joint on Manor Road, and yodeler Kenneth Threadgill who had a gas station turned beer joint way out on North Lamar.

When the folk music scene began to sweep the country in the late fifties and early sixties, Austin was one of the main centers for it in Texas. Threadgill held Wednesday night hootenannies at his place, with regulars including Mance Lipscomb, Bill Neely, two English profs named Stan Alexander and Bill Malone, and a coed from Port Arthur whose name was Janis Joplin.

Rock had its share too. The Conqueroos, Shivas Head Band, and the Thirteenth Floor Elevators were among the Austin bands that made the pilgrimage to San Francisco — and back again.

By the late sixties and early seventies there were a number of small clubs playing all kinds of music: Threadgill's, where hard-core, Jimmie Rodgers-style country and black country blues shared the microphone with collegiate folkies and incipient rock and rollers; Castle Creek, which catered to folk singers old and new; the established country dance clubs like the Broken Spoke and the Split Rail; and clubs with primitive light shows like the Vilcan Gas Company, which showcased a mixture of bluesmen like Lightning Hopkins and acid rock bands in the San Francisco style.

There was also a community of musicians who played together in interchangeable combinations. Most were young, most were from Texas, most were playing rock, folk, or jazz, but most had been raised on gospel and country. And they didn't want to deny or lose their musical roots.

A similar kind of mixture of styles and pride in being Texan was going on in the audiences.

Kickers and hippies, rednecks and students still didn't mingle too much, and a long-haired man wearing sandals and beads literally put his life in his hands if he went into the wrong club. But a change was coming.

The club that symbolized the change was the Armadillo World Headquarters. Taking what had been an old National Guard armory and defunct roller skating rink, several guys prominent in the Austin music scene took it over and made it a beer garden/concert and dance hall. They opened in 1970.

Although a lot of the acts they booked at first were rock bands, they always had the intention of making the Armadillo a center for the arts. And over the years, acts as various as the Austin Ballet, Ravi Shankar, and Bette Midler played the 'Dillo.

By 1972, they realized that audiences, at least Austin audiences, were also interested in country music. So, wanting to broaden their audience, they began to look for a performer they thought would be the best one to premiere country music at the Armadillo.

But they had to choose their acts carefully. They started making lists of performers they thought would fill this dual purpose, people like Bill Monroe, Lester Flatt and Earl Scruggs, Waylon Jennings, Jerry Lee Lewis, Hank Williams, Jr., and Dad. They were looking for people who were either unique or "progressive," people who projected a strong Texas image, or at least who projected an image they could relate to.

They weren't interested in anybody who was solid in the Nashville mold, in other words.

They knew of Dad mainly as a songwriter rather than performer. But his songs and the fact that he was a Texan put him on the list.

When they heard that Dad was back in Texas, his name was moved closer to the top of the list. But they couldn't find him.

Then one day a hippie chick came by the 'Dillo. In those days, you have to understand, the 'Dillo was a major stopping point for folks hitchhiking around the country. It was open night and day, almost like a crash pad. She started talking to Mike Tolleson, one of the owners, and told him she had been picked up by some guys driving a Winnebago. They were in Willie Nelson's band, she told Mike.

"Really? We've been trying to find those guys."

"Yeah," she said, "they had some of the greatest pot. I spent three or four days with those guys and stayed high constantly. And they are great people."

That was the first time Mike realized that maybe Dad and the band might smoke a little weed. In fact, it was the first time Mike realized that a country band might be into drugs of any kind.

"Wow," Mike told me, "I thought, 'They are exactly who we are looking for.' " Here was someone they thought could draw the country audience and please their traditional rock and roll people.

"We saw our place as a cultural center, a concert hall. And we thought we had a unique opportunity to bring the hippies and the rednecks together."

And Dad saw it too.

Mike and his partners started putting out the word that they wanted to book Dad. They still didn't know how to reach him.

But Dad heard. One night he walked into the Armadillo's beer garden. Eddie Wilson, one of the partners, was there, and Dad told him that he'd heard they were looking for him.

"That's right."

Well, he'd like to play there, Dad told him. And they picked a date right then.

Dad's first show at the Armadillo World Headquarters was on August 12, 1972.

☆ ☆ ☆ ☆

And it was exactly what they thought it was going to be. They had the strangest mix in the audience they had ever had. But everybody loved it.

Dad played all of his old songs, the ones that had been hits for other people. The hardcore, kicked-in-the-head country fans loved it, of course. But so did the young rock and rollers. If ever a new movement happened at one particular time, it happened that night.

Dad didn't actually create something from scratch. There was a lot of spirit to fuse country and rock in the air at the time. Austin had a number of bands and performers like Michael Murphy, Gary P. Nunn, Asleep at the Wheel, Freda and the Firedogs (Marcia Ball), Greezy Wheels, and Jerry Jeff Walker who were experimenting and developing country rock.

I was a big Leon Russell fan. To me he has always been a country rocker. I got Dad to listen to the *Mad Dogs and Englishmen* album, and he liked it. And I got him to go with me to a Leon Russell concert, and he liked that. He liked it so much, in fact, that he went up and introduced himself to Leon after the show.

And it turned out that Leon had been a session musician on some of Dad's early recordings for Liberty. Not only that, Leon told Dad that his favorite song was "Family Bible."

In the spring of 1972, some promoters put together something called the Dripping Springs Reunion on a ranch outside of the town of the same name in the Hill Country around Austin. It featured bluegrass groups, traditional country acts like Loretta Lynn, Tex Ritter, and Roy Acuff, and "rebels" like Kris Kristofferson, Waylon Jennings, and Billy Joe Shaver.

The idea was to have a kind of country Woodstock. Well, the weather was bad and the promoters lost a bundle. But between fifteen and twenty thousand people showed up. Old and young, couples and singles, dressed and in various stages of undress. It was a sign of things to come. And one of the signs was a picture in the *Austin American-Statesman* of Leon Russell, Coach Royal, and Dad.

If you put the Dripping Springs Reunion together with Dad's gut sense of what was going on and add that to the way people, kids especially, responded to all of the country rock action going on in Austin, you get the new Willie Nelson era.

Which was really nothing more than the old Willie Nelson being appreciated by a bigger audience. A much bigger audience.

All of a sudden, Dad started getting booked at college auditoriums. By the end of 1972, Dad and the band logged over 160,000 miles on the road, and the next year they played in every state of the union.

Dad began to spread the word. He got Waylon Jennings to come down and play the 'Dillo. When Waylon walked in and saw all the longhairs, he thought, "What's that crazy sonofabitch got me into now?"

"Goddamn, Willie."

"Trust me. If they don't go for it, you're going down with me."

And the rest, as they say, is history.

Or as Dad told Waylon, "I think we found something."

NINETEEN

Changes in Austin

"It's not supposed to be that way."

Dad may have found something, but I was still lost.

Nothing seemed to be going right for me. I couldn't deal with Travis High School. It was big, for one thing. And there was a lot of racial tension, which was quite a change for someone fresh from a little Tennessee mountain high school.

You have to remember that this was in the early seventies and nobody — white, black, or brown — got along with each other. If you had to go to the restroom, you went with a teacher's aid so you wouldn't get stabbed.

It was no fun. So I quit going. And this time I had a car, so I could really skip school.

☆ ☆ ☆ ☆

My relationship with Connie was changing too. For one thing, Connie had had Amy, so she had two babies to care for.

The mayhem hadn't stopped. Since she and Dad had been together, she had had two children and had gone from Houston to Ridgetop, to Bandera, to Ridgetop, to Houston, to Austin in less than three and a half years.

That's not what you would call a stable life.

I'd gone through the same mess and I wasn't handling it very well. And, of course, I was right in the middle of those rebellious teenage years anyway.

Sometimes it was funny. I remember once while I was still at Travis High School, Pattie Monnett and I skipped school and went downtown. And who should drive up but Dad.

"Hello, girls," he said pleasantly.

172

"Oh hello, Dad. What brings you down this way?"

I looked to Pattie for support. No help there. She started laughing hysterically, the way she always did when she was nervous.

I was caught, but I tried to bluff it out.

"You girls need a ride?"

"Oh no, Dad. Not today. I love you though and thanks anyway."

Dad smiled. "I love you too. Now get in the car."

I went to school for the next couple of days. But I started skipping again as soon as I thought I could get away with it.

And so did Billy. He was fourteen and he spent his time playing hooky and wrecking motorcycles.

Looking back, there were probably a number of reasons on both sides for the change between me and Connie. Whatever the reasons, both Billy and I began to feel like we weren't wanted. Maybe with the birth of Amy, her own children took all her energy and Connie didn't have time for us — the "other" family. Paula Carlene and Amy were young and couldn't take care of themselves, while Billy and I were teenagers and trying to be independent. And we were just as obnoxious about it as most teenagers. Maybe she felt that she'd tried to be a friend and mother to us but Billy wouldn't cooperate and I was starting to act contrary, so it wasn't worth the trouble.

But I felt shut out. It didn't help that Dad was on the road so much.

When we moved from the apartments on East Riverside Drive to a duplex in Lake Austin Estates, Dad and Connie lived on one side with Paula Carlene and Amy. Billy and I lived by ourselves in the other.

They were two separate households. We rarely ate together or did things together as a family.

I didn't really mind at first. I could go to bed when I wanted and get up when I wanted. I could eat what I wanted, when I wanted, or not eat if I didn't want to.

But I knew it wasn't right. Not for a fifteen- or sixteen-year-old. I would go over to my friend Pattie's house and see that they all sat down to dinner together, see that Pattie's mom made her come home at a certain time.

One incident summed up the whole situation. I went next door to Dad and Connie's side of the duplex around suppertime and just walked right in. Connie chewed me up one side and down the other for not knocking first.

I thought, "Okay. That makes it plain as day that we aren't living in the same home. And it makes it crystal clear that I am not welcome here."

I don't want to be anyplace where I'm not wanted. So I just started to stay away.

☆ ☆ ☆ ☆

I started hanging out with a boy who lived down the road. His name was Roy Owen. He was a year older than me and he was sweet. He liked me and wanted to be with me. And his mother was nice to me too.

I spent as much time as I could down at Roy's house, a lot like the way I would spend time at Moon Mullin's or Aunt Bobbie's when things got bad at Ridgetop.

Before long, I moved in with Roy. We shared the same room, the same bed, everything.

I had hardly had any boyfriends at all up to this point and I hadn't had any sex beyond kissing. Not only that, I didn't know anything about sex. Oh, I knew how it was done. I knew I was supposed to lie down on my back and the man—or boy—was supposed to get on top. But I didn't know anything about birth control. I didn't know anything about how to have fun. I didn't know anything.

There I was, barely sixteen and living with Roy, and I had no idea of what I was doing. I'd never let Roy see me naked. I made him stay out of the room until I had changed for bed and gotten under the covers. And then I made him turn out the light.

He wasn't too happy about that. "You've got to get over this thing about me seeing you naked," he'd tell me. But not me. Nobody was going to see me naked.

I suppose it was a wonder that I didn't get pregnant. But I didn't. I hardly thought about it.

That's the way it went for quite a while. I'd divide my time between living at "home" and living with Roy. I'd stay with Roy until I began to feel like it was getting too serious—Roy kept talking about getting married—then I'd go back to the duplex and try to hang out there.

Sooner or later, though, something Connie did—or I thought she did—would piss me off. Or I'd miss that welcome feeling, that "gee we're glad to see you" feeling I would get from Roy and his mother, so back down the road I'd go.

By this time, I'd virtually quit school.

Nobody said a word. Connie pretty much ignored me, and Dad was, of course, on the road.

☆ ☆ ☆ ☆

That was the year Dad and the band played every state in the union. It was also the year that Dad's first album for Atlantic, *Shotgun Willie,* came out.

If in *Yesterday's Wine* Dad summed up where he had been, what he had learned, and where he was going, then in *Shotgun Willie* he told the world he was moving down the trail — fast.

Like *Yesterday's Wine*, it was sort of a concept album. It included Johnny Bush's "Whiskey River," a couple of Bob Wills tunes, and two by his new friend, Leon Russell: "You Look Like the Devil" and "A Song For You."

But the title song, according to legend, was written at the Holiday Inn in New York while they were recording. Dad was sitting in the bathroom at the motel, and he picked up a wrapper for a sanitary napkin. It read "Preferred By Particular Women" and "Another Individual Service Provided By Holiday Inn."

For some reason, Dad was inspired. And he wrote:

Shotgun Willie sits around in his underwear
Bitin' on a bullet and pullin' out all his hair.
Shotgun Willie's got all of his family there.

The first time Dad played it for me, I was still living in the duplex. He called me in and said, "I've got a new song. Wanna hear it?"

"Sure. Hit it, Dad."

By the end of the first verse, I was laughing. So was Paula Carlene. Even Dad started laughing, although he was red with embarrassment when he was done.

I looked at him and said, "That song is so dumb it's bound to be a big hit."

The album outsold anything he had ever done before.

Then Dad got another idea. Inspired by the potential he had seen in the Dripping Springs Reunion of the preceding year, Dad decided that he was going to put on an outdoor show.

And the Willie Nelson Fourth of July Picnic was born.

Dad's idea was to have a giant, outdoor all-day concert with as many acts as he could find.

And the acts that came to that first picnic on July 4, 1973, made up a *Who's Who* of country music talent—although not necessarily Nashville establishment. Waylon Jennings was there. So was Charlie Rich (whose "Behind Closed Doors" was going to win song of the year that year), Sammi Smith, Johnny Zero, The Geezinslaws, Doug Sahm, Michael Murphy, Tom T. Hall, Kris Kristofferson, and Rita Coolidge. And a whole lot of folks I can't remember.

But it was Dad's show.

One reason, of course, was that he put it on. He got the talent, and he divvied up the ticket sales into regions—one person was responsible for Houston, another for San Antonio, another for Dallas, and so on. The folks at the Armadillo handled the tickets for Central Texas and did the site preparation and advertising.

But there wasn't a whole lot of money to work with. Not that it didn't hurt the advertising. Radio coverage and word-of-mouth did that, not to mention the posters done by the Armadillo artists which are now collector's items. But a lack of capital kept site preparation down to primitive levels.

They decided to use the same ranch that had been the scene of the Dripping Springs Reunion.

"From Highway 71 take Highway 290 west through Dripping Springs. Then follow the signs," instructed the Armadillo's posters.

There were only three dirt roads leading into the ranch, which was about five or ten miles off of 290. Helicopter shuttles flew the performers between Austin and the picnic.

It was a good thing too. Because they never imagined in their wildest dreams how many people were going to show up.

The temperature hit 102 that day. Anywhere from fifty to eighty thousand people paid $10 apiece—or at least a lot of them did—for the privilege of sitting on an overgrazed hillside while a hot wind coated them with caliche dust as fine as talcum powder and the hot Texas sun baked every bit of exposed flesh.

And there was plenty of exposed flesh for the sun to work on.

I was there, and I constantly marveled at the number of people and what they were willing to put up with. There were hippie girls running around with nothing on but a pair of cutoffs and a pair of sandals. I also saw a couple of hippie guys running around without either cutoffs or sandals.

But the ones I really couldn't believe were the Texas society girls. Today they'd be called yuppies. I watched a couple of them who had come from El Paso equipped with lawn chairs and a cooler. They set up the chairs where they could see the stage, which meant they weren't anywhere near shade. Down they sat, pulled out a pre-rolled joint, and passed it back and forth while they listened to the music.

It was what they were wearing that got me. They had on skimpy halter tops, leaving a lot of white skin just begging for the sun to burn it. They had on short-shorts, *panty hose*, high heels, and mascara. Just the thing for a concert in the middle of a cow pasture on a Fourth of July in Texas.

And you know, they were so cool, I don't think their mascara ran.

They were some of the lucky ones who were already inside. The traffic got so bad that a lot of folks spent hours in their cars barely moving. Cars were overheating and traffic was stalled in all directions. Mike Tolleson has a photograph from the Austin paper that shows him at an intersection of the three access roads, futilely trying to direct traffic that had no place to go.

People drank up all the beer they'd brought with them before they got to where they could park their cars. There was no beer available on the grounds. In fact, the water was running out. There weren't enough restrooms to handle the demand, and first aid facilities were stretched to the breaking point.

But even so, the hillside was covered with people who stayed and stayed and stayed.

The music began around noon. Charlie Rich played around 5:30, Waylon around 6:00 or 7:00. It was dark by the time Kris and Rita came on. And when Tom T. Hall took the stage, the power went out.

Still, people stayed. Not all them, of course, but a lot. They stayed until the power got fixed and Tom T. finished his set. And they stayed to hear Dad close the show.

That first picnic proved one thing for sure. From El Paso to Houston, from Corpus Christi and the Rio Grande Valley to Dallas and points north, folks were ready for the kind of show Dad and his friends put on. Thirty years after he first played a guitar for money, Willie Nelson was a draw. With a capital D.

From a business point of view, however, a few kinks needed to be straightened out. They barely broke even.

☆ ☆ ☆ ☆

There were a few kinks in my life too.

I was back living with Roy one day in the late spring when I ran into my brother Billy, who was messing around with some friends.

"We moved today, you know," he told me.

"That's interesting. Where did we move to?"

"Over off of Westlake Drive."

"Show me where. I'd like to see if they bothered to move my stuff."

So Billy took me to the new house. And they had bothered to move my stuff. There was a room for me.

I started back to Roy's when I ran into Dad. He was back off the road.

"Hello, Susie," he said, "how's school?"

"I'm not going to school," I said, "I just got a job at Mr. Gatti's."

"Why?"

"So I can pay for my car," I said. Which was bullshit. Dad paid for my car. "And besides, I don't like school."

"Would you like to go for a drive with me?" he asked. "You can drive."

"Sure. Why not?"

We got into the car and I drove west, further into the Hill Country. Dad didn't say much. He had brought along a guitar and was kind of picking quietly.

After a little while he said, "Why don't we go see Freddie?"

My cousin Freddie lived outside of Denver at that time.

"Sure. Why not?"

So we drove up to Denver and then turned around and drove back. We talked a bit, but mostly Dad sang.

Dad knew I was having a lot of trouble figuring things out, and singing was his way of talking to me, of giving me advice. Some of the songs he sang were off of his yet-to-be-released *Phases and Stages* album.

"Phases and stages, circles and cycles, scenes that we've all seen before—listen, I'll tell you some more."

It was a true, complete concept album. It was about relationships—about divorce and finding the ability to live and love again. The first side tells the woman's story, side two, the man's.

One song on the man's side of the record was written especially for me. I believe that, although I never asked Dad. But he really looked at me when he sang:

> It's not supposed to be that way;
> You're supposed to know that I love you.
> But it don't matter anyway
> If I can't be there to control you.
> And, like other little children,
> You're gonna dream a dream or two.
> But be careful what you're dreamin',
> Or soon your dreams will be dreaming you.
> It's not supposed to be that way;
> You're supposed to know that I love you.
> But it don't matter anyway
> If I can't be there to console you.
> And when you go out to play this evenin',
> Play with fireflies 'til they're gone.
> And then rush to meet your lover,
> And play with real fire 'til the dawn.

That's how Dad has always talked to us kids. In his songs. He only yelled at me once in my whole life.

He would just sing and cry. And I cried too, because I knew I was hurting him.

If I could change anything about those years, I'd change it so I could talk to him about the things that were bothering me. I knew how happy he was with Connie, and I didn't want to hurt him by telling him I thought that she was the cause of a lot of my troubles. So I just kept on doing what I'd been doing, letting Dad think that I didn't give a damn, that I just wanted to screw up.

When he sang:

> Walkin' is better than runnin' away,
> And crawlin' ain't no good at all.

I almost told him everything. But I stopped. I didn't want to cause him any more problems.

The last verse of "It's Not Supposed To Be That Way" goes like this:

> If guilt is the question
> Then truth is the answer.
> I've been lying to me all along.
> There ain't nothin' worth savin'
> Except one another
> And before you wake up I'll be gone.

I knew that Dad was trying to understand.

I decided to break up with Roy and move back into the house with the family.

☆ ☆ ☆ ☆

When we got back to Austin, Dad drove me over to Roy's house to pick up my things.

"Susie's going to live at home," Dad told Mrs. Owen, who said fine. Being a mother, she understood.

But Roy was heartbroken.

He used to drive up to see me, to talk to me through my bedroom window. When he got about a mile from the house, he would turn off the car lights and then when he got closer, he would turn off the engine and coast to a stop.

I was torn. I didn't love Roy—I had enough sense to know that—but I felt bad because I had made him feel bad. And things weren't going all that well at home.

We had started off with a bang. Connie had taken me shopping to buy all new furniture for my bedroom. But when Dad wasn't there, and he wasn't there very much at all, I got that same old shut-out feeling all over again.

I knew that I would feel welcome back at Roy's house. I mean, there he was outside my window almost every night telling me how much he loved me and how much he missed me. I had always gotten along well with Mrs. Owen too.

So I moved back to Roy's.

And one day, when he asked me to marry him for the umpteenth time, I said yes.

I don't know how much of my saying yes was because I was tired of saying no, or how much of it was because I needed to get away from home. Maybe I thought that I wasn't going to ever have a normal home where I felt welcome and comfortable, so I figured that I'd just have to make one for myself.

We got married on September 7, 1973, in West Lake Hills.

It was a big event. Coach Royal and his wife were there. Mama had come down from Waco along with Nannie and Pa. Dad even wore a tuxedo.

I remember standing at the back of the church with Dad waiting for everything to start.

"What have you gotten yourself into this time, Susie girl?" I was thinking. Dad sensed my feelings and bent over to whisper in my ear.

"This church has got a back door."

"No, Dad. Nannie's had her hair done. You've spent a lot of money for this thing. Mama would have a screaming fit."

Just then the organist started playing the "Wedding March."

Dum-dum-de-dum . . .

"Well, I guess we better start walkin' then."

And so I became Mrs. Roy Owen.

I was sixteen.

☆

TWENTY

E Pluribus Willie

"To keep the hair out of my eyes."

I

t seems as if almost everything Dad did after the first Fourth of July picnic was the right move. He took off like a Fourth of July rocket, and he would reach a height and send out a shower of stars and you would think: "That's it. He's reached the top. He can't go any higher."

But he would. Dad just kept on going.

Maybe he's reached the top now. But I wouldn't bet on it.

I missed a lot of those skyrocketing years. After we got married, Roy joined the Air Force. He lasted a lot longer than Dad had in the service. When he was through basic training, he was stationed at Nellis Air Force Base in Las Vegas. I went with him.

☆ ☆ ☆ ☆

One of the first things that happened after the first picnic was Dad's election to the Nashville Songwriter's Association Hall of Fame. That was in October 1973.

At the banquet after his induction, Dad started singing his hits. You know Dad. Once he gets a guitar in his hands, it's hard to get him to stop. Dad sang hit after hit after hit. The crowd just sat there, many of them probably realizing for the first time just how big Dad's song catalog was, and why he really belonged in the Hall of Fame. Finally, a voice hollered from the back of the room, "Hell, Willie. What song *didn't* you write?"

Not long after that, he held another picnic. This time it was at Abbott. The Abbott Homecoming, in November, to benefit the Abbott PTA.

That was the picnic where Mama Nelson, who must have been

close to ninety, came up to the stage to get a bouquet of roses from Dad.

"You need a haircut," was the way she thanked him.

And he probably did. At least compared to the way he used to look.

At his first picnic, Dad's hair was short and he wore a cowboy hat. But not long after that, he began to let his hair grow. And he stopped shaving. The jacket for the *Phases and Stages* album, for example, shows him with shoulder-length red hair and a beard. And a cowboy hat.

Soon he added an earring. And the hair grew longer, so he added a headband.

Ralph Emery interviewed him in 1975, not long after the *Red Headed Stranger* album was released.

"Why do you wear a headband, Willie?" Ralph asked.

"To keep the hair out of my eyes."

What he was doing was bringing the kickers and the hippies together by the way he dressed, not just by the places he played. He changed what he wore, but not what he played or the way he played it.

The music producer Fred Foster tells the story of when Dad and Faron Young did an album together in 1980. It was recorded at Dad's studio at the Pedernales Country Club, after the *Stardust* album.

"They needed another song and wanted it to be an original," Fred told me, "so Willie went away and came back the next day with 'Forgivin' You Was Easy.' And you know, it was a song just like he wrote back in 1960 or 61."

☆ ☆ ☆ ☆

His songs were selling as well as or better than they did in the early sixties, only this time *he* was singing them.

Shotgun Willie did better than any of his eighteen previous albums. *Phases and Stages* sold over 400,000 copies, which wasn't bad in an era when 100,000 was a good showing for a country album. What made it even more remarkable was the fact that Atlantic was in the process of dismantling their country division when it was released, and they just kind of threw it out there to sink or swim on its own.

But with Atlantic getting out of the music business, Dad had to find another label.

He cut a deal with Columbia. Only this time he got complete artistic control. Columbia would put the records out, but Dad would record what he wanted, with musicians that he wanted to record with, and he'd record where he wanted to. Dad even got control over the record jackets.

His first album on Columbia was *Red Headed Stranger*.

As I've mentioned several times before, I grew up with Dad singing that song. He finally got to release it as a concept album.

He and Connie were driving back to Austin from Colorado when they developed the idea for the whole album. They did it like a movie treatment and, as a matter of fact, the movie version of the *Red Headed Stranger* was released in 1987. With Dad as the red-headed stranger, of course.

Fred Foster was one of the first people ever to hear the song. It was back in 1954, when he was working as a promo man around the Washington D.C. area and down into Virginia and the Carolinas.

Fred knew a lot of writers, and one of them was a man named Carl Stutz, who lived in Richmond, Virginia, and sang on WRVA. He met Carl one day and Carl told him he had a couple of songs he wanted Fred to hear. But first Carl explained how he came across the songs.

It seems this proper southern lady named Edith Lindeman, who was the society editor for the local paper, approached him one day. She understood that he was a songwriter. She had written some poems, and would Mr. Stutz look at them and see if any had potential to be set to music?

Songwriters and performers get questions like this all the time, and Carl was none too happy to be asked again. But he didn't want to be out-and-out rude, so he said he'd look at a couple.

She reached into her briefcase and pulled out a single sheet of typewritten paper. Carl looked at it and read:

> Little things mean a lot
> Blow me a kiss
> Say I look nice when I'm not
> Touch my hair when you pass my chair
> Little things mean a lot.

Carl was impressed. But he didn't want to show too much emotion in case it didn't hold up on a later reading, so he asked, "What else do you have?"

She handed him a second sheet of paper and he read:

The red headed stranger from Blue Rock, Montana
Rode into town one day.
And under his knees was a raging black stallion
And trailing behind was a bay.

Carl told her, "That's fine. Let me see what I can do with these and then we'll see what else you've got."

That night he wrote the melody to "Little Things Mean a Lot." But "Red Headed Stranger" proved to be more difficult because he knew it required something special. He worked on it for three days until he came up with a tune.

When he sang the songs to Fred, well, Fred was knocked to his knees.

Fred said that "Little Things Mean a Lot" would be perfect for Kitty Kallen, a big-band singer who had had a Top-20 hit with "Are You Looking For a Sweetheart?" She cut "Little Things" and it went to number one, selling over a million — and that was in 1954.

Fred didn't have any idea who could cut "Red Headed Stranger" because there was nothing approaching that sort of music on the market at the time.

He didn't know that Arthur "Guitar Boogie" Smith of Charlotte, North Carolina, had cut the song, which was the version Dad had heard and played when he was a disc jockey in Fort Worth.

Fred later went into record producing and had several artists, including Eddy Arnold, cut "Red Headed Stranger." But none of them came off. And that really bothered Fred. One, because Carl Stutz was such a good friend. And two, because he was so affected by the song.

"So nobody on this planet was any happier than I was when Willie brought out 'Red Headed Stranger,'" Fred later told me.

☆ ☆ ☆ ☆

Dad always said that since us kids all liked the "Red Headed Stranger" when we were little, he figured the big kids would like it too.

But he had never felt the time was right to record it before. It was too long for a single, for one thing. And it was a ballad — music to sit and listen to in your living room, not music to dance to.

But now Dad sensed the time was right. The rediscovery of country roots was really taking hold in Texas and spreading across the country. And "Red Headed Stranger" was a serious western about lost love and violence, a western that had more in common with *The Wild Bunch* or *The Good, The Bad, and The Ugly* than it did with Roy Rogers or Gene Autry.

And that's the kind of album Dad put together.

The people at Columbia didn't like it. Dad had recorded it at Autumn Sound Studios in Garland. It had a loose, gospel feel to it, an understated simplicity that sounded like it had been cut on the front porch. The top executive wanted to smooth it up, put some strings behind it. Something.

Dad refused.

Some middle-level folks at Columbia did like it, and they worked hard to promote it. They made sure that country music critics got copies of it. And they sent it to rock critics too.

"Blue Eyes Crying in the Rain" was released as a single. Much to everyone's surprise, including Dad's, I think, it went soaring up the charts. By July, it was number one.

One friend of Dad's couldn't figure it out. "After all the great songs you've written and recorded," he told him, "how could you get to number one with a thirty-year-old piece of shit like that?"

Others saw it differently.

Ray Pennington thought it was a "stone smash" the first time he heard it.

Wesley Rose called Dad to thank him for recording the song just the way his father wanted it done.

But whatever anyone thought, there was no disputing that Dad had reached a new high.

☆ ☆ ☆ ☆

Dad's insistence on doing things his way and his determination to follow his dreams through all those years had a lot to do with the unprecedented success he was starting to have. But there were a lot of other things going on that helped make the time right for him.

Jimmy Dean, Johnny Cash, Roger Miller, and Glen Campbell all had prime-time, major network television shows during the sixties that helped expand the record-buying public for country music.

Perry Como, The Lovin' Spoonful, and Ringo Starr of the Beatles had recorded in Nashville. So had Bob Dylan. Kris Kristofferson, Rhodes scholar and suspected hippie, had written songs that were classics by any measure.

In the early seventies, ABC's Monday Night Football was giving wives across the nation one more reason to hate the NFL. But Don Merideth was captivating the football audiences with his Texas twang, and he developed the habit of singing "Turn Out the Lights" whenever the winner of the game was apparent. He'd finish by saying: "What's the matter? Don't you know about Willie Nelson?"

There were others in Nashville who were seen as being the same type — rebels, who wouldn't bend to the establishment, who insisted on doing their music their way.

"Outlaw music" was a term coined by a public relations person and gossip columnist named Hazel Smith. A disc jockey from a small country station in North Carolina called her and asked what to call this music by Dad, Waylon, Tompall Glaser, and Kris that people kept asking for. He was going to play nothing but their records on his Sunday afternoon show, and he needed something to call it — he needed a hook.

Taking her cue from Waylon's 1972 hit, "Ladies Love Outlaws," she said, "Call it outlaw music."

There were times when Dad and Waylon and everybody else wished Hazel had kept her mouth shut. But outlaw music served its purpose for a while. It separated the beards and blue jean wearers from the Nudie suit wearers in the public mind. It played off of the cowboy image while stressing the anti-establishment/rebel themes in ways that both hippies and kickers could identify with.

Although Waylon Jennings would sing "Don't you think this outlaw bit has done got out of hand?" and though it contrasted strangely with Dad's aura of laid-back serenity, one of the most successful country albums of the seventies was the *Outlaws* album.

The Outlaws was an RCA Victor release that Waylon and Tompall produced. It featured Waylon and his wife Jessie Colter, Tompall, and Dad. They used old songs that Dad had cut when he was still with RCA, "Yesterday's Wine" and "Me and Paul," and Waylon and Dad sang a duet on "Good-Hearted Woman" that they had co-written. The duet was created by the magic of engineering: Waylon laid down a vocal track on Dad's old tape.

Outlaws led to "Let's Go To Luckenbach, Texas" and the *Waylon and Willie* album — monsters all. So the "outlaw" stuff had its advantages, even if it did get out of hand.

☆ ☆ ☆ ☆

And there were the picnics.

Dad didn't stop with the Abbott Homecoming. In 1974 he held his second Fourth of July picnic at the Texas World Speedway in College Station.

This one was a three-day affair that lasted through the sixth. The posters listed forty-three separate acts "and more" ranging from Bill Monroe and Kenneth Threadgill to Kinky Friedman and Ricky Nelson.

Waylon was there. So were Bobby Bare and Sammi Smith. Leon Russell was master of ceremonies, but many criticised that Leon spent too much time performing and not enough time being an emcee.

The third one, in 1975, was in Liberty Hill, to the northwest of Austin. It advertised Willie, His Family and Friends, for just one day, on the fourth. The Pointer Sisters were one of the acts. Attendance figures ranged from fifty to ninety thousand, and all reports agreed that the fans clogged every road leading in and out of town.

Gonzales, eighty miles to the southeast of Austin, won the privilege of hosting the Bicentennial picnic. Billed as "The Nation's Largest Annual Music Event," it was a three-day festival that bracketed the fourth. Headlines after the fact read:

COMPLAINTS FILED AGAINST PROMOTERS
PICNIC-GOERS DISPLAY BODIES, UNUSUAL TALENTS, PERSISTENCE
NAKED, DRUNK PEOPLE EVERYWHERE
WILLIE NELSON'S PICNIC A SMASH

It was also miserable for many. The concert was held in a low spot in a pasture, and many people had camped out in front of the stage. It rained the night of the fourth, turning the site into a quagmire of mud, spilled beer, and floundering bodies.

Between the weather, the complaints, and the lack of profits, Dad decided against a picnic in 1977.

☆ ☆ ☆ ☆

He may have had a few problems with some of the picnics, but by the mid-seventies, Dad could do very little wrong.

The Texas House of Representatives presented Dad with a Certificate of Citation in 1975, and the Texas Senate passed a resolution declaring July 4, 1975, "Willie Nelson Day in Texas." In 1978 he was commissioned an honorary Texas Ranger and an admiral in the Texas Navy on the same day.

Souvenir dollar bills were printed with Dad's picture and the slogan "E Pluribus Willie" on them. In Texas, it became the gospel according to Matthew, Mark, Luke, and Willie. He was on the cover of *Rolling Stone*. In 1978 he and the band played the White House for President Carter.

But through it all, Dad kept his perspective and his sense of humor. "Stick with me kid," he told one of the band, "and you'll be wearing horse turds big as diamonds."

Even though he was becoming a superstar, he still enjoyed being with the fans.

Chet Atkins told me a story of being with him at an outdoor concert one time. He took pity on Dad because he was constantly surrounded by fans. They wouldn't give him any peace. At least, that's the way it looked to Chet.

He went over to Dad and asked if he could speak with him for a minute.

Dad excused himself and went over to Chet, who explained that he was just trying to give Dad a break.

Dad thanked him, talked with Chet for a short while, then went back over and talked with the fans.

"He just likes to be with them," Chet said.

☆ ☆ ☆ ☆

I was busy with my marriages. I left Roy in 1975 and married my second husband in 1977.

I would see Dad whenever he came to Las Vegas, of course, just like when I lived there with Mama. But there was a difference: now he was a headliner and played the big halls.

Around this time, a major female country star was playing a big date in Las Vegas. She was in the middle of her act when all of a sudden Dad walked onto the stage, whispered in her ear, and then disappeared.

As soon as the number was finished, she told the band, "Willie just invited us to come jam with him." So she cut her set short, walked out, and they all went to join Dad. David Zentner, who played in her band at the time, didn't know what the management of the casino thought about that, but you can bet they weren't pleased.

I remember seeing Dad once in Las Vegas when I was about seven or eight months pregnant with my daughter Rebecca. Mother Harvey was there too. She was about my height, five foot one, and really heavy—mainly from all the booze she had put away over the years.

Dad was going out the door, and he paused to say goodbye. As he looked at us he gave his sly Willie Nelson grin.

"Y'all look like bookends."

By that time, things weren't going well with me. I was just eighteen, and all of the foreboding I had had about Roy at the church were coming true. I didn't love him. He may have loved me, or thought he did, but he was running around on me. I walked into a casino one time, eight months pregnant, and found Roy with another woman.

He didn't seem to have much to do besides putting in his time on the base and then running around with his Air Force buddies, sampling the delights of Las Vegas.

He was young, it's true. And Las Vegas was too much of a temptation for any nineteen-year-old to ignore. But this one had a pregnant wife at home.

I didn't like it. I didn't like it one little bit.

And I vowed to do something about it as soon as I could.

☆

TWENTY-ONE

Losing direction

"Take that money and go buy some groceries."

R ebecca was born on October 18, 1975.

Eight months later, I left Roy.

I hadn't told Roy a thing. The first he knew that I was leaving was when he came home one night and found us gone. I left on Father's Day.

Now that was cold. I admit it. But running around on me when I was pregnant wasn't an act of warm-hearted compassion on his part. Besides, I was young, I was mad, and I knew what I wanted to do. And what Roy wanted didn't make much difference.

☆ ☆ ☆ ☆

I called my friend Pattie Monnett in Austin and told her how unhappy I was. Could she fly to Las Vegas and help me drive back to Austin?

Of course she could. When she arrived, I got her a room at one of the downtown hotels for the night. After Roy reported for work at the base, I got in my Pinto and drove down to a U-Haul dealership. As soon as I got back, Pattie and I began throwing stuff into the trailer every which way—dishes, clothes, baby things, it didn't make any difference.

The trip back to Austin was an experience. I drove to Phoenix in 100-degree heat that we couldn't do anything about because if we turned on the air conditioner, the car would overheat. I was exhausted, so I asked Pattie if she could drive for a while.

I soon found out that driving wasn't Pattie's strong suit. She was going up a steep hill—actually, it was a mountain—in third gear.

"Put it in first," I told her.

191

Pattie was laughing hysterically. It turns out she has never driven a stick shift before. So we changed seats, with cars backed up behind us for a mile and honking. I got us moving and asked Pattie to look at the map and tell me where to go.

Pattie didn't know how to read a map. Neither did I.

So we made it back to Austin by calling her parents every 100 miles or so for new directions. When we pulled into the driveway at her parents' house, the battery died.

By this time, Dad and Connie were living on the ranch on Fitzhugh Road. I didn't want to go there because I didn't feel welcome. And I guess I was right, because I was never invited.

Mr. and Mrs. Monnett gave me enough money to get to Waco, where Mama was living with her third husband Mickey. I got a job at the Waco Apparel Factory, and Mama watched Rebecca while I worked. As soon as I got my first check, I got an efficiency apartment.

Mama was good to me. She bought me groceries, helped me with my apartment, and watched Rebecca. But she had little ones of her own, and helping me was just too much. So, after a bit, Nannie and Pa started watching Rebecca.

Nannie has been an inspiration to me since I was a little girl. And she helped me get a better job at the Owen Illinois Glass Plant, where I made $150 a week.

I still saw Mama a lot, but she wasn't always what I needed after a day at the factory. She'd come over to visit, usually with her hat on crooked, which meant that she'd been drinking, and before long she'd start picking a fight.

And we'd usually have one, because I take after her in a lot of ways. I say what's on my mind and I generally don't back down. And when Mama drinks, she never fails to tell me what's on her mind. So we got into some classic rows.

Nannie used to take my side a lot of the time and chew Mama out for playing favorites with her children — or, in my case, making it clear that I was not a favorite. Having her own mother against her didn't do much to improve Mama's temper any.

One of the things that Mama got on to me about was leaving Roy.

"That boy really loves you," she'd tell me. "I don't see how you could do him the way you did. You better go back to him while you've still got a chance."

By this time, Roy was out of the service and back home at his mother's house in West Lake Hills. And he was calling Mama and me every day, begging to get me and Rebecca to come back to him.

I was getting it from Mama in person and from Roy over the phone, and I finally gave in.

Roy drove up to Waco to pick us up. On the way back, I had a chance to think clearly. And I told Roy what I thought.

"I'll go back with you. I'll cook your dinner, clean your house, and wash your clothes. But it isn't going to work."

"Why not?"

"For one thing, we're too young. We've already changed a lot from the people we were when we got married. And you don't want to work. You may be young, but I can already see that in you. You haven't ever had a good job. The Air Force was the best job you'll ever have because you don't want a good job. You just want to have somebody take care of you — your mother, your grandfather, your grandmother, or me, it doesn't matter. And besides, I don't love you."

"Aw, you don't mean that. You're just upset. It'll work out."

But it didn't. You can call it fate, or you can call it a self-fulfilling prophecy, but it didn't work out.

I went back for about three months. And I got a job as a receptionist for a dentist. I used to tell Dad when we smoked together in my psychedelic closet that I wanted to be a receptionist when I grew up. So I must have been grown up at nineteen, because now I was a receptionist.

But I wanted something else too. I wanted a place of my own. After two months of work, I was able to put down a deposit on a little efficiency apartment on Oltorf. And Rebecca and I left Roy again — this time for good.

☆ ☆ ☆ ☆

You'd think that I probably wanted a little time to be alone with my daughter, to sort things out and get my feet on the ground. I thought so too.

But it wasn't too long until I did it again.

Good old Pattie and I went to a singles bar called Mother Earth with this guy she had dated named Tony Brewster. One thing led to another, and we followed him to his apartment. When Pattie went to the bathroom, Tony came over and sat by me. When it came time to go home, he walked us to the car and asked for *my* phone number.

You'd think that would have made Pattie mad, right? No way. We'd shared guys. Pattie would get tired of whoever she was dating and, since I was a mother and rarely went out, she would pass them on to me.

That's how I met my second husband. Pattie always tells me, "I only asked you to go out with him, not marry him."

I may have started out in life with Dad's problem of not being able to say no, but after Roy and Tony, I learned, believe me.

Tony was tall and good looking, the son of a career army sergeant from Virginia and an Italian woman his dad had met overseas. He was a natural-born salesman with a smooth line that wreaked havoc in all the singles bars. And he put his talents to work as a professional salesman. He sold anything — insurance, mobile homes, drugs, the proverbial refrigerators to Eskimos, you name it. But mainly, he sold himself.

He sold me with his pitch — sort of. I always had this nagging feeling in the back of my mind that something wasn't right.

"Uh-oh, Susie," I'd catch myself thinking, "you're about to do it again."

But I kept on doing it.

Tony couldn't sell Dad, though.

By this time, Dad was the biggest thing that country music had ever seen. *Red Headed Stranger* and *The Outlaws* had gone platinum, and *Stardust* had just been released. Tony was just thrilled to be going with the daughter of Willie Nelson. To him, it was just one more bit of evidence that proved he was cool.

Being cool was Tony's main goal in life. He had to have the right clothes, do the right drugs, go to the right places, date the right chicks, and hang out with the right people.

Being Willie Nelson's daughter made me one of the right chicks. If he could hang out with Willie Nelson, Outlaw Willie and all the drugs and wild parties which were part of the image, then he would be cool beyond belief.

He was constantly on me to introduce him to Dad.

"Your dad's cool. I've got to meet him."

So I arranged it.

Dad was playing at his own place, the Austin Opera House, and he was staying in a room at a motel on Town Lake about six blocks away. He often did that before a show, even if it was in Austin.

I took Tony down to meet him.

Dad was sitting on the bed as he watched Tony go into his Mr. Cool act. Drugs were part of his scene.

"Would you like a toot before you go on, Willie?" he asked. Without waiting for an answer, Tony pulled out his vial and shook out some cocaine on the mirror he carried in his wallet.

Dad didn't say anything. He just watched as Tony chopped it up with his razor blade and laid out a couple of lines.

Tony reached in his pocket for his money clip and pulled out a $100 bill—it *had* to be a $100 bill, of course—then rolled it into a tight cylinder and handed it to Dad.

"You first, Willie."

Dad looked at him.

"Son, I don't toot speed and I don't toot coke. You shouldn't either. Take my advice. You take that money and go buy some groceries."

Tony was crushed. So of course he got mad.

"Come on, let's get out of here. I thought you said your dad was cool. He's not cool. He's just a tight-ass old man." And he stormed out.

I got up to follow. Dad stopped me just before I got to the door.

"He's no good, Susie. If you marry him, I'm not coming to the wedding."

"I know, Dad."

But I went on out the door to catch up with Tony.

☆ ☆ ☆ ☆

I knew Dad was right, but I still couldn't say no.

We kept on living together and moved to an apartment on Cameron Road, not far from where I worked.

Tony worked odd hours. He sold a lot of insurance to soldiers at Fort Hood, so he would be gone for a couple of days, maybe even a week at a time. I think he spent as much time on drug deals as he did selling insurance.

So when he was home, he was around the house all day. I would come home during my lunch hour and fix him a meal.

One day I hurried home from the dentist's office and fixed tuna sandwiches for lunch. Just the way I used to fix egg salad for my cousin Freddie when I skipped school at Ridgetop—with onions.

Tony didn't like onions. He took one bite, spit it back out on the plate, and began chewing me up one side and down the other.

For some reason, I was in a feisty mood that day.

"If you don't like the way I fix tunafish salad, you can fix it your own damn self," I yelled back.

And he hit me. He wound up and hit me in the face so hard it knocked me out of the chair. I got up crying and ran to Pam Page, our next-door neighbor. She was a fire-breathing women's libber who Tony didn't like at all.

The feeling was mutual. "If I was Susie," she'd tell him, "I'd throw you out in a New York minute. No way I'd put up with your bullshit."

Of course, I didn't get any sympathy from her.

"Serves you right for letting that low-life sonofabitch hang around."

So, still sobbing, I called my sister Lana.

"Tony hit me because I put onions in the tunafish salad," I wailed.

"That's the silliest thing I ever heard," said Lana. "Get rid of the bastard."

But did I listen?

Not me.

We were married in Hampton, Virginia, on March 25, 1977. True to his word, Dad didn't come to the wedding. In fact, the only member of my family who attended was my two-year-old daughter.

"Well, Rebecca," I told her just before we marched down the aisle, "I think we're fixing to make a big mistake."

☆ ☆ ☆ ☆

We bought a house in Round Rock, a town just north of Austin. Tony got a job selling mobile homes, and I quit my job because the commute got to be too much.

So I settled into trying to be a good housewife. To tell the truth, I liked the housewifely life. I liked fixing meals and keeping the house clean. I liked decorating and trying to get a yard established. If I could have been Beaver Cleaver's mom or Harriet Nelson at that time, I would have reached the height of my ambition.

Unfortunately, I wasn't married to Ward Cleaver or Ozzie Nelson. I had to put up with Tony Brewster.

Tony was a white glove man like Chuck Andrews had been. I guess he picked it up from his father, the sergeant. He would come home and inspect the house, and if he found dust on the window sill, or if the sofa hadn't been vacuumed, there would be hell to pay.

Dad's career kept on climbing, but my being married to Tony

continued the separation from him that had begun when I married Roy.

I did know that the albums were selling well. By 1979, four had gone platinum: *Stardust* and *Waylon and Willie* joined *Red Headed Stranger* and *The Outlaws*.

And I knew Dad had started in the movies. His first part was as Robert Redford's manager in *Electric Horseman*. His best scene was just after Redford had ridden off on a prize stallion into the wilds of Nevada, thereby ending any need for a manager.

"What should we do?" someone asks Dad.

"I don't know about you," he answers, "but I'm going to get a quart of tequila and find me a girl who can suck the chrome off a trailer hitch."

Dad then starred in his second movie, *Honeysuckle Rose*, the story of a country and western singer who played golf in cow pastures, a lot like Dad, who lived on a ranch near Austin, a lot like Dad, and who had an affair with the girl singer in the band, a lot like — well, maybe, maybe not.

It did all right at the box office and was well-reviewed by *The New Yorker*'s Pauline Kael. But the soundtrack album did even better: it made platinum number five. And "On the Road Again" was a hit single.

Bill Wittliff wrote a script based on the *Red Headed Stranger*, and negotiations for filming it, starring Robert Redford, began. They fell through, and it would be 1985 before Dad and Bill put the project together themselves, with both producing, Bill directing, and Dad starring.

In the meantime, Dad starred in *Barbarosa*, about a legendary bandit of the Texas border. Bill wrote that too.

In 1979 Dad won the Country Music Association's entertainer of the year award. Typical of Dad, in his acceptance speech he said that there were a lot of entertainers of the year, every year, and that he accepted it on behalf of Little Jimmy Dickens and all the others he had listened to when he was growing up.

Things may have been going great for Dad, but they weren't going so well for me.

☆ ☆ ☆ ☆

From time to time, Dad would ask me how Tony and I were getting along. I'd tell him the truth. Then it wouldn't be long after that when Tony would tell me that he'd been told through the grapevine to straighten up. And he would. For a while.

Tony and I were starting to have real trouble. He was doing drugs, a lot of drugs. Speed mainly. And he wasn't working. He'd quit his job at the mobile home lot. "Why should I have to work?" he'd say. "You're Willie Nelson's daughter." And then he'd complain about the house and tell me how stupid I was, how he was the best thing that had ever happened to me.

And then he'd hit me.

Things got so bad that I'd try to leave.

One time we got in a fight at the bar in the Marriott Hotel. He hit me and I ran away, through the kitchen and out the back door. I called some friends to come get me and I spent the night with them.

But I went back.

As things got worse at home, I began to find more things to do away from the house.

I became very active in the Baptist Church, especially the choir. I got to be a soloist, and that's when I first started to get the idea that maybe I could do something with singing.

I also discovered dance.

I had enrolled Rebecca in a local dance class run by a woman named Lillian Coltzer. I had always admired dancers, especially ballerinas, ever since I was a little girl. To me, a ballerina was everything a woman should be — beautiful, elegant, and graceful.

I had never gotten to dance and I was bound and determined to give Rebecca everything I had missed. But when I took her to enroll, I found out that the school also had beginning classes for adults.

So I enrolled too.

And I loved it.

After a few classes, I asked Lillian if she thought I could be a dancer.

"Honey, you can be anything you want to be." But she also said that I had real talent, that I was a natural.

That did it. I started spending all my time dancing. I worked to get in shape. I turned the garage at home into a ballet studio. I took every lesson Lillian offered. I even went to Julliard for a summer program.

Lillian hired me to teach the little kids classes because I was so good with children. She was around seventy at the time and was looking to slow down. What she really wanted to do was find someone who would buy the school from her, and she thought she had found the perfect candidate in me.

I was staying away from home as much as I could, because I enjoyed dancing and because Lillian was always telling me how far I could go. I mean, who would you rather be with? Someone who tells you that you are stupid and always puts you down, or someone who is always building you up?

My dancing wasn't making Tony any happier. But I kept on dancing. I even did a ballet recital at Georgetown, on point, when I was seven months pregnant.

That's right. Pregnant again. Because despite all our troubles, despite the beatings, and despite trying to leave several times, I was still basically trying to be a dutiful wife. Just like the folks down at the church were telling me to be.

And that's how I came to be eight months pregnant when I went to my second Willie Nelson Fourth of July Picnic.

☆

TWENTY-TWO

Fate steps in

"Are you Mrs. Robert Anthony Brewster?"

T he fourth picnic in Gonzales had caused a lot of problems. A citizens group tried to get it stopped altogether. When that didn't work, they were able to hold the permit down to twelve hours.

Technicalities about the permit didn't have much of an effect either, since the picnic lasted two days — longer if you counted the folks who camped out early and stayed late. On top of that, the Sheriff's Department reported seven stabbings and two rapes. Add the miserable weather, and you could see how folks might have decided that this picnic business had done got out of hand.

Because of all this, Dad didn't have a picnic in 1977.

"A whole lot of people were relieved to hear we weren't goin' to have a picnic this year."

☆ ☆ ☆ ☆

But he couldn't stop for long. The next year he held outdoor concerts in Tulsa and at the Cotton Bowl in Dallas. And he had a three-night gig, July 3–5, at his own Austin Opera House.

In 1979, after he had bought the Pedernales Country Club southwest of Austin, he decided to use the golf course as a concert site. That one was a success, despite the neighbors' fears and objections and the mountain of trash that was left behind. Dad did notice that the crowd had stomped the greens down until they were like putting on a parking lot.

But he decided to hold the 1980 picnic at the country club anyway.

I described in the first chapter how that picnic was a revelation to me. Even though I had sort of kept up with Dad's career during the seventies, it was mainly from a distance. Oh, I knew he was making movies, and I had gotten to be good friends with Amy Irving, his

200

co-star in *Honeysuckle Rose*. I knew he had played at the White House. I had seen him receive the entertainer of the year award on television. I had been to a few concerts at the Opera House, and I had even gotten to go along once or twice when he played in Las Vegas.

I knew he was doing better financially. You couldn't miss that, what with the ranch on Fitzhugh Road, the house in Colorado, one in Malibu, the cars, the customized Silver Eagle buses, the number of people in the crew who had never met me — who didn't even know I existed.

But none of it had really sunk in before. I knew it, but I didn't know it.

To me, he was still the same old Dad.

The music was the same, with a lot of the same people around — Paul English, Bee Spears, Jody Payne, and Aunt Bobbie.

In a lot of ways, everything seemed to be pretty much like it had been during the Bandera days. Maybe because the people I saw, when I saw anybody connected with Dad, were the people I had known from the old days.

Dad was just Dad. He had always written music. He had always made records. He had always played the guitar and sang. And the songs he recorded and played in his show were the same songs he had sung to us after dinner. At least, a lot of them were.

So even though I was aware that a lot of changes had taken place, the picture I had of Dad and his career was the one of him at Ridgetop and Bandera.

He was no big deal. He was just Dad.

It wasn't until I was backstage at that picnic, looking out at the thousands of screaming, adoring fans, that it all came into focus for me. All of those people who loved Dad and didn't even know him. And Dad didn't know them, but he loved them right back. At that moment, he was the most important thing in the world to them, and they were to him.

That's when I realized that my Dad was important. And I realized what he had been doing all these years.

Knowing what it was all about didn't necessarily make up for all the times when he wasn't there when I needed him or wanted him. But it sure put things in a different perspective. And it made me put myself in a different perspective.

It made me realize that I could be something more than a submissive wife who was trapped in a marriage with a man she couldn't tolerate.

So I flew back on the helicopter, with my mind made up to do something about it.

☆ ☆ ☆ ☆

Of course, there's always a big step between the deciding and the doing. I knew what I wanted, but I didn't have the foggiest idea of how to start.

For one thing, there was the baby who was six weeks away from being born. And I didn't know how to get rid of Tony.

Things were getting worse and worse between us. I didn't feel I had anybody to talk to who could be any help. The church was very supportive, but their advice was to stick it out. I didn't know what the answer was, but sticking it out wasn't it.

I couldn't figure out what to do.

Me. Susie the schemer. The one who had managed to get us living with Dad. The one who had gotten rid of Shirley, and then Helen. The one who was the deep thinker and who always had a plan about how to fix things, to make things right. I didn't have any idea of how to go about making my own situation right.

One of the problems was that, while I wanted to get rid of Tony, I didn't want a divorce. I know that sounds silly, but that's the way I felt. There was no way I could go through that again. I just wasn't going to be the one to do that like I had with Roy.

The solution, as much as there was one, was for Tony to leave. So I started acting meaner towards him than I ever had before. When I was there. I still spent as much time as possible at the church or at the dance school. But I really got on to Tony about all the drugs he was doing, and about the fact that he wasn't working—especially that he wasn't working.

One night I came home late from the church and Tony was home, waiting for me. He was mad and irritable. He had been out the night before and had put a lot of speed up his nose. Now he was down from the high—he always went down farther than the white stuff ever took him up—and he was in a really bad mood.

"You're late and I'm hungry. Where's my supper?"

I was in no mood to put up with him. "Maybe if you'd get off your ass and get a job I'd fix you your supper. But as long as you're not going to work you've got plenty of time to fix supper your own damn self."

He hit me.

I mean, he really hit me. There I was, going into my ninth month of pregnancy, and he hit me so hard I fell against the wall and slid to the floor.

At first I couldn't believe it. Then I started to cry. I got up, threw a few things into a suitcase, and left for Dad's ranch on Fitzhugh Road. Luckily, Rebecca was with her father at the time.

Because of his popularity, Dad hadn't lived at the ranch for years. When he wasn't on the road he lived at the country club or in Colorado. So the ranch became a kind of weekend getaway place for us kids or anybody else who needed a place to stay.

Before Dad moved out, he had installed a high security fence all around, complete with a closed-circuit television so you could see who was at the gate.

I let myself in with my key and I locked everything behind me. Along about two in the morning, the bell rang. It rang and rang until I finally went to the closed-circuit television screen to see who was there. As if I didn't know.

It was Tony all right. He pleaded for me to let him in, but I didn't.

He finally went away, and I stayed out there for a week.

But then I began to realize that I was going to have a baby pretty soon and I couldn't stay there forever.

So I went back home. To Round Rock and Tony.

☆ ☆ ☆ ☆

Tony was contrite. For a while.

We got along about as well as we had at the beginning. Tony even went to church with me. I couldn't believe it. I thought to myself, maybe it's going to be all right after all.

I had my doubts, but I went to the hospital to have Anthony with the hope that maybe things would work out.

After the delivery, I felt awful. I had what was probably the world's worst case of post-partum depression. I didn't want to see the baby, ever.

When the nurses asked if I wanted to see Anthony, I told them no. They would describe him to me and I wouldn't listen. I hated his father and I didn't want to have anything to do with him, including his son.

That was the worst period of my life.

Finally, a number of friends, including Amy Irving, brought me out of it. Once I held him and saw how beautiful he was, my natural mothering instincts took over.

I even consented to see Tony.

And being a father seemed to bring about a change in him. He was sweet to me. He promised he would clean up his act. He even promised to go back to work and returned to selling insurance at Fort Hood.

"We'll see," I thought. But I went back to the house in Round Rock with my new baby, anyway.

Tony did try to straighten up. He'd slip back into his old ways, but never too far. Then he'd straighten up for a while.

This wasn't a happy time for me. With Tony having periods of trying to be a good husband and father, and with me still as determined as ever not to be the one who got the divorce, I didn't see how I was ever going to get out of the situation and make something of my life. I was torn between wanting a happy, complete family and wanting to escape from a dead-end road. I prayed for the answers.

That fall and into the holiday season I went about the business of taking care of my children and trying to figure out what to do.

I was pretty much paralyzed. Then fate took a hand.

☆ ☆ ☆ ☆

Tony's birthday was on New Year's Eve. The day before, he went up to Fort Hood to check on his insurance business and a band that he was managing. He was going to be cool and get into the music business one way or another. Maybe he was also going to check on his drug deals, I don't know. But I do know he hadn't given that up completely.

I remember he asked if he could drive the new Volvo Dad had given me. I told him no.

He didn't come home that night. That wasn't unusual, so I didn't pay it much mind. Probably partying in honor of his birthday.

But then the DPS, the Texas state troopers, came by and asked if I was Mrs. Robert Anthony Brewster.

I was.

They had some bad news for me. My husband had been killed by a car full of drunk teenagers.

It was ironic. After all he had done during the years I had known him, Tony was driving home stone-cold sober to be with his family when he got killed by a bunch of drunk kids. And they all survived.

He was just twenty-three.

It didn't seem fair. Maybe if we'd had a little more time . . .

Tony's mother and two sisters flew down from Virginia for the funeral. Mr. Brewster (we called him Papa Jack) lived in Austin already. He was aware of our troubles, but he always tried to give us both positive advice. I had to call him and tell him the sad news. I felt so sorry for him. He was a nice man, and he grieved because he had lost his only son.

After the service, two close friends, the Malickis, drove me to the ranch on Fitzhugh Road. On the way back, as I held little Anthony, who wasn't yet six months old, I finally realized it was all over between Tony and me.

He was gone.

I began to cry. I felt so guilty because of all the bad thoughts I had had about him. I thought about the way it had been at the beginning and the way he had tried to turn things around after Anthony was born. Was I still in love with him?

As the car pulled through the big iron gates to the ranch, I decided to take up Dad on his offer and stay there for as long as I needed to pull myself together.

Going for it

"Do you know any songs?"

☆ ☆ ☆ ☆

Dad told me to stay at the ranch as long as I needed to. It was my home. He and Connie were both so good to me then.

My relationship with Dad stayed pretty much the same. He had been on the road, playing Las Vegas and singing the national anthem at the Democratic National Convention — at President Carter's invitation — among other places when Anthony had been born. So he didn't get to see his new grandson until he was four months old.

☆ ☆ ☆ ☆

Dad was definitely busier than he had ever been. By now he had a Lear jet, which Paula Carlene and Amy named Air Willie, to help him get to all of his engagements. It was nothing for him to fly into Austin, play eight or nine holes of golf with Darrell Royal on the pro-am day of the Legends of Golf tournament, then fly to Atlanta for a concert, and then be in Denver in time to do an interview he had promised to do.

He could also use that jet to get away from things. I dated Dad's pilot for a while, and he told me that more than once Dad would have them fly to Biloxi or someplace where they would spend a couple of days just hanging out in beer joints.

And Dad had his fleet of customized Silver Eagle buses by this time. His is the "Honeysuckle Rose," and the others for the band and road crew are "Me and Paul" and "Willie's Boys."

He had reached a stage where he could do just about anything he wanted to, including own a state-of-the-art recording studio where he has recorded a lot of his duet albums. Duets are one of his things now, and he has recorded with a whole host of people: Ernest Tubb, Ray Price, Roger Miller, Faron Young, Johnny Cash, Kris Kristofferson,

Waylon Jennings, Webb Pierce, Ray Charles, and, of course, Julio Iglesias ("To All The Girls I've Loved Before").

He also recorded the *Poncho and Lefty* album with Merle Haggard. According to Townes Van Zandt, who wrote "Poncho and Lefty," it was an afterthought. They were all done recording and the band was packing up and putting their equipment on the bus when Lana, who was a friend of Townes', got Dad's attention and told him he ought to record it.

Dad said okay, so the band unpacked everything and went back into the studio where Dad and Merle recorded what turned out to be the title cut to the album and a monster single. Not only that, they made a prize-winning video of it, and Townes played one of the *federales*. Lana produced it. And earlier she had produced another prize-winning video for Dad, "Tougher Than Leather," from the album of the same name.

Dad kept on reaching heights that no country singer had ever dreamed of before. Not only did he have complete artistic control over his recordings, he could sing whatever he wanted to with whoever he wanted to.

And he continued his movie career. *Barbarosa* came out in early 1982. And the same year, he was in a made-for-television movie called *Coming Out of the Ice*, starring John Savage, that had nothing to do with the West or with music. It was about some Americans who had been living in Siberia and how they finally made their way back home.

And he did a movie called *Songwriter* in which he played a singer/songwriter who went through a number of things that were surprisingly close to things Dad had done. And he did a made-for-television remake of the classic John Ford western, *Stagecoach*, with his old buddies Waylon, Kris, and Johnny Cash.

☆ ☆ ☆ ☆

Despite all of this, performing stayed number one.

And it was getting to be number one with me too.

It started with my dancing. I had bought into the dance school and was teaching the little ones and learning as much as I could so I could take over one day.

But one of the first things I did after Tony was killed was take over as manager of his group, the Jo Bangles Band.

They weren't bad.

With my connections, I was able to book them through Buddy Lee Attractions, and they began playing dates in places they had never thought about before.

My family connections gave me a good foot in the door, I'll admit. But still the band showed up on time and put on a good show. And I was able to get them booked into bigger and bigger places.

I even got them booked into Billy Bob's in Fort Worth. It was the biggest place they had ever played, and we did it as a favor to Dad.

The singer was having a lot of trouble with me being the manager and the boss, so to speak. I saw what needed to be done and I wasn't shy about telling them to do it. He decided just when we got to Billy Bob's and started to set up that he wasn't going to take any more orders from a woman, and a young woman at that.

What set it off was that he was being rude to the sound men during the check — Billy Bob's has some of the best sound men in the world — and I jumped in and chewed him out. I told him that we were there as a favor to my dad and we weren't going to let him, or anybody else, down by not being ready on time and doing the best we knew how.

He threatened to quit if I didn't shut up.

"Okay. Quit," I told him.

And he did.

There we were with a show to do in a couple of hours and no singer.

"What are we going to do?" asked Jimmy Flores, who played the sax.

"I'll sing."

They all looked at me like I was crazy. Maybe I was.

But I worked on a couple of songs with them.

Now I'm not saying I was great, because I wasn't. This wasn't a movie where a new star is born. We hadn't had much time together, and anyway there's a whole lot of difference between being allowed to solo in the Westside Baptist Church down the street from your home in Round Rock and singing professionally at any level. I had a lot to learn. I still have a lot to learn.

But we went on. We were just a warmup act and we didn't have a lot of time. Between the instrumentals and the two or three songs I did, we got through all right. We may not have turned any heads, and we sure didn't have any record company executives offering us contracts, but we opened on time and did our job to the best of our ability. We acted like professionals.

And I discovered that I liked being on stage. I felt more at home there than anywhere else.

The first real show I was in was a big outdoor concert in Lake Wells, Florida, about two weeks after my impromptu debut at Billy Bob's. Buddy Lee Associates out of Nashville had booked us. Joe Harris was an agent at the Buddy Lee agency, and he kind of took me under his wing.

It was a big show with a lot of acts, including Hank Williams, Jr. as a headliner. There were more than 20,000 people there, and it was kind of like one of Dad's picnics.

At Billy Bob's we had only done a thirty-minute opening set for Rick Nelson. That works out to about five or six songs, although I don't remember doing that many. I guess I was in shock. But at Lake Wells, we were expected to do an hour or more. That means fifteen to seventeen tunes.

I had a crash course. I would drive up from Round Rock to Temple every night, and the band and I would practice in a little Mexican bar near where Jimmy Flores lived. Then I would drive back to Round Rock, singing the songs as I drove.

The time came to go to Lake Wells. They flew us first class. Lake Wells didn't have a major commercial airport, so they flew us by Lear from Orlando to the River Ranch, where the concert was being held.

When we got there, they led us to a big bus. We had it all to ourselves, a well-stocked wet bar and what looked like all the food in the world.

The band just about flipped. They had only heard about stuff like this. They had never seen it before.

The promoters had made a big deal about Willie Nelson's daughter being on the show. So they were treating us like stars.

I went into the bathroom and kept practicing my songs in the mirror. I'd only had about a week to learn them, and I was still memorizing the words from pieces of paper.

We were scheduled to go on at noon, and by the time I got backstage, I practically had the hives. Everybody associated with the promotion treated me like a star. It was "Would you like a drink, Miss Nelson?" or "Here's your towel, Miss Nelson." I was so nervous I was in a trance.

The band went out and did an opening number, and then I went out on stage. The band carried me through. They were so tight that they knew how to improvise whenever I forgot a line or otherwise got into trouble. I'd run into a mental blank and Jimmy Flores would sense it immediately and take off on a saxophone solo. Then I'd say, "And let's hear a big hand for the great Jimmy Flores."

We got through it. And as we were coming off, the crowd gave us a standing ovation.

I couldn't believe it. Maybe they were all drunk. It was only noon, but it was possible.

But we actually got a standing ovation. Joe Harris stopped me in the wings and told me we had to do an encore.

I looked at him like he had lost his mind.

Surely he didn't expect me to get out in front of all those people when I didn't even know another song.

"I don't know any more songs."

Joe laughed. "You're just nervous." And he pushed me toward the stage.

He didn't believe me. Jimmy Flores did, though. When I told him to go back out there he stuttered, "But Susie, you don't know any more songs."

"Never mind that. Go back out there and play something while I think," I said as I pushed him toward the stage.

So Jimmy and the rest of the band went back on stage and played "Big Mamoo" while I thought.

They stopped. I walked out on the stage. It was quiet, strangely quiet, after all the noise and applause of the moment before.

I went to the microphone and stood looking out at the sea of faces. I still didn't have any idea of what I was going to do.

Then Dad's voice drifted into my mind. "Sing a gospel song," is what he would have told me.

So I picked up the mike and I said, "I want to thank you all for the great reception you have given us. I know we wouldn't be here if it wasn't for my dad. And I'd like to finish our set with a gospel song Dad wrote before I was born and which he used to sing to me when I was just a baby. It's called 'Family Bible.' "

The band is looking at each other like I've lost my mind. They had never heard of "Family Bible," let alone played it. But the piano player started a chord pattern and I started singing, moving around close to each of the other guys so they could pick up the melody line.

And that was the best number we did.

We left the stage to another standing ovation.

Then it was back to the bus, then the Lear, then the first-class flight to Austin. And then reality. Back to poverty.

☆ ☆ ☆ ☆

I had been with the Jo Bangles Band for about a year when I went to Dad's New Year's Eve concert at the Summit next to the Astrodome in Houston.

Besides playing Las Vegas and in huge stadiums, Dad had a couple of concerts recorded live for the HBO cable network. One was done at the Austin Opera House in the summer of 1985, but the first was at the Summit in 1981 and went out live.

It was a year to the day after Tony had been killed. Before the show started, I went back to Dad's bus to talk to him.

There were a lot of people around him, like always. I waited patiently, and finally he turned around and saw me.

"Well hello, darlin'," he said with a smile.

I was nervous. I hardly ever got to see him, and I was worried about how he would react to what I was about to tell him.

Would he laugh? Would he be embarrassed? Would he be mad?

"Hi, Dad." I paused and looked at the floor. Then I started stuttering. What little cool I had when I walked onto the bus had just run out.

"Dad, I need to talk to you in private."

"Sure, darlin'. Is anything wrong?" And he put his arm around me.

"No, Dad. I just have something I need to talk to you about." By this time, there were even more people crowding around, and I knew that time was running out. I got nervous again. But I knew it was now or never — or at least it would be a long time before I got to see him again.

So I just blurted it out, before God and everyone: "Dad, I want to sing just like you do. For the people. I know I can do it."

I looked at the floor, too embarrassed to look up by now. I knew everyone had heard.

Dad leaned over and whispered in my ear.

"Do you know any songs?"

I started laughing. Then everyone on the whole bus started laughing.

Dad put his arms around me and gave me a kiss. I hugged him back. He looked into my eyes — neither of us paid any attention to the people watching us — and he said, "Go for it, kid."

Without a word, I walked off the bus with my eyes focused on the floor.

I started to cry as soon as I was back on the ground. And as I walked to my seat, I vowed to learn everything I could about this man I called my father. I needed to find out where he got the wisdom to trust his own judgment. I needed to learn how he got the strength to follow his dreams for all those years, ever since he was a little boy pickin' and singin' for nickels at the Abbott barber shop. So that I could follow mine.

A little over a year later, on his fiftieth birthday, I gave him a biographical essay and asked him what he thought.

"Go for it, kid."

☆ ☆ ☆ ☆

I went for it. And I'm still going.

I've kept up my music career. I also kept up with my dancing for quite a while, but finally I just had too many irons in the fire and I had to sell the school.

And I kept working on Dad's biography.

It was a real joy to meet and talk with so many people about Dad. I talked to people from Abbott who knew him when he was a little boy. And I talked to people who knew him at various stages in his career — present and former members of his band, people he knew from the early days in Nashville, people who knew him in the early days in Austin from the first Armadillo concert on.

But one of the best things for me was that I got to reestablish my relationship with Shirley. I knew that if I was ever going to understand what went on at Ridgetop, I was going to have to talk with Shirley.

I hadn't seen her, except for a brief how-do-you-do in Las Vegas that I didn't even remember, since she had left Tennessee.

So I wrote her a letter explaining that I was writing this book and asked if I could talk with her. We finally made arrangements for me to visit her in Chillicothe.

So on Labor Day of 1986, I arrived at the airport in Kansas City. We recognized each other instantly. But the first thing she said to me was, "Where's your blonde hair?" It had been blonde when I was a little girl, and that was the way she remembered me.

I answered with "You're so short" because I remembered this big, tall lady with a loud voice. Shirley is only a little bit taller than I am, and I'm just five foot one.

We didn't stop talking for three straight days.

Not only did we patch up our relationship like it had been during the early good days at Ridgetop, it was better now because we were both adults.

Shirley is a Catholic, and for years she had been praying that one of us—Lana, Billy, or me—would come to her so she could explain things as she saw them. So, in a way, she had been waiting for my letter for more than fifteen years.

Not only did we become friends again, we became singing partners too.

Shirley hadn't performed professionally since she quit the road after marrying Dad, but she did sing at nursing homes and the like around the Chillicothe area. And she still wrote songs.

It started when I asked her if I could record some of her songs. I was leaving for Nashville next, and I wanted to take some new material along.

She thought about it for a while. Shirley is very protective of her songs, "my babies" she calls them, but after sleeping on it for a night, she said yes.

I went to Nashville to get more interviews for this book and to rehearse for a concert at the National Congress of American Indians Convention in Phoenix. The girl I had hired to do the backup vocals turned out to be a royal pain, and I fired her after the first rehearsal.

I needed somebody fast. I went back to my room and called Shirley.

"Mom #2, I need you. Catch a plane to Nashville and then come do a show with me in Phoenix."

Shirley had been asleep and she told me she'd call me back in the morning. Fifteen minutes later the phone rang in my hotel room.

"Can I bring my bass?"

Shirley had never heard me sing before, and this made me very nervous. I knew she would tell me the truth, no matter how it hurt.

She listened with a critical ear, and after the Arizona performance she told me she thought I could make it.

Even after working on the road for five years, nothing ever pleased me more. I guess I'm just a natural-born ham. And Dad's dream has become my dream too.

Hank Cochran had listened to Shirley and me sing together when I interviewed him for this book. He liked our sound together so well that he produced an album. We cut it in January 1987. And so, twenty-seven years later, Hank is helping another Nelson get along in the music business.

Shirley and I worked so well together in the studio that we were able to get the voice tracks done in two or three takes. It got to be a joke in the studio. The engineer would say, "It's been twenty minutes. Aren't you done yet?"

And when I told Dad about Shirley and me, he thought it was great.

"Shirley's a fine, fine singer," he told me. "Nobody sings harmony any better than she does."

TWENTY-FOUR

Through my eyes

"No .. I don't. But I sure appreciate your remembering me."

And Dad?

Dad just keeps on rolling along.

In March 1987 he realized one of his dreams when the movie of the *Red Headed Stranger* premiered in Austin. It was shot for less than $2 million, using a western town that Dad had built at the country club and at other locations around the Austin area. They brought it in two days ahead of schedule, and both Dad and the writer Bill Wittliff are very pleased with it. Bill thinks he included every important theme that was in the album, and Dad says that it is better than he ever imagined it could be.

☆ ☆ ☆ ☆

The picnics are continuing, but now with a difference.

After the 1980 picnic, Dad decided not to hold another one at the country club because he didn't want the golf course "turned into a strip mine." The next year he did a series of three outdoor concerts in Syracuse, Newark, and Atlanta. He didn't do any in 1982 or 1983.

The Fourth of July picnic was back in Austin in 1984 and 1985 at a field just south of town and just off of IH-35.

Then a comment Bob Dylan made at the Live Aid concert in 1985 started something. The concert, one of the largest live events ever organized, was given to solicit contributions to help feed starving people in Africa. As Dylan was getting ready to sing, he said, "Maybe they could just take . . . one or two million, and use it, say, to pay the mortgages on some of the farms that the farmers owe to the banks."

And Dad's first Farm Aid concert was born.

Of course, Dad says, "I have no idea how it got started. I was just sitting on the bus . . ."

Farm Aid I was held that September at the University of Illinois football stadium in Champaign. And Farm Aid II was held on the Fourth of July in 1986 at Manor Downs, a quarterhorse track about ten miles east of Austin.

After the first one, Dad knew he was on to something. "I figured people would respond, but not nearly as well as they did, and as that money started rollin' in, I had to rethink my position. I realized I had to do a lot more than make some calls and go out and sing. My name was attached to that money, so by necessity I had to take responsibility and decide that I would be the one who writes the checks. So that's what happens; nothing goes out without my signature on it. And so far as I know, every quarter of that money has gone to benefit the family farmer in some way."

The Farm Aid concerts have raised more than $14 million so far, and Dad, as chairman of the board, has made all the final decisions on how it was spent. Says Caroline Mugar, the director, "We just do the research . . . and make recommendations. Then Willie decides."

Dad is dead serious about Farm Aid. He works closely with Texas Agricultural Commissioner Jim Hightower and many others in the farmers' movement to determine the best ways for the money to be used. Most of it goes to support services like hotlines, crisis and counseling centers, and so forth. The concerts don't raise enough money to directly help the very serious economic situation that American farmers are in—they raise millions and the problem requires billions and billions—but they do help provide vital immediate necessities.

As Dad says, "We're trying to get the word out that the problem still exists. Farmers are still going out of business every day. They still need money, they still need legal help, and more than anything they still need more pay for their product."

Farm Aid has sponsored the groundbreaking of the Farmers and Ranchers Congress, given scholarship grants to the Future Farmers of America Foundation (on the condition that the recipients be needy candidates from small-farm families), helped a group of South Texas minority farmers market their produce directly, run the Family Farm Defense Fund, which provides attorneys and legal advice to people engaged in farm defense cases, and provided emergency aid.

"It may sound crazy to be giving food to farmers," says Dad, "but the reality is that many of them have a freezer full of meat, but no money to buy bread."

☆ ☆ ☆ ☆

Through my eyes
I've discovered what you mean to me
Though there were times I couldn't see
You were only making plans and dreaming dreams.
Through my eyes
I see a very special Dad
And now I realize
The things I couldn't understand just had to be
Through my eyes
Warm and tenderness I see
There in your eyes, now
Look in mine and see love shining back to you.
Through my eyes.

Shirley, Mom #2, wrote that song especially for me, and we recorded it on our first album. It truly says a lot for me.

I am still continually amazed by this unique, gentle man who is my father.

After the 1980 picnic, for example, when I really began to get a sense of how big a star he had become, I'd sometimes find myself looking out my window and see him coming to the house. "That's Willie Nelson coming to my house," I'd think. Then I'd catch myself and remember that that was only Dad.

He is a man of enormous talents. That is obvious. But he is also a man with an enormous capacity to love and to give. The Farm Aid concerts are just the most recent and best publicized examples of a lifelong generosity of spirit.

Dad makes millions every year, but he basically lives from month to month. And the reason is that he supports a lot of people. I don't know how many, but it wouldn't surprise me if more than 1,000 people are directly dependent on Dad for their livelihood, or a big part of it.

Not just the band and the crew. But friends and family who are in no way connected to the business. People like Mama—Dad bought her the house in Waco. People like me and Billy.

David Zentner told me Dad always helps folks who are down on their luck, and he does it in a way so that they can save face. "Look. You dropped something," Dad'll say and hand the person $500 or $1,000.

And this has been his way all of his life. He would share what he had. The $600-a-month child support was his figure, not Mama's. Of course, she didn't say no. And one of the reasons he was always close to the edge during the Ridgetop years was because he bought houses for and supported Mother and Ken Harvey, Pop and Lorraine, and Aunt Bobbie.

Of course, Dad also spends a lot on luxuries for the people around him and on himself. He likes cars — he drives a Mercedes — and gives expensive cars to family and friends almost like party favors.

He doesn't seem to think about the future, and that bothers me. I'm a pretty good businesswoman, at least I think I am, and I have already started planning for Rebecca and Anthony's economic security.

But I have to stop and remember that Dad is different. He grew up during the Depression, when nobody had any money. By living through that, he knows he can live without money again if he has to. Dad's attitude seems to be that you might as well enjoy the moment, because you don't know what the future will bring. And he wants everyone else to enjoy the moment too.

That is one of the reasons for his serenity. He once told an interviewer that he learned through the years that what felt right at the time was usually the best thing to do. Dad has a combination of serene acceptance of whatever happens — a fatalism — combined with a fierce determination to pursue his dream. "Don't let him fool you," Waylon once said. "If you get in his way, Willie'll run right over you."

He is one of the most laid-back, hardest-working people in the world.

There are things I would change if I could. I wish he had been home a lot more when we were growing up, and I wish our home life had been more stable in other ways too. I'm still working out a lot of the feelings that emerged in those days.

And I wish Dad would face things directly more often. He has a habit of avoiding confrontation. I wish he'd just tell people what to do more. I sometimes even wish he had told me what to do more.

But people aren't perfect. We all have our strengths and our weaknesses. And I sure wouldn't want Dad to change if it meant changing his good qualities.

I wouldn't want anything to change his loyalty. He has an enormous capacity for being loyal and, as a consequence, people are loyal to him. Paul English, for example, stuck with Dad through the lean years, selling his rent property and going without his pay in order to help Dad follow his dream.

His loyalty and consideration for others extends to everyone around him. Since he doesn't worry about things he can't control, he doesn't get on to people who work for him. No matter how hectic or screwed-up things get, Dad can always give you that famous Willie Nelson smile.

He is almost apologetic whenever he asks anyone to do something for him. "It's almost like he works for you," his pilot once told me. He's still the same appreciative boy from Abbott who used to ask Eldon for a ride to the baseball game in West.

In a way, Dad has never left Abbott, never forgotten where he came from. He still drops in on his boyhood friends from Abbott, and he still remembers and keeps in touch with all of the folks who helped him on his way up.

Of course, he never has lost his touch with the fans. He will sign autographs as long as there is anybody asking for one. And he'll play as long as anyone wants to listen. He has said over and over again that he can't understand performers who think they are bigger than their fans, who won't sign autographs, who cut the shows short or don't even show up. "I always figure that if my audience shows up, I ought to show up too," he says.

The size of the audience doesn't make any difference. He'll put on the same show for one person crowded around the bandstand as he will for 70,000 screaming fans.

Dad is an extraordinarily popular figure, a hero and an idol to millions around the world. Very few people in history have the kind of following that Dad has. For some people, going to one of Dad's concerts is like a religious experience.

I think the source of his great and enduring appeal is the fact that he truly believes that in the grand design of the universe, he is no more important, no more unique, no better, than any other individual human being on the planet. He communicates a true belief in equality, in tolerance, that we are all in this together. That's what his music is all about. And that's what makes him so approachable.

Paul English tells a story that sums Dad up about as well as any I've heard.

After a concert, a woman in her late fifties came up to Dad. "I met you in San Antonio five years ago," she told him, "but I don't suppose you remember me." It was said in kind of a challenging way, in a you-think-you're-hot-stuff tone.

"No, I'm sorry, but I don't," he answered, "but I sure appreciate your remembering me."

That's my dad.

And I love him.

Index